THE HOLY SPIRIT

A COMPREHENSIVE STUDY OF THE PERSON AND WORK OF THE HOLY SPIRIT

JOHN F. WALVOORD

ZondervanPublishingHouse
Grand Rapids, Michigan

A Division of HarperCollins*Publishers*

The Holy Spirit: A Comprehensive Study of the Person
and Work of the Holy Spirit
Copyright © 1954 by Van Kampen Press
Copyright © 1958 by Dunham Publishing Company
Copyright assigned to Zondervan Publishing House, 1965
First Paperback Edition, 1991

Requests for information should be addressed to:
Zondervan Publishing House
Grand Rapids, Michigan 49530

Library of Congress Cataloging-in-Publication Data

Walvoord, John F.
   The Holy Spirit : a comprehensive study of the person and work of
the Holy Spirit / John F. Walvoord.
      p.   cm.
   Reprint. Previously published: Wheaton, Ill. : Van Kampen Press,
1954.
   Includes bibliographical references and index.
   ISBN 0-310-34061-6
   1. Holy Spirit.   I. Title.
BT121.W27   1991
231'.3–dc20   91-20458
                                                                     CIP

Printed in the United States of America

HB 03.22.2024

PREFACE

During many years of teaching the doctrine of the Holy Spirit in the classrooms of Dallas Theological Seminary, it was discovered that no text was entirely satisfactory as a presentation of all the essential truth in this area. The lectures on the Holy Spirit, first delivered orally, were reduced to writing in a series of articles appearing in *Bibliotheca Sacra,* beginning in April, 1940. These were published privately in 1943 by Dallas Theological Seminary in revised form for use as a classroom textbook under the title, *The Doctrine of the Holy Spirit.* The interest aroused by the limited circulation of this private edition, now exhausted, has prompted the present publication.

Those familiar with either the articles or the book will find all the essential material reproduced in the present revised publication. The entire book has been revised, some chapters entirely rewritten, and improvements in clarity achieved. Added material has been included on points previously obscure. The original purpose to present a comprehensive treatment of the entire doctrine, omitting nothing essential to its presentation, has guided the revision. The comprehensive table of contents, a complete Scriptural index and topical index, make the volume a ready reference work.

Except for the section on the history of the doctrine, the appeal has been to the teaching of the Scriptures rather than to the dogma of the church as is shown by the more than fourteen hundred Scripture citations. It has also been the policy to limit citations of other works to those which make a real contribution and not to clutter the mind of the reader with every possible variation of the doctrinal point in question. The underlying purpose has been to instruct the reader in the doctrine of the Spirit comprehensively, particularly fortifying him against the many popular misconceptions that exist. Special attention has been given to such important and misunderstood subjects as the work of the Holy Spirit in the Old Testament, the baptism of the Spirit, spiritual gifts, the filling of the Spirit, and the eschatology of the Spirit. The author knows of no work which attempts to deal adequately with all these aspects of the doctrine. In addition to the doctrinal treatment, the chapter on the history of the doctrine of the Spirit gathers the essential material in brief and readable form which will enable the reader to grasp the great movements in the church in relation to this doctrine.

To Lewis Sperry Chafer, founder and first president of Dallas Theological Seminary, the author is indebted for his own introduction to the doctrine of the Spirit and for inspiration in the preparation of the earlier written form. His *He That Is Spiritual* and his *Pneumatology*, volume six of his *Systematic Theology* published in 1948, have been of inestimable help in preparation of this work. The many questions, suggestions, and constructive criticism of the advanced students in theology who have heard the lectures at Dallas Theological Seminary during the past fifteen years have had their part in shaping the material. The work has taken form amidst the pressure of many other duties, and without the enablement of the Holy Spirit the task could not have been completed. The author wishes to thank those who have given permission to quote copyrighted materials. The American Standard Version has been used in Scripture quotations, except as indicated, as best suited to theological study.

To those who seek to know the "things of the Spirit of God" this book is prayerfully commended.

JOHN F. WALVOORD

PREFACE TO THE THIRD EDITION

In preparing this third edition, it has seemed advisable to add an appendix on "The Contemporary Doctrine of the Holy Spirit." Though the purpose of the volume as a whole is to discuss the theology of the Holy Spirit as held by those who believe in Biblical infallibility, it has become important for students of the doctrine to know something of the interpretations current in liberal, neo-orthodox, and crisis theology. The doctrine of the Holy Spirit in contemporary theology is the key to interpretation of modern thought, and for this reason is an essential factor in theological discussion. Though it was found impractical to include the appendix in the indexes and bibliography, the outline provided in the table of contents will make the material easily available. This edition, like those which preceded, is issued in the hope of making known the precious truth of the person and work of the Holy Spirit.

April, 1958

John F. Walvoord

ACKNOWLEDGMENTS

The author gratefully acknowledges the kindness of authors and publishers in giving permission to reproduce material in this volume as follows:

Wm. B. Eerdmans Publishing Co. — *The Inspiration of the Scriptures*, 1937, by Loraine Boettner; *The International Standard Bible Encyclopaedia*, 1937, edited by James Orr.

The Judson Press — *Systematic Theology*, unabridged edition, copyright 1907, by A. H. Strong; renewal 1935 by The Judson Press.

The Macmillan Company — *Reinhold Niebuhr, His Religious, Social, and Political Thought*, 1956, edited by Charles W. Kegley and Robert W. Bretall.

Moody Press — *The Holy Spirit of God*, 1913, by W. H. Griffith Thomas.

Thomas Nelson & Sons — American Revised Version and the Revised Standard Version of the Holy Bible. Used by permission of the copyright owners, The National Council of the Churches of Christ in the U.S.A.

Fleming H. Revell Co. — *Studies in the Holy Spirit*, 1936, by James B. Green.

St. Martin's Press, Inc. — *Holy Spirit in the Ancient Church*, 1912, by H. B. Swete.

Charles Scribner's Sons — *The New Being*, 1955, by Paul Tillich.

Joseph F. Wagner, Inc. — *Discourse on the Holy Ghost*, 1942, edited by Lester M. Dooley.

The Westminster Press — *Revelation and Reason*, 1946, by Emil Brunner, translated by Olive Wyon; *The Holy Spirit in Christian Theology*, 1956, by George S. Hendry; *Karl Barth's Church Dogmatics*, 1953, by Otto Weber, translated by Arthur C. Cochrane.

Zondervan Publishing House — *Reigning in Life*, 1937, by J. East Harrison.

TABLE OF CONTENTS

PART ONE

THE PERSON OF THE HOLY SPIRIT

CHAPTER I

THE PERSONALITY OF THE HOLY SPIRIT

IT IS A fundamental revelation of Scripture that the Holy Spirit is a person in the same sense that God the Father is a person and the Lord Jesus Christ is a person. The Holy Spirit is presented in Scripture as having the same essential deity as the Father and the Son and is to be worshipped and adored, loved and obeyed in the same way as God. To regard the Holy Spirit in any other way is to make one guilty of blasphemy and unbelief. We tread therefore on most holy ground in thinking of the Holy Spirit of God and the truth involved is most sacred and precious.

The personality of the Holy Spirit has been subject to denial and neglect through the centuries of the Christian church and is seldom understood by twentieth-century Christians. The heretic Arius who stirred up a rebellion against the Scriptural teaching concerning the person of Christ and the person of the Holy Spirit denied the eternity of Christ and the personality of the Holy Spirit. For him the Holy Spirit was only the "*exerted energy* of God" manifested in the created world.[1] While his view was repudiated at the Nicene Council in 325, it foreshadowed the defection from Scriptural teaching which was to follow. Socinius and his followers in the sixteenth century held that the Holy Spirit was merely the eternally proceeding energy of God.[2] This laid the foundation for modern Unitarianism. Variations in the doctrine of the Holy Spirit have been many through the centuries, but in the main the great body of conservative and orthodox Christians have regarded the Holy Spirit as a Person according to the revelation given in the Scriptures.

I. His Attributes Affirm Personality

Every aspect of the doctrine of the Holy Spirit contributes to His personality, but a study of His attributes in themselves demonstrates the truth of His personality beyond question. Personality is commonly

---

[1]Richard Watson, *Theological Institutes*, I, 630.
[2]Cf. William G. T. Shedd, *Dogmatic Theology*, I, 328, "Socinians deny the distinct personality of the Holy Spirit; they concede eternity, because they regard the Spirit as the influence or effluence of the eternal God."

defined as containing the essential elements of intellect, sensibility, and will.[3] All of these elements can be found in the Holy Spirit. His intelligence is manifest in all His mighty works. It is expressly claimed for the Holy Spirit, "The Spirit searcheth all things, yea, the deep things of God. For who among men knoweth the things of a man, save the spirit of man which is in him? even so the things of God none knoweth, save the Spirit of God" (1 Cor. 2:10-11). He is the Spirit of wisdom (Eph. 1:17) and the Spirit of wisdom and understanding, the Spirit of counsel and might, the Spirit of knowledge and of the fear of Jehovah (Isa. 11:2). His sensibility is revealed in that the Spirit can be grieved by sin (Eph. 4:30). His will is shown in the sovereign bestowal of spiritual gifts on men which is accomplished "as he will" (1 Cor. 12:11). Sustaining these essential elements of personality is the whole broad doctrine of the deity of the Holy Spirit. If God possesses personality, and the Holy Spirit is a person of the Trinity, it follows that He has personality. A denial of His personality is a denial of the doctrine of the Trinity.

II. His Works Affirm Personality

The most tangible and conclusive evidence for the personality of the Holy Spirit is found in His works. The very character of His works makes it impossible to interpret the Scriptures properly without assuming His personality. In view of the discussion of His works in detail which follow, it is necessary only to mention illustrations here. All the works of the Holy Spirit are such that personality is required. His work in creation (Gen. 1:2), empowering (Zech. 4:6), teaching (John 16:13), guidance (Isa. 48:16; Rom. 8:14), comforting (John 14:26), prayer (Rom. 8:26), convincing the world of sin, righteousness, and judgment (John 16:8), restraint of sin (Gen. 6:3; Isa. 59:19; 2 Thess. 2:7), and His commands (Acts 8:29; 13:2; 16:7) make it evident that the Holy Spirit is a true person. A mere influence or emanation does not create, empower, teach, guide, pray, or command. In the history of the church, opponents of the personality of the Holy Spirit have found it necessary also to deny the inspiration and accuracy of the Word of God in order to sustain their teaching.

III. Use of Personal Pronouns Affirms Personality

In normal discourse, personal pronouns such as *I, thou, he, they* are used of persons. While personification occurs in literature fre-

[3]Lewis Sperry Chafer, *Systematic Theology*, I, 191.

quently, it is always quite apparent and does not leave the meaning in doubt. Personal pronouns are used of the Holy Spirit in such a way that personality is affirmed. In the New Testament the Greek word *pneuma* is neuter and would normally take a neuter pronoun. In several instances, however, the masculine pronouns are found (John 15:26; 16:13-14). The only explanation for the masculine is that the pronouns refer to a person. Relative pronouns are used in the same way in Ephesians 1:13-14. These indirect evidences confirm that the Holy Spirit is commonly regarded as a person in the Scripture. As Charles Hodge states: "He is introduced as a person so often, not merely in poetic or excited discourse, but in simple narrative, and in didactic instructions; and his personality is sustained by so many collateral proofs, that to explain the use of the personal pronouns in relation to Him on the principle of personification, is to do violence to all the rules of interpretation."[4]

IV. The Holy Spirit the Personal Object of Faith

Christians who have an intelligent comprehension of the truth regard the Holy Spirit as an object of their faith. This is done unconsciously rather than deliberately, their relation to the Spirit drawing out this response. According to the Scriptures it is possible to sin against the Holy Spirit (Isa. 63:10), grieve Him (Eph. 4:30), reverence Him (Ps. 51:11), and obey Him (Acts 10:19-21). It is impossible in the light of these Scriptures to regard the Holy Spirit intelligently without viewing Him as the personal object of faith. This is further confirmed by the baptismal formula in Matthew 28:19 where the Holy Spirit is associated on an equal basis with the Father and the Son, whose personality is generally accepted. Likewise the apostolic benediction of 2 Corinthians 13:14 indicates an equality of personality of the Trinity.

The only tenable position for those who accept the revelation of Scripture is to believe in the full-orbed personality of the Holy Spirit. This certainly has been the position of orthodox Christians from the beginning. As Charles Hodge expresses it, "The personality of the Spirit has been the faith of the Church from the beginning. It has few opponents in the chaotic period of theology; and in modern times has been denied by none but Socinians, Arians, and Sabellians."[5]

---

[4]Charles Hodge, *Systematic Theology*, I, 524.
[5]Charles Hodge, *ibid.*, I, 522.

Chapter II

THE DEITY OF THE HOLY SPIRIT

THE DEITY of the Holy Spirit has been a cardinal doctrine of the Christian faith from the beginning. The Arian controversy in the fourth century of the Christian era settled for all time the orthodox doctrine on both the personality and the deity of the Spirit. Arius, who held that the Holy Spirit was a created being, though he originally adhered to the personality of the Spirit later denied both His personality and His deity. His views were denounced by his contemporaries, and Arius was branded a heretic. From that day to this, orthodox Christianity has affirmed the deity and personality of the Spirit. As Hodge expresses it, "Since the fourth century his true divinity has never been denied by those who admit his personality."[1]

In the sacred Scriptures, the evidence for the deity of the Holy Spirit is superabundant. In general the doctrine is supported by the names and titles of the Holy Spirit, His identification and association with God, His procession and relation to the holy Trinity, His divine attributes, and His many divine works. These combine to confirm and enhance the significant contribution of each to the whole and harmonize in a great symphony of Scriptural testimony.

I. The Titles of the Holy Spirit

An examination of the Scriptural revelation on the Holy Spirit will indicate that He is nowhere assigned a formal name, such as we have for the Second Person, the Lord Jesus Christ, but is rather given descriptive titles, of which the most common in Scripture and in ordinary usage is the *Holy Spirit*. As His person is pure spirit, to which no material is essential, He is revealed in the Scriptures as the Spirit. The descriptive adjective *holy* is used to distinguish Him from other spirits which are creatures.

A study of the references to the Holy Spirit by various titles in Scripture will reveal some significant facts. The basic words in the original are also used in reference to entities other than the Holy Spirit. In the Old Testament, however, *ruach* is used over one hundred

---

[1] Charles Hodge, *Systematic Theology*, I, 527.

times for the Holy Spirit. The matter of interpretation enters into the problem. Cummings lists eighty-six references to the Holy Spirit in the Old Testament.[2] The American Standard Version of the Bible by means of initial capital letters indicates considerably more than this. In any case, the instances are numerous and well scattered throughout the Old Testament. Cummings notes that the Pentateuch has fourteen references, none in Leviticus, that Isaiah has thirteen and Ezekiel fifteen, and that the references are scattered throughout twenty-two of the thirty-nine books of the Old Testament.[3] The concise summary of Cummings on the significance of these references may well be quoted:

"It is impossible to say that the passages increase in number, or in clearness, with any special characteristic of the books of Scripture. They seem to bear no special relation to chronology, as they appear chiefly in Isaiah (750 B.C.), in Ezekiel (590 B.C.), and in the books of Moses. Nor can we trace any relation to the comparative spirituality of the books, though Isaiah stands so high in the list; for whereas Ezekiel stands first, the Judges has seven, Psalms has only six, Deuteronomy only one, and 2 Chronicles four. But it is possible to discern that each of the inspired writers has caught some special aspect of the Holy Spirit's person or work, which is reiterated in his pages. In Ezekiel, for instance, it is the action of the Holy Spirit in transporting the prophet bodily to the places where he is needed, which accounts for *six* of the passages out of fifteen. In Judges it is the in-breathing of courage or strength which is alluded to in every one of the seven passages. In Exodus it is as the Spirit of wisdom that He is specially—and exclusively—regarded. It is His office as the Giver of prophetic inspiration which is most constantly spoken of in the books of Samuel and the Chronicles. In Isaiah, and in the Psalms, the twofold teaching concerning Him is His connection with the Messiah on the one hand, and what may be called His personal qualities, such as being grieved, or vexed, by ingratitude or rebellion, on the other."[4]

In the New Testament, the references to the Holy Spirit are even more numerous. The New Testament word for the Spirit, *pneuma*, is found in two hundred and sixty-one passages, according to Cummings, scattered throughout all the major New Testament books.[5] To

---

[2] J. E. Cummings, *Through the Eternal Spirit*, p. 50.
[3] *Loc. cit.*
[4] *Ibid.*, pp. 51-52.
[5] *Ibid.*, p. 60.

quote Cummings, "The Gospels contain fifty-six passages; the Acts of the Apostles, fifty-seven; St. Paul's Epistles, one hundred and thirteen; and the other books, thirty-six."[6] From these facts, it may be clearly seen that there is consistent reference to the Holy Spirit from Genesis 1:2 to Revelation 22:17, and the inference is plain that a constant ministry of the Holy Spirit is maintained suitable for each dispensation. The titles of the Holy Spirit as commonly translated are subject to significant classification which furnishes an interesting background for the doctrine.

Titles of the Holy Spirit revealing His relationships. Of the many titles and variations in reference to the Holy Spirit, sixteen reveal His relationship to the other Persons of the Trinity. Eleven titles are found relating the Holy Spirit to the Father: (1) *Spirit of God* (Gen. 1:2; Matt. 3:16); (2) *Spirit of the Lord* (Luke 4:18); *Spirit of Our God* (1 Cor. 6:11); (4) *His Spirit* (Num. 11:29); (5) *Spirit of Jehovah* (Judg. 3:10); (6) *Thy Spirit* (Ps. 139:7); (7) *Spirit of the Lord God* (Isa. 61:1); (8) *Spirit of your Father* (Matt. 10:20); (9) *Spirit of the Living God* (2 Cor. 3:3); (10) *My Spirit* (Gen. 6:3); (11) *Spirit of Him* (Rom. 8:11).

Five titles are found relating the Holy Spirit to the Son: (1) *Spirit of Christ* (Rom. 8:9; 1 Pet. 1:11); (2) *Spirit of Jesus Christ* (Phil. 1:19); (3) *Spirit of Jesus* (Acts 16:7); (4) *Spirit of His Son* (Gal. 4:6); (5) *Spirit of the Lord* (Acts 5:9; 8:39). In some of these instances it is not clear whether the reference is to the Spirit from Christ, the Holy Spirit, or the Spirit of Christ Himself. The Greek form is the same. Most of them are probably references to the Holy Spirit.

While there is some distinction in meaning in the various titles, the chief significance is to bring out the relationship of the Holy Spirit as the Third Person of the Trinity, all affirming His deity and procession.

Titles of the Holy Spirit revealing His attributes. Abundant revelation is given in the titles of the Holy Spirit to disclose His attributes. At least seventeen of His titles indicate the divine attributes of His Person. (1) The unity of the Spirit is revealed in the title, *One Spirit* (Eph. 4:4). (2) Perfection is the implication of the title, *Seven Spirits* (Rev. 1:4; 3:1). (3) The identity of the Holy Spirit and the Essence of the Trinity is affirmed in the title, *the Lord the Spirit* (2 Cor. 3:18). (4) The eternity of the Spirit is seen in the

---

[6]*Loc. cit.*

title, *Eternal Spirit* (Heb. 9:14). (5) *Spirit of Glory* connotes His glory as being the same as the Father and the Son (1 Pet. 4:14). (6) *Spirit of Life* affirms the eternal life of the Spirit (Rom. 8:2). Three titles affirm the holiness of the Spirit: (7) *Spirit of Holiness* (Rom. 1:4), a possible reference to the holy human spirit of Christ; (8) *Holy Spirit* or *Holy Ghost* (Ps. 51:11; Matt. 1:20; Luke 11:13), the most formal title of the Spirit and most frequently used; (9) *Holy One* (1 John 2:20).

Five of the titles of the Holy Spirit refer to some extent to Him as the author of revelation and wisdom: (10) *Spirit of Wisdom* (Ex. 28:3; Eph. 1:17); (11) *Spirit of Wisdom and Understanding* (Isa. 11:2); (12) *Spirit of Counsel and Might* (Isa. 11:2); (13) *Spirit of Knowledge and of the Fear of the Lord* (Isa. 11:2); (14) *Spirit of Truth* (John 14:17). The transcendence of the Spirit is indicated (15) in the title, *Free Spirit* (Ps. 51:12). The attribute of grace is found in two titles, (16) *Spirit of Grace* (Heb. 10:29), and (17) *Spirit of Grace and Supplication* (Zech. 12:10).

Titles of the Holy Spirit revealing His works. Many of the titles referred to as indicating His attributes also connote His works. In the discussion of the titles revealing His attributes, it may be noticed that the *Spirit of Glory* (1 Pet. 4:14) engages in a work to bring the saints to glory. The *Spirit of Life* (Rom. 8:2) is the agent of regeneration. The *Spirit of Holiness* (Rom. 1:4), the *Holy Spirit* (Matt. 1:20), and *Holy One* (1 John 2:20) is our sanctifier. The *Spirit of Wisdom* (Eph. 1:17), the *Spirit of Wisdom and Understanding,* the *Spirit of Counsel and Might,* the *Spirit of Knowledge and of the Fear of the Lord* (Isa. 11:2) speak of the several ministries of God in teaching, guiding and strengthening the saint. The *Spirit of Truth* (John 14:17) has a similar idea. The Spirit as one who manifests grace is revealed in the titles, *Spirit of Grace* (Heb. 10:29), and the *Spirit of Grace and Supplication* (Zech. 12:10).

In addition to these, two other titles are given the Holy Spirit, affirming His works. (1) The *Spirit of Adoption* (Rom. 8:15) has reference to His revelation of our adoption as sons. (2) The *Spirit of Faith* (2 Cor. 4:13), while perhaps impersonal, and in this case not referring to the Holy Spirit as such, if admitted as a reference, it indicates the ministry of the Spirit in producing faith in us.

Another title of the Holy Spirit, which does not involve the name *spirit,* however, is that of *Comforter,* from *parakletos,* meaning, according to Thayer, when used in its widest sense, "*a helper, succorer, aider, assistant;* so of the Holy Spirit destined to take the place of Christ with the apostles."[7] It is found frequently in the New Testament (John 14:16, 26; 15:26; 16:7). It reveals the Holy Spirit as one who is always ready to help the Christian.

The many titles of the Holy Spirit with their manifold meanings speak eloquently of the beauties of His Person and the wonders of His attributes. The many aspects revealed speak of His infinite Person, equal in power and glory with the Father and the Son.

II. His Identification and Association With God

Identification with Jehovah. The deity of the Holy Spirit is shown not only by His titles but by His identification with Jehovah of the Old Testament. A comparison of Acts 28:25 and Isaiah 6:1-13 will show that the One described by the titles of both *Adonai* and *Jehovah* in Isaiah is identified with the Holy Spirit in Acts. Isaiah 6:9-10 is quoted in Acts 28:26-27 as spoken by the Holy Spirit while Isaiah attributes it to Jehovah and Adonai. A similar instance is found by comparison of Hebrews 10:15-17 with Jeremiah 31:31-34. What Jehovah declares in Jeremiah is attributed to the Holy Spirit in Hebrews. The title of Jehovah, reserved in Scripture for the true God, is therefore used of the Holy Spirit.

Identification with God. Other titles of deity in the Old and New Testament are also used of the Holy Spirit. The Spirit of Jehovah and the God of Israel are identified in 2 Samuel 23:2-3. Very commonly in the Old Testament the Holy Spirit is spoken of as God, the first instance occurring in Genesis 1:2. In a similar way, in the New Testament the Holy Spirit is considered God in many instances. The Christian indwelt by the Holy Spirit is said to be indwelt by God (1 Cor. 3:16; 6:19; Eph. 2:22). Blasphemy against the Holy Spirit is said to be an act against God (Matt. 12:31-32). The sin of Ananias in Acts 5:1-4 is declared to be both a sin against the Holy Spirit and against God.

Association of the Holy Spirit with the Father and the Son. The Holy Spirit is repeatedly associated with the Father and the Son on equal terms, which would indicate His deity. In the baptismal formula of Matthew 28:19, the Father, Son, and Holy Spirit are related on an equal basis. In fact, the use of the singular, *name*, seems to mean that the full name of deity is "Father, Son, and Holy Spirit." Another instance of such association is found in the apostolic benediction recorded in 2 Corinthians 13:14. In this frequently quoted

---

[7]J. H. Thayer, *Greek-English Lexicon of the New Testament*, p. 483.

verse, the persons of the Trinity are displayed as equals and accorded equal honor. It would certainly be difficult to justify such usage on any other basis.

Instances of such association can be multiplied. For instance, the inspiration of the prophets is traced to God in Hebrews 1:1, but to the Holy Spirit in 2 Peter 1:21. In other words, it is common practice to associate the Holy Spirit with God and with the Father and the Son.

III. THE PROCESSION OF THE HOLY SPIRIT

The doctrine of procession has to do with the being and eternity of the Holy Spirit in His relation to the Father and the Son. As a division of the doctrine of the Trinity, it affirms that the Holy Spirit is the Third Person of the Trinity, the same in substance and essence, and equal in power, eternity, and glory. The proper statement of the doctrine is that the Spirit proceeds eternally from the Father and the Son. Jacobs calls the activity of the Father and Son in this regard "spiration."[8]

The fact of the procession of the Holy Spirit. The doctrine of procession is based on Scripture and on inference. The early creeds of the Christian church gave attention to the proper statement of it. The Nicene Creed, for instance, states: "And I believe in the Holy Ghost, the Lord and giver of life, who *proceedeth* from the Father and the Son, who with the Father and Son together, is worshipped and glorified."[9] The Athanasian Creed speaks of it more briefly, "The Holy Ghost is of the Father and of the Son, neither made, nor created, not begotten, but *proceeding*."[10] In more recent times, the *Articles of the English Church* state the doctrine: "The Holy Ghost, *proceeding* from the Father and the Son, is of one substance, majesty, and glory, with the Father and the Son, very and eternal God."[11] The *Westminster Confession of Faith* has a similar statement: "In the unity of the Godhead there be three persons of one substance, power, and eternity; God the Father, God the Son, and God the Holy Ghost. The Father is of none, neither begotten nor proceeding; the Son is eternally begotten of the Father; the Holy Ghost eternally proceeding from the Father and the Son."[12]

---

[8]H. E. Jacobs, *A Summary of the Christian Faith*, p. 54.
[9]Cited by Watson, *op. cit.*, p. 628. The phrase "and the Son" was added in 589.
[10]Cited by Watson, *loc. cit.*
[11]Cited by Watson, *loc. cit.*
[12]*The Constitution of the Presbyterian Church in the U. S. A.* (1946 edition), p. 19.

The abundant creedal evidence while not possessing the infallible inspiration of the Bible may be taken as conclusive proof that the large portion of evangelical Christendom accepts without question this doctrine. While the statements vary, the fact of the procession is clearly stated in all as being eternal, distinguished from generation.

The wide acceptance of the doctrine by theologians and church creeds is caused by specific Scriptural testimony to it. While in its precise nature the character of the procession is inscrutable, it provides a definition of the relationship of the persons of the Trinity. Important Scripture texts such as John 15:26 and Psalm 104:30 have been accepted as explicit proof. In John 15:26, the Comforter whom Christ promised to send is referred to as, "the Spirit of truth, which proceedeth from the Father." The word for "proceedeth" (*ekpo-reuetai*) is in the present tense in the original, which has been accepted without much opposition as indicating the eternal and continuous relation of the Spirit to the First Person. Psalm 104:30 is a similar reference, "Thou sendest forth thy spirit."

Additional proof of the fact of the procession of the Holy Spirit is found in the frequent reference to the Spirit as being "of God" or "of Christ" (1 Cor. 2:11-12; Gal. 4:6; Rom. 8:9). From these two avenues of proof, it may be concluded that the procession is a Scriptural doctrine.

The eternity of the procession of the Holy Spirit. Among the several conclusions which form a part of the doctrine of procession is the fact that the procession of the Holy Spirit is eternal. There has not been uniformity of opinion in the whole of Christendom on the subject, the question being raised early in the history of the church along with the other questions in the field of theology proper. The Greek Orthodox and the Roman Catholic churches have failed to reach agreement to this day on the subject, the Greek Catholic Church affirming that the procession is to be identified with the incarnation of Christ, in the sense that both occurred at the same time, while the Roman Church affirms the eternal nature of the procession. Protestant churches have followed the Roman view.

That the procession of the Spirit is eternal is borne out by the Scripture passages none of which recognize any point in time. The inference from John 15:26 is certainly that of an eternal relation. The most obvious difficulty with the view of the Greek Church is that the Holy Spirit is operative in the Old Testament, and the procession was then a fact (Ps. 104:30). The work of the Holy Spirit in creation and all subsequent operations involves the procession of the Spirit.

The very nature of procession points to its eternity. Procession like the eternal generation of Christ is not a matter of creation, commencement of existence, or analogous in any way to physical relationships common in the human realm. It proceeds rather from the very nature of the Godhead, being necessary to its existence. Without the Holy Spirit, the Godhead would not be what it is. The procession of the Holy Spirit cannot be compared to the incarnation, as the incarnation was not essential to deity, though it serves to reveal the attributes of love and righteousness as they combine in grace.

The relation of procession and generation. Theologians have borrowed the Scriptural distinctions as to the eternal relation of the Second and Third Persons to the First Person. In speaking of the Son, the Scriptures affirm His generation eternally (Ps. 2:7), while in speaking of the Spirit, the word *proceed* is used, as we have seen. No human mind can improve on these distinctions, even if it be admitted that the terms are inadequate to comprehend all the truth which they represent. Generation must be guarded from all purely anthropomorphic ideas, and proceeding must be made eternal. The terms cannot be reversed. Though Christ may be said to have proceeded from the Father, it cannot be said of the Spirit that He is generated.

Procession from the Father and the Son. Most of the controversy historically concerning the doctrine of procession centers in the question of whether the Spirit proceeds from the Son as well as from the Father. The early creeds such as the Nicene (325) and its revision at the Council of Constantinople (381) did not state procession from the Son though it was commonly believed.[13] The Council of Toledo, which represented only the western church, added the phrase *filioque,* meaning, "and the Son," to the statement of procession in 589. This aroused the opposition of the Greek church, which had not been consulted, who denied this teaching thereafter. The Greek church argued that the major text, John 15:26, affirmed only procession from the Father. The western or Roman church argued that the Spirit obviously proceeded from the Son as well as the Father. Their Scriptural support included Galatians 4:6, "the Spirit of his Son," and Romans 8:9, "the Spirit of Christ." They further argued that the Spirit is sent by the Son as much as by the Father (John 16:7).

---

[13]According to Smeaton, Athanasius, Didymus, Epiphanius, Gregory Nyssen, Basil, Augustine and others all taught this doctrine and no voice was raised against it until Theodoret in 431. Cf. George Smeaton, *The Doctrine of the Holy Spirit,* pp. 317-19.

It also helps to justify the divine order in the Trinity, of First, Second, and Third Persons, which if the Spirit did not proceed from the Son would tend to make difficult a real distinction between the Son and the Spirit in this divine order. The argument for the procession from the Son as well as from the Father became the orthodox point of view of both Roman and Reformed churches.

Relation of procession to the work of the Holy Spirit. While the doctrine of procession may seem somewhat of a technicality except to theologians, it has a vital bearing upon the work of the Holy Spirit as revealed in the Scriptures. In the case of Christ, His eternal generation involved the work of the Son which was accomplished in time, fulfilling the purpose of redemption. As Christ became an obedient Son in doing the Father's will, so the Holy Spirit in procession became obedient to the Father and the Son. This subordination without detracting from the eternal glory and divine attributes which characterized all three Persons is taught specifically in the Scriptures (John 14:16, 26; 15:26; 16:7). The ministry of the Third Person is performed in His own power and gives testimony to His eternal deity and glory, but it is accomplished on behalf of the Father and the Son. Hence, the Spirit is sent into the world to reveal truth on behalf of Christ (John 16:13-15), with the special mission of making the things of Christ known and magnifying the Father and the Son. He is not seeking His own glory any more than the Son sought His own glory while in the period of humiliation.

In the work of both the Son and the Spirit, an illustration of the respective doctrines of eternal generation and procession can be seen. While the Father sends the Son and the Spirit, the Son never sends the Father, but does send the Spirit. The Spirit neither sends the Father nor the Son, but is subordinate to Their will which at all times is His own will, and accomplishes His work in the earth. While the nature of procession is largely inscrutable, it is an expression in human words based on the Scriptural revelation of the relationship of the persons of the Trinity to each other.

IV. The Attributes of the Holy Spirit

The Scriptural revelation concerning the attributes of the Holy Spirit points unmistakably to the conclusion that the Holy Spirit possesses full deity. This can be demonstrated in at least seven particulars.

(1) The Holy Spirit is revealed as possessing life (Rom. 8:2). The context indicates spiritual or eternal life is in view, which, originally, was the possession of God alone, now bestowed on some of

His creatures through regeneration. (2) The attribute of personality has abundant witness as already demonstrated. (3) The Holy Spirit is omnipresent (Ps. 139:7), an attribute only God may possess. (4) Omniscience belongs to the Holy Spirit (1 Cor. 2:10-11), and (5) omnipotence, as illustrated in His work of creation (Gen. 1:2). (6) Holiness is frequently assigned the One who is distinctively known as the Holy Spirit (Luke 11:13). (7) The eternity of the Spirit is revealed also in Scripture (Heb. 9:14). The nature of the attributes are such that they could not all be communicated to a creature. From the explicit revelation of the attributes of the Holy Spirit, it may be concluded that His deity is fully sustained in Scripture.[14]

V. The Works of the Holy Spirit

The deity of the Holy Spirit is demonstrated also in His works. As the work of the Holy Spirit constitutes the bulk of the present treatment in this volume, it is necessary only to illustrate the character of this argument here. All of the works of the Holy Spirit bear the marks of His deity. By way of illustration, the work of the Spirit in creation may be cited (Gen. 1:2). Obviously the work of creation is a work of deity. The work of the Spirit in regeneration is another illustration (John 3:6). Only God can give spiritual life to those spiritually dead. The sanctification of the believer can also be mentioned (2 Thess. 2:13). Only God can make the unholy holy in any real sense. Anyone who accepts Scriptural testimony at its face value comes easily and quickly to the conclusion that the Holy Spirit is God as revealed in His works.[15]

Of the deity of the Holy Spirit, we may conclude with Charles Hodge, concerning the Holy Spirit, "He is therefore presented in the Scriptures as the proper object of worship, not only in the formula of baptism and in the apostolic benediction, which bring the doctrine of the Trinity into constant remembrance as the fundamental truth of our religion, but also in the constant requirement that we look to Him and depend on Him for all spiritual good, and reverence and obey Him as our divine teacher and sanctifier."[16]

---

[14]L. S. Chafer mentions also the attributes of divine love, truthfulness, and faithfulness as attributes proving the Spirit's deity. Cf. L. S. Chafer, *Systematic Theology*, VI, 24-25.

[15]L. S. Chafer lists seventeen works of the Holy Spirit as proving deity: creation, striving, inspiration, generating Christ, convincing, restraining, regeneration, illumination, work as Paraclete, witnessing, anointing, baptism, sealing, filling, intercession, sanctification, and as an earnest. Cf. L. S. Chafer, *op. cit.*, VI, 26-46.

[16]Charles Hodge, *op. cit.*, I, 528.

CHAPTER III

THE TYPOLOGY OF THE HOLY SPIRIT

FOR THE most part typology is a neglected area of systematic theology. Devoted to enrichment and illustration of doctrine otherwise revealed, typology obviously has some limitations. It is not intended to establish doctrine in itself. It is susceptible to misuse in that its interpretation is open to personal bias and human opinion to a greater extent than explicit statements of Scripture. Like other figures of speech in the Bible such as allegory, emblems, metaphors, parables, similes and symbols, it is useful only when used with care. Some would sharply limit the use of typology to those explicitly mentioned as such. A study of this area of typology will lead to the conclusion that this constitutes only a small fraction of the typology actually intended in the Scripture. Accordingly in the present study of the typology of the Holy Spirit, attention will be directed to types which are commonly recognized even if not specifically mentioned as such in the Bible.

The importance of typology as a means of illustrating spiritual truth has not been recognized as it should. Lewis Sperry Chafer speaking of this writes: "It is needful to remember that behind every form of utterance there is a reality of truth, which truth must not be underestimated because of the form in which it is presented. All these varied forms of speech which the Bible employs are directly chosen and utilized by God the Holy Spirit. They in no way represent mere literary notions of men."[1]

Typology plays a relatively minor role in the doctrine of the Holy Spirit as compared to Christology where types abound. Such types as are used of the Holy Spirit serve to emphasize and illustrate a doctrine which might otherwise be difficult to understand fully. The types are here treated in alphabetical order.

I. CLOTHED WITH POWER

In Luke 24:49, Christ instructed His disciples, "And behold, I send forth the promise of my Father upon you: but tarry ye in the

---

[1]L. S. Chafer, *Systematic Theology*, VI, 47.

city, until ye be clothed with power from on high." It seems clear
that Christ was predicting the experience of Pentecost when they
were filled with the Spirit. The use of the figure of clothing for this
work indicates its outward character, its covering of human weakness, and its function as an official vestment identifying a person as
a divine representative. The use of clothing as a figure to reveal
spiritual truth is found frequently in Scripture (2 Cor. 5:3; Eph.
4:24; 6:11-17; Col. 3:10, 12; 1 Thess. 5:8; Rev. 19:8, 13-14). As Marsh
points out in his thorough discussion of this type[2] the Scriptures
distinguish between spiritual garments which we put on ourselves
(Rom. 13:12; Eph. 4:24; 6:11, 14; Col. 3:10, 12; 1 Thess. 5:8) and
those which God puts on us. Our clothing with power is that which
God puts on us. It is to provide complete enablement for the appointed
task. It is related to the filling of the Spirit as the outer evidence of
the inward work of the Spirit. It is therefore power manifested in
individuals and circumstances touched by the ministry of the apostles.

II. THE DOVE

The use of the dove as a type of the Holy Spirit is indicated in
the description of the baptism of Christ. On that occasion all four
Gospels mention that the Holy Spirit descended upon Christ in
the form of a dove (Matt. 3:16; Mark 1:10; Luke 3:22; John 1:32).
Aside from this reference, the type is not explained in Scripture. The
only other mentions are the instances where Christ spoke of being
"harmless as doves" (Matt. 10:16) and the reference to selling of
doves in the temple for sacrifice (Matt. 21:12; Mark 11:15; Luke 2:24;
John 2:14, 16).

In the Old Testament, the dove is mentioned principally as an
acceptable sacrifice and is a type of Christ rather than of the Spirit.
The dove released by Noah after the flood is sometimes taken as typical of the ministry of the Holy Spirit in the various dispensations.
Mackintosh finds it typical of the "renewed mind . . . which seeks
and finds its rest and portion in Christ."[3] As a distinct type of the
Holy Spirit the only clear reference is in the Gospels.

From the nature of a dove when used as a type of the Spirit, it
may be inferred that at least four aspects of the Holy Spirit are in
view: (1) beauty; (2) gentleness; (3) peace; (4) heavenly nature
and origin. The dove by its general characteristics is well suited to
be a type of the Holy Spirit.

---

[2]F. E. Marsh, *Emblems of the Holy Spirit*, pp. 229-41.
[3]C. H. Mackintosh, *Notes on Genesis*, 4th ed., p. 104.

III. The Earnest of the Spirit

The accepted meaning of the Greek word *arrabon*, translated *earnest* in its three occurrences in the New Testament (2 Cor. 1:22; 5:5; Eph. 1:14), is that of a pledge or token payment. Thayer defines it, "Money which in purchases is given as a pledge that the full amount will subsequently be paid."[4] The Holy Spirit Himself rather than His gifts is the Earnest. He is the token and pledge that all the Father has promised while not ours now as to actual enjoyment is nevertheless our possession and will be ours to enjoy later. F. E. Marsh illustrates it in this manner: "'All things are ours,' not as to actual or full enjoyment, but as to possession or security; just as a child who is heir to property left to him, and is allowed a certain part of it until he becomes of age, when he may enter into and enjoy the whole, is assured the property is none the less his, although he has not come into full possession."[5]

Of what is the Spirit the Earnest? The Scriptures make it clear. All the future blessings of God are assured by the presence of the Holy Spirit. His presence is our guarantee. Our inheritance, our salvation, our glory, our fellowship with God, our likeness unto Him, our freedom from sin and its evils, all are represented in the token payment of the Person of the Spirit.

IV. Fire

Fire is used in Scripture in many typical senses just as other figures frequently have more than one application. For instance, the dove is a type of Christ as well as a type of the Spirit. Marsh in his classic work on emblems mentions six symbolic uses of the word *fire* apart from reference to the Holy Spirit: (1) symbol of Lord's presence (Ex. 3:2); (2) the Lord's approval (Lev. 9:24; 1 Kings 18:38; 2 Chron. 7:1); (3) the Lord's protection (Ex. 13:21; Zech. 2:5); (4) the Lord's discipline and testing (Mal. 3:3; 1 Pet. 1:7; Heb. 12:29; Rev. 1:14); (5) emblem of God's Word (Jer. 5:14; 20:9); (6) God's judgment (Lev. 10:2).[6]

The seventh use of fire is in reference to the Holy Spirit. On the Day of Pentecost, in connection with the work of the Spirit on that occasion "there appeared unto them tongues parting asunder, like as of fire; and it sat upon each one of them" (Acts 2:3). Immediately

---

[4] J. H. Thayer, *Greek-English Lexicon of the New Testament*, p. 75.
[5] Marsh, *op. cit.*, p. 242.
[6] Marsh, *ibid.*, pp. 114-15. Cf. also p. 113 where Marsh lists in different fashion fourteen meanings or uses of the word *fire*.

the Scriptures record they were filled with the Spirit (Acts 2:4). The Scriptures do not interpret this event as far as the mention of fire is concerned. Judging by previous usage, the appearance of fire carried with it the thought of the Lord's presence, approval, protection, and cleansing and sanctifying for the ministry before them. It was like the descent of the cloud upon the newly constructed Tabernacle in the wilderness and the newly built temple of Solomon (Ex. 40:34; 1 Kings 8:10-11) which at night had the appearance of fire. It was designed to set them apart for the service and testimony which was before them.

The reference to baptism by fire in Matthew 3:11-12 does not seem to be related to the Holy Spirit. The immediate context following relates to the second advent of Christ and the burning of the "chaff" with "unquenchable fire" (Matt. 3:12). The baptism of the Spirit which begins the present age is set in contrast to the baptism of fire which will begin the millennial age.

V. Oil

Oil played an important part in the lives of God's people in both the Old and the New Testament. Uniformly, when used in a typical way, it has reference to the ministry of the Holy Spirit. In the Tabernacle the pure olive oil kept the lamp burning continually in the holy place, speaking eloquently of the ministry of the Holy Spirit in revelation and illumination. Apart from the oil and light it gave, the glories of Christ portrayed in the embroidered linen, the lampstand, the table of showbread and other items would have been left in complete darkness. The way into the holy of holies would not have been made plain (Ex. 27:20-21).

In the sacrifices oil was used as an important ingredient. In the meal offering (Lev. 2:1-16) oil was mingled with the flour and also poured upon it. Lewis Sperry Chafer writes: "All this anticipates in type the life and ministry of Christ in His unique relation to the Holy Spirit, which relationship He maintained while here on earth— a relationship in which Christ's humanity was sustained and His actions empowered by the Holy Spirit."[7] Oil was also used in the ceremony for the cleansing of lepers (Lev. 14:10-29).

In the induction of the priests and the consecration of the Tabernacle, oil was used (Ex. 40:9-16; Lev. 8). The oil was used not only for Aaron, representing the Spirit in relation to Christ our High Priest, but also for his sons, representing the Spirit in relation to the

---

[7]L. S. Chafer, *ibid.*, VI, 47.

believer. The Tabernacle and all the things within were also anointed
with oil including the altar. It speaks of the ministry of the Spirit
in all aspects of the work of redemption. Oil was used also in the
induction of kings to their office (1 Sam. 10:1; 16:13; 1 Kings 1:39;
Ps. 23:5; etc.). It connects the work of the Spirit with the functions
of the kingly office.

Oil was also a commonly used food (Rev. 6:6), sometimes as
medicine (Mark 6:13; James 5:14), and even as a means of commodity
exchange (1 Kings 5:11). In these instances no typical meaning is
necessarily intended. In connection with the parable of the ten vir-
gins (Matt. 25:3-8), while the oil used in the lamps was in keeping
with ordinary custom, probably a typical and spiritual meaning is
intended as a work of the Spirit. Mention can also be made of the
expression "oil of gladness" (Ps. 45:7) quoted in Hebrews 1:9 of
the joy of the Spirit.

In its typical meaning, as illustrated in both the Old and New
Testaments, oil is used to represent the concepts of holiness, sanctification, revelation, illumination, dedication, healing, and sustaining.
As the type is the shadow of the reality, it serves to reveal the abundant
ministry of the Holy Spirit to the believer.

VI. Seal

Three times in the New Testament the Holy Spirit is represented
as a seal of the believer's redemption (2 Cor. 1:22; Eph. 1:13; 4:30).
It seems evident that the Holy Spirit is Himself the seal rather than
the one who does the sealing. His very presence indwelling the
believer is the sign and seal of the ultimate fulfillment of God's
redemptive purpose in that individual. The word *seal* indicates (1)
security, (2) safety, (3) ownership, (4) authority. Marsh suggests
in addition (5) "Among men a seal signifies a finished transaction";
(6) that the seal constitutes a mark of recognition; (7) that the seal
implies secrecy and (8) obligation; and that "the seal leaves an impression upon the wax which corresponds to it."[8] All this finds beautiful fulfillment in the life of the believer. It provides security and
assurance that God will fulfill His promise of redemption.

VII. Servant

The Holy Spirit in His ministries often assumes the work of a
servant. Just as the Lord Jesus Christ was sent into the world to be

---

[8]Marsh, *ibid.*, pp. 29, 33-34, 36.

a Servant, so the Holy Spirit also serves. Out of the Old Testament a typical illustration of this is afforded in the story of the servant of Abraham seeking a wife for Isaac. While not authorized by explicit Scripture, the similarities are obvious. Like the servant of Abraham, the Holy Spirit is seeking a bride for Isaac the only begotten Son, a type of Christ. Like the servant, He is successful and presents the bride at the close of the day. The details of the story, the journey into the far country, the bride given gifts, the bride deciding for herself, and the journey to Isaac in which the bride forsakes all others combine to unfold a typology that illustrates the present work of the Spirit of God.

VIII. WATER

The abundance in which water has been created makes it a good type for that which is infinite. In this sense it is used of God's all-powerful judgment as illustrated in the flood and the Red Sea. A second important use is that signifying the Word of God, which is infinite in truth and in extent of revelation (John 3:5; Eph. 5:26). Water is also used poetically of distress and tribulation (Ps. 69:2, 14). Of point here is its typical meaning in connection with the Holy Spirit, the infinite Third Person, constituting the third important typical aspect of water in the Scriptures.

Two important Scripture references use water as a symbol of the Holy Spirit and His ministry. In John 4:14, in connection with our Lord's dealing with the Samaritan woman, it is revealed, "Who-soever drinketh of the water that I shall give him shall never thirst; but the water that I shall give him shall become in him a well of water springing up into eternal life." This passage coupled with the further revelation in John 7:37-39 is best interpreted as relating to the Holy Spirit. This is expressly stated in the second passage: "If any man thirst, let him come unto me and drink. He that believeth on me, as the scripture hath said, from within him shall flow rivers of living water. But this spake he of the Spirit, which they that believed on him were to receive: for the Spirit was not yet given; because Jesus was not yet glorified" (John 7:37-39; cf. Song of Sol. 4:12, 15; Prov. 5:15-16; Isa. 41:17-18; 43:2, 19-20; 58:11; Jer. 31:12). The well of water of John 4 becomes the spring of rivers of water in John 7. Thus is predicted the ministry of the Holy Spirit begun at Pentecost and continuing through the present age. The figure includes the eternal life springing from the Spirit, and the power, abundance, and cleansing of His ministry. It constitutes not only a revelation, but a challenge to let the indwelling Spirit of God make our hearts the origin of this outflow of spiritual blessing.

IX. WIND

Wind is well suited to be a type or symbol of the Holy Spirit in that the characteristics of wind are similar to those of the Holy Spirit in many respects. The power, invisibleness, immaterial nature, and sovereign purpose of wind in creation have their counterpart in the person and work of the Spirit. Wind is often mentioned in Scripture in perfectly natural contexts, of course, from Genesis 8:1, the first mention, to Revelation 7:1, the last. Three passages stand out, however, as using wind as a symbol of the work of the Spirit.

In John 3:8, wind is used as an illustration of the work of the Spirit in the new birth: "The wind bloweth where it will, and thou hearest the voice thereof, but knowest not whence it cometh, and whither it goeth: so is every one that is born of the Spirit." In this passage the immaterial character of the Spirit as invisible yet sovereignly accomplishing the divine work is presented.

In Acts 2:1-2, wind is a symbol of the coming of the Spirit: "And when the day of Pentecost was now come, they were all together in one place. And suddenly there came from heaven a sound as of the rushing of a mighty wind, and it filled all the house where they were sitting." While the wind is not explicitly connected with the Spirit, the outer phenomena were clearly intended to imply the work of the Spirit which was accomplished. Just as the wind "filled all the house where they were sitting," so "they were all filled with the Holy Spirit" (Acts 2:4). It speaks of the mighty power of the Spirit and God's sovereignty in the coming of the Spirit.

A third instance which may be related to this type is found in 2 Peter 1:21 where in connection with the inspiration of the prophets of old it is declared, "men spake from God, being moved by the Holy Spirit." While the word *wind* does not appear in the verse, the imagery is that of a "ship . . . driven by the wind."[9] The motive power and direction of the prophets was the Spirit of God so that the prophecy was of God.

All of the types and symbols taken together present much of the ministry of the Holy Spirit given explicitly in the Scriptures. By the Spirit the yielded believer is clothed with power from on high, sanctified and made secure by His presence, anointed and set apart for service.

---

[9]Chafer, *op. cit.*, VI, 53.

By the Spirit the Word is illumined so that we can understand the perfections of Christ. Abundant in power and sovereign in purpose, the Spirit deals with our lives. Every important work of the Spirit is prefigured in the types and symbols. To such an infinite and glorious person we can yield our hearts and lives in worship, love, and obedience.

PART TWO

THE HOLY SPIRIT IN THE OLD TESTAMENT

CHAPTER IV

THE HOLY SPIRIT
IN THE ETERNAL PURPOSE OF GOD

THE GREAT Dutch theologian of the last century, Abraham Kuyper, in beginning his classic work, *The Work of the Holy Spirit,* struck a note which every careful student of the doctrine of the Holy Spirit will echo when he wrote, "The need of divine guidance is never more deeply felt than when one undertakes to give instruction in the work of the Holy Spirit—so unspeakably tender is the subject, touching the inmost secrets of God and the soul's deepest mysteries. We shield instinctively the intimacies of kindred and friends from intrusive observation, and nothing hurts the sensitive heart more than the rude exposure of that which should not be unveiled, being beautiful only in the retirement of the home circle. Greater delicacy befits our approach to the holy mystery of our soul's intimacy with the *living God*."[1]

The subject of the work of the Holy Spirit is frequently based on explicit revelation, the contemplation of which affords the devout soul exquisite delight. Some aspects are revealed in less detail, requiring on the part of all who study them most careful interpretation to avoid error. Frequently a great field of truth is revealed in a few scattered Scriptures. All must share some feeling of futility in endeavoring to display the beauties of infinite truth, the field being so vast, the danger of warping or slighting the truth ever being present.

Two great dangers in interpretation are apparent as illustrated in the literature on the subject. First, we are ever prone to interpret Scripture through experience, instead of interpreting experience through Scripture. The factor of human experience is very close to some aspects of the doctrine of the Holy Spirit, but experience may not be normal, and if normal may not be properly interpreted. Much harm has come through arbitrary doctrines established in the last analysis on experience rather than revelation. A second danger, in the opposite extreme, is to limit the doctrine of the Holy Spirit to facts accepted by all. Much that is spiritual is not subject to proof sufficient to satisfy all. Inductions carefully made, and in keeping

---

[1] Abraham Kuyper, *The Work of the Holy Spirit,* p. 3.

with all known revelation, are often necessary to bring out all the beauty of doctrine. The Scriptures have been expressly formed to be apparent to those who are taught by the Holy Spirit Himself while a closed book to cold reason and precise logic. One who appreciates these dangers comes with a renewed sense of dependence on the Holy Spirit Himself to teach the intimate truths relating to His works.

It is natural that more attention be given to the New than to the Old Testament, with which we are primarily concerned at present. The Old Testament, however, affords an important introduction to the revelation of the New Testament. The similarities and contrasts bring out the truth of the New Testament in greater beauty. The doctrine of the Holy Spirit is not complete until viewed as a whole from eternity to eternity. It may then be seen that His work is all part of one majestic purpose of God to display His own attributes and work His own will.

It is fundamental to any doctrine that it be related to the sovereign purpose of God. The doctrine of the Holy Spirit is no exception. Behind the work of the Holy Spirit in time is the work of the Holy Spirit in eternity. While possibly distinct from the doctrine of the work of the Holy Spirit in the Old Testament, in that its major revelation is found in the New Testament, the work of the Holy Spirit in eternity past is considered here as a proper introduction to His work in the Old Testament period. No attempt will be made, therefore, to limit the discussion to the Old Testament in this foundational subject.

All events of every classification are properly included in the one eternal decree of God. For the purpose of analysis and study, however, they may be conceived as falling into certain divisions, among them the work of the Holy Spirit. While theologians have given surprisingly little attention to this important aspect of the eternal decree, all who accept the sovereignty of God will agree that the work of the Holy Spirit is vital and essential to the whole and may be safely inferred. An examination of this field of truth will reveal at least four major phases of the work of the Holy Spirit as directly involved in the plan of salvation.

I. OBEDIENCE OF THE HOLY SPIRIT

The doctrine of procession states that the Holy Spirit proceeded from the Father and the Son as the Son proceeds from the Father. Based on this eternal relationship of the persons of the Trinity, it may be inferred that in the eternal plan of salvation the Holy Spirit undertook to be obedient to the First and Second Persons. The obedience of the Holy Spirit as revealed in a number of Scriptures

(John 14:16-17, 26; 15:26; 16:7, 13) is not confined to any one dispensation, but it is rather the norm for every age. The Scriptures of the Old and New Testaments never reverse the order of obedience. As the Son is always obedient to the Father, so the Spirit is always obedient to the Father and the Son. This must not be taken to imply any inferiority of the Holy Spirit as to His person, but rather a willing subordination in keeping with His person and the unity of purpose of the Godhead. This subordination of the Holy Spirit is essential to all His ministry and characterizes all that is revealed. As it behooved Christ to be obedient even unto death, so it is harmonious with all that we know of God and His work that the Holy Spirit should be the unseen obedient servant of God, speaking of Christ rather than Himself, glorifying the Father rather than His own Person directly. Yet, as Christ in humiliation brought to Himself the added glory of being the Saviour, so the Holy Spirit will ultimately bring to Himself the glory of being ever subordinate to the will of the Father, thus glorifying the eternal Godhead and fulfilling the fundamental purpose which underlies all the details of events.

II. PART IN CREATION AND PROVIDENCE

From the use of *elohim* in the creation narrative, it may be assumed that the Holy Spirit had a part in creation. This inference is sustained by explicit Scriptures which will be subject to later discussion. It is in keeping with all that is revealed about Him in Scripture. Not only in creation, but also in preservation of creation the Holy Spirit undoubtedly has His part. While the distinct features of this work are not revealed, we may assume that One who is immanent in the world bears a sustaining relation to it. All this is a part of the original undertaking of the Holy Spirit.

III. MINISTRY TO THE SECOND PERSON

Under all circumstances the Persons of the Trinity are mutually sustaining, being one in essence. During the period of kenosis, however, a special problem arises in relation to the Second Person. As a part of the eternal purpose of the Persons of the Trinity, the Holy Spirit undertook all the ministry necessary to sustain the Second Person during the period in which the outward display of glory and power was laid aside in some measure. In the plan, the Third Person undertook to beget the Second Person (the Son) of the Virgin Mary, to fill Him, and to supply all necessary enablement to sustain the Son in the sphere of His humiliation and empower Him for His life among men. This important subject in its several aspects will be considered in detail in a later section.

The fact that the Holy Spirit undertook this ministry is not explicitly revealed, but may be concluded from the nature of the eternal purpose which is based on specific revelation (Acts 2:23; Rom. 8:29; 1 Cor. 2:7; 2 Tim. 1:9; Titus 1:2). As essential to the program of redemption and the salvation of the elect, the Holy Spirit must have assumed this part of the plan. In its place, it is as essential to the whole as any other major aspect of the purpose of God.

IV. Ministry to the Saints

Major emphasis is usually given the part of the Father and the Son in the eternal plan of God, the part of the Holy Spirit being assumed but seldom defined. Both A. A. Hodge[2] and Charles Hodge[3] fail to discuss the part of the Holy Spirit in their treatment of the "covenant of redemption." While the Scriptures direct attention particularly to the Father and the Son in the divine purpose to provide salvation, the part of the Holy Spirit in applying the benefits of grace secured through the death of Christ is of great importance. All the work of the Holy Spirit is related to the sovereign purpose of God in salvation, but some features of His work are especially significant and may be traced briefly here.

Eternal life. The impartation of eternal life is essential to the fulfillment of the plan of redemption. The Scriptures reveal all three persons of the Trinity as being related to it. The First Person becomes the Father of the believer (1 Cor. 8:6; Eph. 4:6). The life of the Second Person becomes the possession of the believer (John 11:25; 14:6; 1 John 5:12). The Third Person is said to regenerate (John 3:5; Titus 3:5). The efficient agent in regeneration is manifestly the Third Person. His work is essential to the bestowal of eternal life.

Revelation. The whole field of impartation of divine wisdom to man is peculiarly the area of ministry of the Holy Spirit. It is God's eternal purpose to make Himself known, and it is the work of the Holy Spirit to carry out this purpose. As in other important ministries, the other persons of the Trinity are vitally related to revelation. Christ, for instance, in His life and ministry revealed God. In every age, however, the Holy Spirit is active in revealing God, even during the lifetime of Christ in the flesh.

---

[2]*Outlines of Theology*, p. 372.
[3]*Systematic Theology*, II, 354-66.

Three phases of revelation are observed in the Scriptures. First, the Holy Spirit gives revelation in the primary sense of making known the will of God and His wisdom. As will be seen in later discussion, this took the form of oral prophecy and various means by which God made known His will to man. This field of revelation had to do with facts about God and creation which would not have been known apart from divine revelation. This form of revelation was especially prevalent before the time of Moses, but is found throughout Scripture to some extent. A second aspect of revelation is found in the inspiration of the written Word. The work of the Spirit here had sometimes to do with revelation in the primary sense, as in the case of prophecy or events prior to human history, and in other cases in infallible guidance in recording the history of man. In it all, the work of the Spirit is observed in the final record which is equally inspired in all parts regardless of source of knowledge, guaranteeing accuracy and finality in revelation. A third phase of revelation has to do with the illumination of the inspired Word, making it known to man, applying it to specific problems. The objective of all forms of revelation is to impart to man the wisdom of God in such measure and in such detail as harmonizes with the purposes of God. This field of doctrine is subject to extended discussion and will be treated more at length in later sections. Sufficient here is the statement that the work of imparting divine wisdom is peculiarly the work of the Holy Spirit and a part of His responsibility.

Indwelling presence of the Holy Spirit. While the Holy Spirit is omnipresent in every dispensation, it is part of His ministry to indwell the saints living in the church age and in the millennium. The personal presence of the Holy Spirit as indwelling the saint is an evident mark of divine grace and the seat of many of His ministries. While both the Father and the Son are said to indwell believers in this age, the preponderance of Scripture revealing the ministry of the Holy Spirit in the believer demonstrates that while the Godhead is present, the ministry thereof is committed in large measure, though not exclusively, to the Holy Spirit. He is Their agent, and through His ministry Their purposes are realized. These truths are in harmony with the nature of the Third Person, and His relation to the other persons of the Trinity.

Enablement for all spiritual service. Throughout various dispensations, a work of the Holy Spirit may be observed in the form of enablement for spiritual service. Because of the fall, man in himself cannot please God or serve Him. The work of the Spirit in every age provides the power and wisdom necessary for various works.

Enablement is especially related to the work of the Holy Spirit in filling individuals. In the Old Testament, this work was sovereign and not universal among believers. In the New Testament, during the church age and the millennium, the ministry of the Spirit in filling the saint is possible for all saints. Differences in kind of enablement and extent of enablement may be observed, in keeping with dispensational distinctions. In it all, a sovereign work of God for man may be observed, an essential part of God's program.

Sanctification. A most important part of God's purpose for man is his ultimate sanctification. The Holy Spirit, according to the Scriptures (Rom. 15:16; 2 Thess. 2:13), has a vital ministry in sanctifying the believer. All three persons of the Trinity are related to sanctification in Scripture, but the Holy Spirit is particularly active in effecting the progressive or experiential aspect of it. Practically all His ministry to the believer is related more or less to the believer's sanctification.

Intercession. The nature of the intercessory work of the Holy Spirit is revealed in only one passage (Rom. 8:26). The limited reference is no token of limited significance, however, as the importance of this ministry is apparent. Not only does the Holy Spirit guide the believer when he prays, but He intercedes on behalf of the believer. As Christ intercedes for the believer in heaven, so the Holy Spirit intercedes for the believer on earth, both being effective, and each mutually sustaining the ministry of the other.

Formation of the church. This ministry of the Holy Spirit, confined to the dispensation of grace, is one of the supreme manifestations of the sovereign purpose of God to effect reconciliation of believers to Himself. By the baptism of the Holy Spirit, the church becomes one in eternal life, united with that intimacy and indivisibility that characterizes the Trinity (John 17:21).

The unfolding of these major undertakings of the Holy Spirit is the task before us, with consideration of the variations and contrasts that prevail in different dispensations. All are involved in the eternal undertaking of the persons of the Trinity. The fulfillment in time of these ministries is evidence of the majestic movement of God's eternal plan. In the discussion of the details of the work of the Holy Spirit which follows, it must ever be borne in mind that each part is essential to the whole purpose of God, that the ministry of the Holy Spirit in its place is just as essential as the work of the Father and the work of the Son, each without the other being incomplete. All sense of emergency or rising to meet contingency must be removed in the work of the Holy Spirit, even though much of it is occasioned by the entrance of sin and the redemptive purpose of God. If viewed from eternity, the work of the Holy Spirit could be seen to reveal the same righteousness, love, omnipotence, omniscience, and grace which characterizes the work of Christ.

CHAPTER V

THE HOLY SPIRIT IN CREATION

IN THE Old Testament revelation of creation, in most instances the creative act is traced to God, without distinction as to persons. In all major works of God, a part is ascribed to each person, though often one person is given prominence and special emphasis. While in the work of creation God the Father is given the most prominence, in the Old Testament most references speak of the Creator as God without personal distinctions, and in the New Testament revelation the creative work is frequently ascribed to Christ (John 1:3; Col. 1:16-17). A very definite relation of the Holy Spirit to creation is revealed in Scripture, however, with sufficient detail to include creation as one of the great undertakings of the Spirit of God.

Two extremes of interpretation must be avoided. In an attempt to establish the work of any one person of the Godhead, some have tended to minimize the work of the other persons, and have made distinctions which do not hold throughout all the revelation of Scripture. If one should take the statements of John 1:3 and Colossians 1:16-17 as excluding from consideration any work by the other persons of the Trinity, one would arrive at the conclusion that all the work of creation was accomplished by the Son. This, however, does not explain other Scriptures ascribing similar works to the other persons. Likewise, while the work of the Holy Spirit can be sustained, it must not be interpreted as destroying or minimizing in any way the work of the other persons. The other extreme is to neglect the diversity of operation of the persons of the Trinity, taking the position that the Father is the Creator, and that the Son and the Spirit are merely agents of the Father. This view likewise does violence to the Scriptures. While the problem of distinguishing the works of the Trinity can never be finally solved, it is in keeping with all Scripture to ascribe the work of creation to all three persons of the Godhead, pointing out only such distinctions as are made in the Scripture revealing the nature of their creative work.

I. PROOF OF THE CREATIVE WORK OF THE HOLY SPIRIT

Specific Scriptures. At least three lines of argument sustain the doctrine of the creative work of the Holy Spirit. The first and most explicit proof is found in references to the Holy Spirit as having a part in creating (Gen. 1:2; Ps. 33:6; 104:29-30; Job 26:13; 33:4; Isa. 40:13). The Hebrew word translated *spirit* is *ruach*, probably arising from the original meaning of *breath* or *wind,* being significant of life and power and the immaterial nature of the Holy Spirit. The same word is used in other connections in the Old Testament. An examination of the various references will reveal a number of interesting facts.

The first reference to the Holy Spirit is in the scene of darkness and chaos described in Genesis 1:2. The Spirit of God is revealed to have "moved upon the face of the waters." John Owen in his classic work on the Holy Spirit speaks of this revelation as definite proof of the creative work of the Spirit. He states: "The word moved [*merachepheth*] signifies a gentle motion, like that of a dove over its nest, to communicate vital heat to its eggs, or to cherish its young. Without him, all was a dead sea; a rude inform chaos; a confused heap covered with darkness: but by the moving of the Spirit of God upon it, he communicated a quickening prolific virtue. The principles of all those kinds and forms of things, which in an inconceivable variety compose its host and ornament, were communicated to it."[1]

Confirming this first revelation is Psalm 33:6, "By the word of Jehovah were the heavens made; and all the host of them by the breath of his mouth." The word for *breath* is the same word translated *Spirit* in Genesis 1:2. The term *Spirit of God* is a proper designation of the Third Person, while the term *breath* is metaphorical, so translated to carry out the meaning of the phrase, *of his mouth.* This passage reveals that all the host of heaven were made by the Holy Spirit.

Psalm 104:30 bears a similar testimony, "Thou sendest forth thy spirit, they are created: and thou renewest the face of the ground." While the context does not indicate definitely that original creation is in view, the use of *bara,* translated "they are created," points to original creation. The passage reveals that the Spirit, upon being sent forth, is engaged in the work of creation, a doctrine in keeping with other passages. Not only is creation in the realm of His works, but the renewal of nature is demonstrated in the sustenance and revival of life in the seasons of the year.

In Isaiah 40:12-14, the Spirit is revealed as the Creator by implication: "Who hath measured the waters in the hollow of his hand,

---

[1]John Owen, *A Discourse Concerning the Holy Spirit*, p. 56.

and meted out the heaven with the span, and comprehended the dust of the earth in a measure, and weighed the mountains in scales, and the hills in a balance? Who hath directed the Spirit of Jehovah, or being his counsellor hath taught him? With whom took he counsel, and who instructed him, and taught him in the path of justice, and taught him knowledge, and shewed to him the way of understanding?" The Holy Spirit is described as the untaught, uncounselled, and omnipotent God, who without need of instruction or assistance measured the waters, the heavens, the dust of the earth, and the mountains. His intimate connection with the plan and management of the universe is apparent.

Job bears his testimony in several passages. In Job 26:13, for instance, as translated in the Authorized Version, "By his spirit he hath garnished the heavens; his hand hath formed the crooked serpent." Translators have struggled with this verse. The American Standard Version translates it: "By his Spirit the heavens are garnished; his hand hath pierced the swift serpent." The Revised Standard Version removes it from the work of the Spirit entirely: "By his wind the heavens were made fair; his hand pierced the fleeing serpent." Conservative scholars find the first clause of the verse a revelation of the work of the Spirit in making the heavens beautiful. Young expresses it, "By His Spirit the heavens He beautified."[2] Job believed that the Holy Spirit had garnished or decorated the heavens and formed the order and beauty of the stars. Expositors have taken the expression "crooked serpent" or "swift serpent" to refer to "the north constellation" of stars.[3] Owen believes it refers to the Milky Way in the heavens, or a more general reference to the stars.[4] While the Scriptures record here an opinion of Job, which could be questioned on the ground that inspiration merely guarantees the accuracy of the quotation, it would seem from the general tenor of Scripture that Job is expressing the truth as revealed to him. The fact that Job as a divinely approved character expresses these ideas gives them the effect of divine authority.

In Job 33:4, Elihu is revealed to have said, "The Spirit of God hath made me, and the breath of the Almighty giveth me life." The same problem of authority exists here as in Job 26:13. It is probable that his statement is true as it is in keeping with the Genesis account

---

[2] Robert Young, *Literal Translation of the Bible*, Job 26:13.

[3] A. R. Fausset, *A Commentary, Critical, Experimental, and Practical, on the Old and New Testaments*, III, 63.

[4] Owen, *loc. cit.*

of creation. Coupled with the other explicit references to the creative work of the Spirit, the Scriptures examined sustain the doctrine and furnish sufficient proof for the spiritual mind.

Use of Elohim. A second important line of proof for the creative work of the Holy Spirit is found in the use of the word *Elohim* for the Creator. The term is properly plural as demonstrated by its use in reference to the plurality of heathen gods. Some have tried to explain away this evidence for the Trinity in the Old Testament, speaking of this use of the plural as the plural of majesty, citing the English idiom of *waters* (plural) for *water* (singular) in poetic expression to give the impression of greatness or extent. In view of the abundant testimony to the Trinity not only in the New Testament but in the Old Testament as well, it is fitting that a name for God should be used which should express the plural idea of the persons of the Godhead. Not a single good reason has ever been advanced for not regarding this plural as genuine. The arguments against it have been Unitarian, Jewish, or from liberal theology. The plural term for God thus found so prominently in the creation narrative constitutes an important contribution to the creative work of the Holy Spirit.

Every use of the term implies a work not only of any one person, but of all three persons. Hence, in Genesis 1:1, where it speaks of *God* creating, it is speaking of the Trinity explicitly, not only conceived of as one essence, but as the Triune God. Every work attributed to God under this term is accordingly an assertion of a ministry of the Holy Spirit. If we had no other reference to the creative work of the Holy Spirit than this use of the plural term, it would justify the doctrine, even though it would not reveal anything distinctive concerning the Spirit.

Argument from immanence. In addition to the explicit references of Scripture and the argument from the plural title of God in the creation narratives, a third line of evidence must be considered as offering further witness to the creative work of the Holy Spirit. The Scriptures reveal the Holy Spirit as being immanent in creation. His presence presumes a great work as, for instance, the presence of Christ in the flesh on earth presumed a work in the flesh for man. The presence of the Holy Spirit is expressly mentioned in Genesis 1:2.

It is clear from Scripture that, in addition to a relation of being the Creator, God bears to creation the twofold relationship of transcendence and immanence. In relation to creation, God is greater than and beyond all finite and material bounds and thus is transcendent. His transcendence is essential to the cosmological argument. His immanence is essential to His work in creation, not only in the original act, but in the preservation of it and in all His providential dealings with it. The deists, of course, held that God is Creator, and that He is transcendent without being immanent. The pantheists on the other hand have affirmed His immanence without His transcendence. Both affirm His relation to creation, however imperfectly, but neither view has stood the test of either reason or Scripture, as both His transcendence and immanence are essential to creation in the last analysis.

In relation to the Godhead, without distinction as to persons, the doctrine of immanence has a vital bearing on the doctrine of creation. It is generally accepted that God was present in the realm of that which He created. If this argument is sustained in relation to the Trinity, it is equally applicable to any person of the Trinity. On the basis of the doctrine of the immanence of the Holy Spirit, we may assume that the Holy Spirit had a part in the creative work. The express declaration of immanence in connection with the creation narrative (Gen. 1:2) is convincing. While this argument might not be sufficient alone, it does add to the strength of other evidence.

From the threefold proof of the creative work of the Holy Spirit, we build the doctrine of His work in creation. Further examination of Scripture texts will reveal a definite character in His creative work.

II. The Nature of the Creative Work

The nature of the creative work of God does not lend itself to distinctions of persons in various works to the extent this is revealed in undertakings of God in the New Testament. A close examination, however, will reveal certain aspects of creation which are specifically referred to the Holy Spirit. In creation itself, four things may be noted.

The order of creation. In Genesis 1:2, the Holy Spirit is revealed to have *moved upon* the chaos revealed in the first part of the same verse. In the revelation which follows, chaos is reduced to a cosmos, or to an ordered, directed world. Psalm 33:6 confirms this aspect by referring the creation of the hosts of the heavens to the Holy Spirit. A number of inferences may be drawn from this passage, but an important one is that the heavens more than any other portion of God's creation reveal His order. The regularity of movement, the perfection of organization, the infinity of control are all found in the heavens.

The design of creation. The testimony of Job is to this effect, "By his spirit he hath garnished the heavens; his hand hath formed the crooked serpent." If the *crooked serpent* refers to the Milky Way, as Owen indicates,[5] it is clear that the formation of the heavens in their design is attributed to the Holy Spirit. A fine distinction may be made, however, between the design itself and the creation of the heavens in this design. The First Person is commonly regarded as the Designer in the original sense, the Second Person as the one who furthers and assists the execution of the design, and the Third Person as the one who finishes and brings to final conclusion the work of God in point. This may be illustrated in the doctrine of salvation in which the Father wills, the Son makes possible through His death, and the Holy Spirit brings to final execution in the lives of the elect. Thus in the creation, the Holy Spirit is revealed to have formed the heavens in their design. It may be inferred that the design of all creation is related to some extent to the Holy Spirit, ever bearing in mind that no work of one person is accomplished apart from the other persons of the Godhead.

The life of creation. Elihu bears witness, "The Spirit of God hath made me, and the breath of the Almighty giveth me life" (Job 33:4). The creation narrative gives us essentially the same revelation, "And Jehovah God formed man of the dust of the ground, and breathed into his nostrils the breath of life; and man became a living soul" (Gen. 2:7). Owen in reference to the creation of man writes: "This was the work of the Holy Ghost. The Spirit of God, and the Breath of God, are the same."[6] It may be also said of the Second Person that He is related to life, as indicated in John 1:4, "In him was life; and the life was the light of men." The Holy Spirit is related to life as the Giver of life. A similar operation may be observed in regeneration, where the life imparted is the eternal life abiding in the Son, and the act of imparting life, the regeneration, is a work of the Holy Spirit. The Holy Spirit probably imparts life to all creation, particularly to man.

In the case of human life, the Holy Spirit gives special significance and quality to life. God had said, "Let us make man in our image, after our likeness" (Gen. 1:26), and in this work, the Spirit imparts life in an operation distinct from the creation of all other life. Owen in speaking of this aspect writes: "Into this formed dust, 'God breathed the breath of life'; (*divinae aurae particulam*) a vital immortal spirit; something of himself; somewhat immediately of his own; not of any pre-created matter. Thus man became a middle

---

[5]*Loc. cit.*
[6]*Ibid.*, p. 57.

creature, between the angels above, and the sensitive animals below. His body was formed as the beasts from matter; his soul was an immediate production of divine power, as the angels were."[7] Human life in the original creation seems, therefore, to have a specific relation to a work of the Holy Spirit, even though Genesis 2:7 speaks of God as the Bestower of life without personal distinctions.

Creation designed for God's glory. A fourth important element in creation is found in the revelation that it is designed to bring glory to God. Reference has been made to Psalm 33:6 with its statement that the hosts of the heavens were made by the Holy Spirit. In Job 26:13, a beautiful picture is painted of the heavens being garnished by the Holy Spirit, as if the final beauty and glory are the work of the Holy Spirit. The psalmist wrote, "The heavens declare the glory of God" (Ps. 19:1), and in this fact we find mention of the result of this work of the Spirit. It is fundamental to an understanding of creation as a whole to comprehend that all things have been brought into being to bring glory to God. The work of the Holy Spirit has the distinctive characteristic of being designed to bring glory to the Father and the Son. Thus, in the present age, in reference to the Holy Spirit, Christ said, "He shall not speak from himself; but what things soever he shall hear, these shall he speak: and he shall declare unto you the things that are to come. He shall glorify me: for he shall take of mine, and shall declare it unto you" (John 16:13b-14). The work of the Holy Spirit ever bears this characteristic, as it reflects the glory of God, the Holy Spirit not being in the foreground.

In the work of creation itself, then, the Holy Spirit is revealed to have a distinct character of operation. He brings order to creation; He is the Giver of life; and shapes creation to achieve its significant purpose of bringing all glory to God.

III. Preservation and Renewal of Creation

In addition to the primary work of creation, which may be considered finished, the Holy Spirit is revealed to bear a most important relation to the preservation and renewal of creation. The doctrine of His immanence is significant in demonstrating a continued work in the world. The Scriptures give explicit revelation on this aspect of His work. We find reference not only to original creation, but to the preservation of that creation. In Psalm 104:29-30, for instance, "Thou hidest thy face, they are troubled; thou takest away their breath, they

---

[7]*Loc. cit.*

die, and return to their dust. Thou sendest forth thy Spirit, they are created; and thou renewest the face of the ground." The passage in addition to affirming the creative work of the Spirit in general adds the thought of the renewal which is constantly seen in the world, particularly in spring. Creation is ordered by God in such a way as to be self-sustaining to some extent, the design of animal and plant life being such that species are self-perpetuating. Behind the outward phenomena, however, is the work of the Holy Spirit, sustaining, directing, and renewing. Much more, then, than an undirected, unintelligent process can be seen in the preservation and renewal of the natural world. As in the spiritual realm, revival and new life are intimately related to the Holy Spirit, so in the natural realm also, the beauty of new life in all its varied forms is a testimony to the work of the immanent Holy Spirit.

An examination of the testimony of the Scriptures concerning the work of the Holy Spirit in creation has demonstrated the importance and extent of this great undertaking of the Holy Spirit. While the emphasis must ever be on the work of the Holy Spirit in the spiritual world, His work in the natural world brings new significance to visible creation. His work in generation and creation and His work in preservation are the introduction to His work in regeneration and re-creation and His work in providence. The natural world is a rich source of illustration of the infinite wisdom, power, glory, and faithfulness of the Holy Spirit, corresponding to the spiritual experience of fellowship with Him, and the enjoyment of His ministry to the saints.

CHAPTER VI

REVELATION IN THE OLD TESTAMENT

I. FORMS OF DIVINE REVELATION

IN HIS sovereign providence, God has revealed Himself to men in various ways. Through the written Word, God has given His revelation in definite and permanent form, to be preserved forever, to be studied, and to be the standard for all truth. Attending the written Word, God had provided a secondary revelation consisting in spiritual enablement to discern the Scriptures and understand their message. In addition to the written Word, Christ Himself, the eternal Word, came to reveal God, and in His life, ministry, death, and resurrection gave tangible form to the infinite attributes revealed in the Scriptures. Apart from the person of Christ and the Scriptures, God has seen fit to reveal Himself in His creation, the order and design of all material things speaking of the infinite hand that made them.

The work of the Holy Spirit in Old Testament revelation is quite distinct from all these important means of revelation. Before the written Word, and during its formation, before the coming of Christ in the flesh, throughout the Old Testament period in particular, God in various ways and according to His sovereign will revealed Himself, His truth, and His program in part to some individuals and groups by means of direct revelation. Sometimes through a prophet, sometimes through events, sometimes through great wonders God made known His will to His people. We possess only a fragment of this great work of God, our only source of authentic information being the written Word and its occasional reference to this form of revelation. The field of truth to be considered is vast, and has been neglected. Of point in this discussion is the work of the Holy Spirit in giving this revelation.

II. THE EXTENT OF OLD TESTAMENT REVELATION

The field of Old Testament revelation includes everything revealed by God in the period prior to the coming of Christ in the flesh. In the limited boundaries of the present discussion, revelation is to be considered only in its primary sense of direct communication of God to man, without the necessary aid of written documents. The sources of information divide into two well-defined categories.

Revelation before Moses. Revelation was given to man before inspiration of Scripture was known. At least two books of the Old Testament, Genesis and Job, deal with periods of time in which there was no inspired Scripture. While the records of these books are inspired, they reveal God's dealings in a period before inspiration. Anything known of God and His ways, any revelation in this period is evidence of a great work of God to make His truth known. The knowledge of Job and his companions about God and His ways is proof that prior to written Scripture God had revealed Himself in definite form. The book of Job furnishes sufficient material in itself for a well-rounded systematic theology. The knowledge of revelation on the part of Job and his friends indicates God had not left Himself without adequate testimony.

Revelation from Moses to Christ. Revelation was also given to men during the period from Moses to Christ, in which portions of the Old Testament were available, and written revelation had its important place. Throughout this period, also, God saw fit to reveal Himself directly to His prophets and speak through them. Only a fragment of their spoken message has been preserved. The methods of revelation indicated in Genesis as God spoke to men from Adam down are not essentially changed throughout the Old Testament. While the written Word had its primary purpose in preserving revelation in infallible accuracy for future generations, direct revelation had to do largely with contemporary problems and need for truth and guidance which would later be afforded by the completed written Word.

III. The Old Testament Prophet

Throughout the Old Testament period, God, in His sovereign will, gave direct revelation in most cases to those who were publicly known as prophets. It is an error, however, to limit revelation to those who were prophets. Prophecy had to do with revelation given forth in the form of a message to the people, while revelation was the reception of that message from God by the prophet. As Kuyper writes, "God spoke also to others than prophets, e.g., to Eve, Cain, Hagar, etc. To receive a revelation or a vision does not make one a prophet, unless it be accompanied by the command to communicate the revelation to others. The word 'nabi,' the Scriptural term for prophet, does not indicate a person who receives something of God, but one who brings something to the people. Hence it is a mistake to confine divine revelation to the prophetic office."[1] The Old Testament prophet, however, was an important medium of revelation as the Scriptures make clear.

A study of Old Testament prophecy will reveal at least seven divisions in the historical development of the prophetic office. While these periods are somewhat arbitrary and often blend from one into the other, their distinctive character can be easily observed.

Revelation before Abraham. In the period before Abraham, revelation was frequently given to man. There were a few who had the distinctive character of prophets as Enoch and Noah, but revelation was more frequently given to those who had no part in the prophetic office. God speaks at various times to Adam and Eve, to Cain, and probably to many others of whom there is no record. The primary idea is that of direct revelation rather than the impartation of a message to be delivered subsequently to others. The extended revelation and the prophetic ministry of Noah is noteworthy. The New Testament adds the ministry of Enoch (Jude 14). It is significant that Enoch revealed detailed and advanced doctrine of which the Old Testament itself bears no record. It can be concluded that there was a far richer prophetic ministry during this period than appears on the pages of Genesis.

Revelation to Abraham. The period of Abraham's life affords an advance in the history of prophecy. Abraham is known distinctly as a prophet to whom God speaks and who is blessed by God (Gen. 20:7). To him is given abundant revelation of his peculiar place in history and of God's great purpose to be realized through him. Notably absent, however, is the command to deliver a message. He received a revelation, but had no message to be communicated to others, except in so far as it is recorded in the Scriptures. Following Abraham, and in the same period, God spoke to Isaac and Jacob confirming the revelation given to Abraham and adding to it.

Revelation to Moses. The lifetime of Moses brings a period of larger prophetic ministry as well as more extended revelation. Not only were the Scriptures of the Pentateuch written during this period, but frequent revelation was needed in the whole course of action relative to freeing Israel from the bondage of Egypt. Moses enjoyed the distinctive call of a prophet when God appeared to him in the burning bush. His office was recognized by all the people.

---

[1] Abraham Kuyper, *The Work of the Holy Spirit*, p. 70.

To him God spoke, not in vague visions, but "mouth to mouth" (Num. 12:8). While the major contribution of Moses as a prophet is his written ministry consisting in the inspired Scriptures, his prophetic office was by no means confined to this aspect. In him we have a full display of the nature of a prophet and his work. Moses was assisted by Aaron and Miriam, both of whom were prophets in their own right, but lower in rank and privilege than Moses (Ex. 7:1; 15:20). Miriam is the first to be noted specially as a prophetess.

Revelation during the judges. The period of the judges is quite in contrast with the lifetime of Moses. It was a period of defeat and demoralization. With the exception of Samuel, the last of the judges and the first of the prophets of the larger prophetic periods, no prophet is mentioned by name during the period of the judges. Deborah is mentioned as a prophetess (Judg. 4:4), and a nameless prophet prepares the way for Gideon (Judg. 6:8). It was a time of "no frequent vision" (1 Sam. 3:1). Occasionally, however, God spoke to individuals, as to Gideon (Judg. 6:12 ff.), and reference without details as to the method of revelation are found indicating God had given special revelation (Judg. 2:20, 22; 10:11-14; 13:3-20; 20:18, 23, 28), but no outstanding prophet appears.

Revelation during the period of the early kings. In the period of the kings of Israel, beginning with Samuel, and ending with the advent of the so-called writing prophets, a definite advance is made in prophetic history. Distinct personalities arise, without peer in their generation as the medium of authoritative revelation. The prophet comes into his own. He is regarded not only as a *seer,* one to whom visions and revelation are given, but also as a divinely chosen representative of God, set apart in many cases to an entire lifetime of prophetic ministry. The birth and childhood of Samuel, while unusual, are illustrative of God's method. Without doubt, the prophetic ministry of Samuel made possible the rise of David and Solomon and the attendant glory of their kingdoms.

During the lifetime of Samuel, the schools of the prophets came into being (1 Sam. 19:18-24). Their rise was probably occasioned by the natural attraction of the prophets to young men of pious minds. Instruction was given by the prophets, and often revelation from God and supernatural manifestations characterized these schools of prophets. Even Solomon was educated by Nathan the prophet, though probably he was never enrolled in a school of prophets.

During the period of the kings, the authority of the prophet is frequently noted. Saul was brought to his downfall because he failed to recognize prophetic authority (1 Sam. 13:13-14). David was openly rebuked by the prophet Nathan (2 Sam. 12) and Gad (2 Sam. 24:13). Ahijah, Jehu, Elijah, and Elisha are also prominent in this period. An occasional prophetess appears, such as Huldah (2 Kings 22:14; 2 Chron. 34:22). Prophetic utterances, however, deal largely with contemporary problems. The extended discourses of Isaiah and Jeremiah did not come until later. The importance of the ministry of prophets of this period was tremendous. They were often greater personalities than kings, with their word and support essential to the success of any ruler. To them, in part, was committed the writing of the history of their periods, though in all probability this was done to a large extent by the scribes and priests, and the prophets played a minor role.

Revelation before and during the Exile. The period of pre-exilic prophetic literature including that written by the exiles Ezekiel and Daniel was the greatest period for prophetic utterance as well as literary effort. During this period the great prophetic books were written, with their partial record of what was said and done by the prophets. The darkening clouds of approaching judgment brought forth the prophetic warnings of the coming exile with the accompanying revelation of the glory of the future kingdom. The great prophets Isaiah, Jeremiah, Ezekiel, and Daniel are examples of the Old Testament prophet at his greatest period. Their testimony was not always heard, but there was abundant evidence of their prophetic gift. In scope and grandeur, their messages exceed any other period. Accompanying the greater prophets was the ministry of others such as Azur, Hananiah, Hosea, Joel, Amos, Obadiah, Jonah, Micah, Nahum, Habakkuk, and Zephaniah. In all probability there were many others whose names have not been preserved, whose contribution was chiefly contemporary. Scant mention is made of the ministry of women prophets, who as in other periods played a less important part. The wives of prophets shared the work of their husbands to some extent as in the case of Isaiah's wife (Isa. 8:3).

Revelation after the Exile. The final period of Old Testament prophecy is found after the Exile. The pens of Ezra and Nehemiah give us the major historical background, and the prophetical ministry of Haggai, Zechariah, and, later, Malachi, forms the principal contribution to this period. In the case of all three of these prophets, their written ministry was probably only a small part of their total work. The reconstruction under Zerubbabel was made possible by the assistance and encouragement of the prophets Haggai and Zechariah. Ezra, following some sixty years later, brought needed revival. Nehemiah who came to Jerusalem shortly after Ezra added the impulse to build the wall and city to which undertaking Ezra gave his support.

Malachi came during the period of Nehemiah, his ministry possibly occurring during the latter part of Nehemiah's life. As the last of the Old Testament canonical prophets, it was fitting for his message to be pointed to the future. He reminds of their sins and paints the prophetic picture of the coming of John the Baptist and of Christ. His prophecy closes with a prediction of the coming Day of the Lord, and an exhortation to watch for the coming of the second Elijah, John the Baptist.

The quality which distinguished all true prophets from other men was their office of speaking for God. Their message was not necessarily prophetic in the sense of speaking of future events otherwise unknown. Often the prophets preached the past, reminding of God's dealings with them. Their message was frequently that of specific guidance in the midst of a crisis, as in the case of Isaiah to Hezekiah when Jerusalem was surrounded. Many times their message was one of warning of judgment to come for sin. Exhortation was given to worship God and obey Him. The prophets because of their sacred office were national leaders, patriots, and reformers; they were the representatives of God, His mouthpiece of revelation whatever the subject. Their lives and ministries did much to shape the history of God's people throughout the Old Testament period.

IV. REVELATION A WORK OF THE SPIRIT

While the impartation of revelation did not necessarily constitute the recipient a prophet, no one could be a true prophet without having received revelation. Behind all the outward display of prophetic gift was the unseen work of the Holy Spirit in imparting the mind of God to His prophets. An examination of the Old Testament record reveals proof for this ministry of the Holy Spirit.

Direct statements of Scripture. Strange to say, the New Testament gives one of the most explicit statements of this ministry of the Holy Spirit in the Old Testament: "For no prophecy ever came by the will of man: but men spake from God, being moved by the Holy Spirit" (2 Pet. 1:21). Old Testament prophecy as a whole is not attributed in this passage to the native ability of man but is traced to its source, the revelation given by God Himself. The Holy Spirit so worked in the hearts of the prophets that they were literally *carried along* as a boat carries its passengers to the proper destination.

They were willing and yielded in most cases to the working of the Holy Spirit, but the source of the revelation was wholly in God.

The New Testament statement is, of course, based on Old Testament Scripture. David bore witness to the work of the Holy Spirit in revelation. "The Spirit of Jehovah spake by me, and his word was upon my tongue" (2 Sam. 23:2). Ezekiel frequently mentions the work of the Holy Spirit in imparting revelation to him (Ezek. 2:2; 8:3; 11:1, 24). Micah traces the power of his prophetic ministry to the Holy Spirit (Mic. 3:8). To those references might be added the many instances in the New Testament where Scriptures are said to be the work of the Holy Spirit (Matt. 22:43; Acts 1:16; 4:25; 28:25; Heb. 3:7; 9:6-8; 10:15). The fact of inspiration presupposes the primary revelation which made it possible. It is significant that the Third Person is given this special work of revelation.

Indirect statements. Many of the references in the Old Testament do not speak of the Holy Spirit directly. A common phrase is, "Thus saith Jehovah." It may be safely inferred that these references, also, indicate a work of the Holy Spirit in revelation. As Owen says, "Where it is said, that God spake by the prophets, or that the word of God came to them, the immediate work of the Spirit is intended."[2] The reference to this work of the Holy Spirit is, therefore, well established on the basis of direct statement in the Old and New Testaments, on the inference from the work of the Holy Spirit in the inspiration of the Old Testament, and on the basis of the many references to revelation as coming from God.

V. Methods of Revelation

At least four methods of special revelation were used by God in making known His mind to His prophets. To what extent the natural and the supernatural combined no one can finally estimate. The emphasis is ever on the result, the revelation given, rather than on the means or the method employed. A study of the methods does indicate, however, the supernatural character of the revelation.

The spoken word. The most prominent means of revelation is that of the spoken word. "Thus saith Jehovah" is found in hundreds of instances in the Old Testament. A comparison of such passages as Isaiah 6:1-10 and Acts 28:25 will demonstrate that the Holy Spirit is the person of the Trinity speaking in these instances. While the Old Testament uses "Jehovah" and "Lord" as the speaker, the New

---

[2]Owen, *op. cit.*, p. 71.

Testament uses the title, *Holy Spirit*. The question of the exact nature of God's speaking cannot be finally settled. It is clear from such New Testament instances as the baptism of Christ, the transfiguration, and the appearance of Christ to Paul that God sometimes speaks vocally and did so on several occasions.

In the Old Testament God spoke in a similar way. At Mount Sinai, for instance, God spoke in such a way to Moses that the people could also hear, with the express purpose of validating Moses as a prophet of God (Ex. 19:9). In the case of the call of Samuel (1 Sam. 3:1-14), the voice of the Lord was mistaken for that of Eli's in the first three instances, so real was it, and so similar to a human voice. Anyone accepting the Scripture terminology as accurate must conclude that God spoke in a way resembling the human voice and used actual words which issued in actual sounds. Of course, God did not need to confine Himself to this method. Between men, the medium of human voice or other means of transmitting words is essential to communication. God is able, however, to speak to the heart of man with such reality that the effect is produced without the need of actual words. Such is the experience of the Christian who is frequently taught by the Holy Spirit the truths of God, and yet he would have difficulty finding words to express all that the Spirit had made known. It may be concluded that God used in some instances a medium of communication similar to a human voice, and in other instances He may have spoken directly to the heart.

It is of great significance that words were used. Revelation was far more than mere guidance of the natural reasoning of the mind. God had a definite message to reveal and communicate to man. The person received this message in accurate terms. It was more than a mere impression or a feeling. The message was tangible and unmistakable. If God had written the message on a scroll and brought it to the recipient, the revelation would not have been more real and accurate. It fulfilled all the purpose of God in making His will known.

Dreams. A secondary means of revelation was that of dreams. This method of revelation was commonly accepted as a normal way for God to speak. Many expressed instances are revealed in Scripture (Gen. 20:3-7; 31:10-13, 24; 37:5-20; 40:5-16; 41:11-13, 15-32; 42:9; etc.). In most instances, the one to whom God speaks is not a prophet, as illustrated in the case of Abimelech, Laban, the butler and baker of Pharaoh, and in the dream of Pharaoh himself. It was considered, however, a valid way for a prophet to receive his message. In the rebuke delivered to Miriam and Aaron for murmuring against

Moses, God said, "If there be a prophet among you, I Jehovah will make myself known unto him in a vision, I will speak with him in a dream" (Num. 12:6). In contrast, God said he would speak to Moses face to face, as proving his greater position as a prophet. In some cases, the revelation was given during a sleep supernaturally imposed, as in the case of Abraham (Gen. 15:12), and Daniel (Dan. 10:9). False prophets were accused of claiming to have received a revelation in a dream when they had not (Jer. 23:25). It is prophesied in Joel 2:28-32 that the future period would involve many instances of this kind of revelation. Peter seems to claim partial fulfillment of this in Acts 2:16-21, though the ultimate fulfillment is reserved for the period of the future kingdom. The important place of this kind of revelation is evident from the many references.

Visions. Closely associated with dreams as a means of revelation were visions. The very term *seer* as applied to prophets had reference to seeing visions. These were no doubt a part of the revelation given in dreams in some instances. In others, however, there is no evidence that the prophet was asleep, the vision occurring during a time when the person involved was fully conscious. Such probably was the case of Isaiah in the two instances noted (Isa. 1:1; 6:1). Ezekiel had a similar experience (Ezek. 1:3). Micaiah's vision of heaven belongs in the same category (1 Kings 22:19). Unlike the method of direct communication by speaking, as in the case of some dreams, visions were not always immediately clear in their import. It may be questioned whether Ezekiel understood his visions. In every case, however, in so far as the vision applied to contemporary problems, it was apparent to the recipient.

Trances. A fourth element, often present in supernatural revelation, was that of trances. In themselves, the trances did not reveal anything. They were incident to the impartation of the message of God, and they often accompanied visions as in the case of Ezekiel (Ezek. 8:3; 11:24). It is difficult to distinguish trances and dreams in some cases as the supernaturally imposed sleep was similar to a trance (Gen. 15:12; Dan. 10:9). It is clear that trances as such were not important in the transmission of revelation.

Such were the methods of revelation used in the Old Testament. As in the case of all supernatural acts, human reason cannot fathom all the details, and human experience cannot rise to the understanding of all that took place. Suffice it to say that God effectively in His own way brought His message to men. His methods were suited to the age in which they were used. They took the place later filled by the completed Bible and the normal ministry of the Holy Spirit to believers in this age. His desire to make Himself known is evident in every dispensation.

VI. NEW TESTAMENT REVELATION

Taken as a whole, revelation in the New Testament is basically the same as in the Old. The eternal God continues to reveal Himself through the Holy Spirit. In a few respects, however, there are new developments in the doctrine of revelation.

Revelation through Christ. In the New Testament the Messiah of the Old Testament is incarnate and in His person and ministry constituted a revelation of God which is distinct. While the Holy Spirit ministered to and through the Lord Jesus, it was a work of Christ essentially. It provided a basis for the larger revelation afforded in the New Testament as a whole. God incarnate in human flesh was a specific revelation of God which exceeded anything which the prophets of the Old Testament could offer.

Revelation in the believer. In the New Testament also, in contrast to the Old, a wider ministry of the Spirit is directed to the individual believer. Beginning at Pentecost the Spirit indwells every believer and constitutes a source of revelation concerning the will of God which before had been limited to a few. The Holy Spirit now guided, taught, and helped believers on a scale not found in the Old Testament. While revelation continued to follow its basic pattern, its effectiveness was greatly enlarged through this ministry of the Spirit.

Revelation through the written Word. The New Testament also contemplates a fuller revelation through the written Word. The record was now complete or in process of completion during the apostolic age. The character of revelation was therefore tied in more explicitly with the written revelation. Instead of dreams, trances, and visions, guidance was normally given through the Scripture, though we have reference in the New Testament to some continued use of these means. As the New Testament came into being, the older forms of revelation seem to have faded from the picture. Today conservative Christians question whether dreams, trances, and visions are any longer a bona fide method of divine revelation, even though it is predicted that dreams and visions will again be used in the time just preceding the second advent (cf. Joel 2:28 ff., Acts 2:16-21). Revelation is regarded in the New Testament as being complete and contained in the Scripture.

Revelation eschatologically considered. Both Testaments, however, testify to the future aspect of revelation in connection with the second advent. This will be revelation of a new character, the personal and visible glory of the Son of God. The present age is the dispensation of the Spirit, and God is known through the work of the Spirit. The future dispensation, while attended by the continued ministry of the Spirit of God, will be that of the Son of God in His glory. This will constitute the capstone to divine revelation.

CHAPTER VII

THE HOLY SPIRIT IN INSPIRATION

I. IMPORTANCE OF INSPIRATION

OF THE many ministries of the Holy Spirit in the Old Testament, few are of more immediate concern to Christians than the work of the inspiration of Old Testament Scriptures. While the particular doctrines of Christianity to a large extent are based on New Testament revelation, it is clear to even a casual observer that the New Testament is based on the Old Testament, and one without the other does not constitute a complete or satisfying revelation. The doctrine of inspiration, having to do with the formation of the Scriptures, does not differ to a great extent in the two Testaments.

The doctrine of the inspiration of the Scriptures has been the historic position of most Protestant churches, as their creeds bear testimony. Whatever the degrees of unbelief latent in either the clergy or the laity, and whatever disagreements there may be between denominational groups on other doctrines, Protestant churches have officially held the doctrine of the inspiration of the Scriptures. This has been subject to extended discussion and argument, however, as various views of inspiration have been proffered. A complete discussion of the doctrine of inspiration cannot be undertaken here.[1]

The importance of the inspiration of the Scriptures, while tacitly denied by some in modern times, is easily demonstrated. It is a matter of tremendous import whether the Scriptures are a supernaturally produced Word of God or whether they are a collection of the works of men, containing errors one must expect in any human work. As Boettner writes: "That the question of inspiration is of vital importance for the Christian Church is easily seen. If she has a definite and authoritative body of Scripture to which she can go, it is a comparatively easy task to formulate her doctrines. All she has to do is to search out the teachings of Scripture and embody them in her creed. But if the Scriptures are not authoritative, if they are to be corrected and edited and some parts are to be openly

---

[1] For a more extended treatment of the doctrine of inspiration, cf. Lewis Sperry Chafer, *Systematic Theology*, I, 61-104.

rejected, the Church has a much more serious problem, and there
can be no end of conflicting opinions concerning either the purpose
of the Church or the system of doctrine which she is to set forth."[2]

It is not the purpose of the present discussion to attempt the
display of the arguments supporting the inspiration of the Scriptures.
The arguments from sources external to the Scriptures will not be
considered at all, and the Biblical evidences discussed only as they
illustrate the work of the Holy Spirit. What the Bible says on the
subject is far more conclusive and plain to the eye of faith than all
the high-flown arguments of unbelievers. As Lewis Sperry Chafer
has written, "That doctrine of inspiration, which the church has held
in all her generations, abides, not because its defenders are able
to shout louder than their opponents, not by virtue of any human
defense, but because of the fact that it is embedded within the divine
Oracles themselves. Since it is so embedded in the Oracles of God,
no saint or apostle could do otherwise than to *believe* the word God
has spoken."[3]

II. The Meaning of Inspiration

The technical meaning of *inspiration* is quite apart from its
common usage in reference to non-Biblical concepts. As B. B. Warfield
points out, "The word 'inspire' and its derivatives seem to have come
into Middle Eng. from the Fr., and have been employed from the first
(early in the 14th cent.) in a considerable number of significations,
physical and metaphorical, secular and religious."[4] We still speak of
being inspired by a beautiful sunset, or of hearing an inspiring
sermon. Such common usages, however, are not parallel to *inspiration*
in a doctrinal sense. Even in ordinary speech, we conceive of inspiration as something that constitutes an influence from without. As
Warfield says, "Underlying all their use, however, is the constant
implication of an influence from without, producing in its object
movements and effects beyond its native, or at least its ordinary
powers."[5]

In Scripture there are few direct references to the word *inspiration*
as far as the term itself is concerned. In the Authorized Version of
Job 32:8, Elihu is quoted, "But there is a spirit in man: and the
inspiration of the Almighty giveth them understanding." This can

[2]Loraine Boettner, *The Inspiration of the Scriptures*, p. 10.
[3]Chafer, *op. cit.*, I, 64.
[4]*International Standard Bible Encyclopaedia*, "Inspiration," p. 1473.
[5]Warfield, *loc. cit.*

hardly be referred to the inspiration of Scripture, however, as it is doubtful if any of the Bible, in its present form at least, was in existence at that time. In the American Revised and Revised Standard Versions "breath" is substituted for "inspiration." The only other reference is found in 2 Timothy 3:16, where the Authorized Version gives this translation, "All scripture is given by inspiration of God, and is profitable for doctrine, for reproof, for correction, for instruction in righteousness." Even here, in the American revision and in the Revised Standard Version the translation is changed to read, "Every scripture inspired of God is also profitable for teaching, for reproof, for correction, for instruction which is in righteousness." The revised translation, while attempting to solve the problem created by the absence of the copula, not at all unusual in the Greek, has greatly weakened the passage, and that, unjustly. The noun *inspiration* would disappear entirely from the English Bible if this translation were allowed, and a misleading impression is created that some Scripture is not inspired.

The difficulty lies chiefly in the word *inspiration* itself. The Greek, *theopneutos,* does not mean inspiring. As Warfield notes, "The Gr. term has, however, nothing to say of *in*spiring or of *in*spiration: it speaks only of a 'spiring' or 'spiration.' What it says of Scripture is, not that it is 'breathed into by God' or is the product of the Divine 'inbreathing' into its human authors, but that it is breathed out by God, 'God-breathed,' the product of the creative breath of God. In a word, what is declared by this fundamental passage is simply that the Scriptures are a Divine product, without any indication of how God has operated in producing them."[6]

From 2 Timothy 3:16, we may conclude that inspiration is the work of God by which or through which the Scriptures are given. After stating the fact of inspiration, however, the same verse draws a most interesting and significant conclusion. Because the Scriptures are inspired, they are, therefore, profitable for doctrine, reproof, correction, and instruction in righteousness. In other words, inspiration guarantees accuracy and gives divine authority to the record. It is hardly necessary here to review the abundant testimony of the Scriptures to this very fact. Christ Himself frequently quoted the Old Testament as the Word of God. The writers claimed inspiration for their own works. The content of Scripture is such that its prophecies must have been the product of divine revelation and their accurate recording the work of inspiration. The witness to inspira-

---

[6]*Ibid.,* p. 1474.

tion is all the more conclusive because the Scriptures never attempt to prove inspiration; they merely state it and assume it, in the same manner as the Scriptures assume the existence of God.

A matter of further observation is that the Scriptures are not only divine, but also human. The words used were those within the vocabulary of the writers. Their own emotions, human knowledge, experiences, and hopes entered into the Scriptures which they wrote, without compromising in the least their inspiration. Without doubt, some portions of Scripture are dictated, as the Scriptures themselves indicate, but most of the Scriptures do not have this characteristic. Regardless of the degree of human or divine influence in the Scriptures, the resultant is equally inspired and equally suited to God's purpose. The examination of the work of the Holy Spirit in inspiration will sustain these evidences for the dual authorship, divine and human, of the Scriptures.

A proper statement of the meaning of inspiration is, therefore, that God so supernaturally directed the writers of Scripture that without excluding their human intelligence, their individuality, their literary style, their personal feelings, or any other human factor, His own complete and coherent message to man was recorded in perfect accuracy, the very words of Scripture bearing the authority of divine authorship. Nothing less than a plenary and verbal inspiration will satisfy the demands of the Scriptures themselves and give to faith the confidence in the Word of God which is essential to faith and life.

III. Inspiration a Work of the Holy Spirit

Much of the material already considered in the study of the work of the Holy Spirit in revelation could be examined anew in connection with inspiration. While revelation had its primary work in making known that which would otherwise be unknown, inspiration has its objective in the writing of the Scriptures, including not only that which is primary revelation, but also the selection of historical facts, their statement, and the record of the mind and thoughts of the writers. That the Holy Spirit should have this particular ministry is entirely in keeping with all the other truth known concerning His work. The evidence sustaining the doctrine of the work of the Holy Spirit in the inspiration of the Scriptures of the Old Testament is subject to a sixfold analysis.

The testimony of the Old Testament writers. The writers of Scripture did not necessarily understand all the meaning of the Scriptures which they wrote, but they were undoubtedly conscious at all times that their writings were a product of inspiration. As

Warfield writes: "The Bib. writers do not conceive of the Scriptures as a human product breathed into by the Divine Spirit, and thus heightened in its qualities or endowed with new qualities; but as a Divine product through the instrumentality of men."[7] The fact of the inspiration of their writings is more assumed than proved. Occasional reference is found to their own consciousness of the work of the Holy Spirit in inspiration. David bears witness to the inspiration of his works, "The Spirit of Jehovah spake by me, and his word was in my tongue. The God of Israel said, the Rock of Israel spake to me" (2 Sam. 23:2-3). Isaiah records the words of the Lord, bearing a similar import, "As for me, this is my covenant with them, saith Jehovah: my Spirit that is upon thee, and my words which I have put in thy mouth, shall not depart out of thy mouth, nor out of the mouth of thy seed, nor out of the mouth of thy seed's seed, saith Jehovah, from henceforth and for ever" (Isa. 59:21). Jeremiah bears witness of the word of the Lord to him, "Behold, I have put my words in thy mouth" (Jer. 1:9). Their writings when produced were immediately accepted as the Word of God by those truly worshiping the Lord. The absence of any formal argument to prove the inspiration of their writings indicates that none was deemed necessary. The character of the Scriptures was sufficient evidence both for the writers and the readers.

Terminology of the prophets. In many of the books of the Old Tesament, recurrent phrases occur which can be explained only by the doctrine of inspiration. The expression, "Thus saith Jehovah" or its equivalent, is found in hundreds of instances. The writer claims in many cases to be directly quoting God, and in others he is the authoritative spokesman. In both cases, supernatural revelation and the inspiration of the writings are claimed.

Titles of the Scriptures. With very frequent reference, the writings of the Old Testament are designated as *the Word of Jehovah, Thy Word, My Word, Words of His Mouth, Words of the Holy One, His Word.* The explicit references of this sort are found over a hundred times in the Old Testament. There can be no doubt that they refer to the Old Testament in its entirety or in its parts as the very Word of God. In some cases, the reference is to direct quotation of what God Himself has said, but in others it is the word of His prophets speaking for God (Ps. 107:11; 119:11; Prov. 30:5). These titles of Scripture in every part of the Old Testament give the stamp of divine inspiration to every book.

---

[7]*Ibid.*, pp. 1479-80.

The testimony of Christ. One of the clearest indications of the work of the Holy Spirit in the inspiration of the Old Testament comes from the lips of Christ Himself. Most of the Old Testament references to the work of God in inspiration do not mention the Holy Spirit specifically, though we have already noted a few instances (2 Sam. 23:2-3; Isa. 59:21). In quoting from the Old Testament, however, Christ is explicit in assigning the work of inspiration to the Holy Spirit. This is important not only in revealing which person of the Trinity undertook this work, but it also constitutes a most conclusive testimony to the doctrine of the inspiration of the Old Testament. An attack on the Old Testament becomes an attack on the word of Christ Himself.

In connection with the encounter of Christ with the Pharisees, Christ asked, "What think ye of the Christ? whose son is he? They say unto him, The son of David. He saith unto them, How then doth David in the Spirit call him Lord?" (Matt. 22:42-43). In quoting Psalm 110:1 which is written by David, Christ affirms that David wrote by the inspiration of the Holy Spirit, finding in this fact the explanation of David's wisdom in calling his own son, "Lord." In the account in Mark, which is undoubtedly the same instance, Christ in presenting the question concerning David's son said, "David himself said in the Holy Spirit, The Lord said unto my Lord, Sit thou on my right hand, till I make thine enemies the footstool of thy feet" (Mark 12:36). In this instance, again, Christ bears witness to the work of the Holy Spirit in the inspiration of this Psalm, and explains its authority by the fact that David spoke by the Holy Spirit.

The testimony of the apostles. The testimony of the apostles is more abundant and equally explicit as that of Christ. Peter, speaking of the fulfillment of Psalm 41:9, says, "Brethren, it was needful that the scripture should be fulfilled, which the Holy Spirit spake before by the mouth of David concerning Judas, who was guide to them that took Jesus" (Acts 1:16). In quoting the second Psalm, God is said to have spoken by the mouth of David (Acts 4:24-25). Paul quotes Isaiah 6:9-10, saying, "Well spake the Holy Spirit through Isaiah the prophet unto your fathers" (Acts 28:25). Similar references are found in Hebrews 3:7; 10:15-16, and elsewhere in the New Testament. All bear witness to the inspiration of the Old Testament by the Holy Spirit, and at the same time the human authorship is sustained.

The analogy from oral revelation. In the discussion of oral revelation, reference was made to 2 Peter 1:20-21 which bears testimony to the supernatural work of God which is the origin of all prophecy: "For no prophecy ever came by the will of man: but men spake from God, being moved by the Holy Spirit." It is a clear statement that all prophecy is possible only by a work of the Holy Spirit. It is, however, not at all necessary to limit the application of this passage to oral revelation. Some portions of the prophetic Word were not delivered orally, but were first revealed in written form (cf. Daniel). In these instances, it is the written record which *speaks,* and the writers were *borne along by the Holy Spirit* in their work even as 2 Peter indicates. If all oral prophecy proceeds from a work of the Holy Spirit, and all written prophecy has the same source, it is reasonable to extend by analogy the work of the Spirit to all the Old Testament, prophetic in the wide sense of being a message from God. The work of the Holy Spirit is thus extended not only to the aspect of revelation but also to the inspiration of the written Word.

The Scriptures are clear, then, both as to the fact of inspiration and as to the agent of inspiration, the Holy Spirit. The proofs are abundant for both. As James B. Green says, "The Law and the Prophets, the teaching of Jesus and the preaching of Paul; these are declared to be the Word of God. It has been estimated that the Bible in various ways asserts its own inspiration some three thousand times. How often does the Bible have to say a thing before men will believe it?"[8]

IV. The Extent of Inspiration

An examination into the records of the Old Testament will reveal literature of all types: history, poetry, drama, sermons, love stories, and insight into the innermost devotional thoughts of the writers. It is a matter of great significance that inspiration extends to all of these kinds of literature, without regard as to form or style, without concern as to the origin or the knowledge embodied in writing. The question naturally presents itself concerning the relation of inspiration to various portions of Scripture.

Every attempt to fathom the supernatural is doomed to a measure of failure. Man has no criterion by which to judge that which transcends our experience. Without trying to explain inspiration, an examination of its application may be undertaken. At least seven types of operation may be observed in the work of inspiration.

The unknown past. Scripture occasionally speaks with authority

---

[8]James B. Green, *Studies in the Holy Spirit,* p. 49.

concerning the past in such detail and upon such themes as would be unknown to man. In the early chapters of Genesis, for instance, Moses portrays events occurring before the creation of man, therefore beyond all possible bounds of tradition. In Isaiah and Ezekiel, reference is made to events in heaven outside the sphere of man's knowledge and prior to his creation. It is clear that these narratives demand both a revelation concerning the facts and the work of the Holy Spirit in inspiration to guarantee their accurate statement. Some have advanced the idea in relation to the accounts of creation that these are similar in many details to pagan accounts of creation. It is possible that revelation was given prior to the writing of Scripture on the subject of creation and that men had added to and altered this revelation in the formation of nonscriptural accounts of creation. The existence of other records of creation and points of similarity of these with the Scriptures in no wise affects the inspiration of Genesis. Whether Moses used documents or not has no bearing on the writing of the Scriptures. Whether documents were used, whether there was knowledge of pagan ideas of creation, or whether tradition had contributed some truth on the subject, the work of inspiration was necessary in any event to distinguish truth from error and to incorporate in the record all that was true and to omit all that was false. Without doubt, the primary source of information was direct revelation, and the documents, if any, and such traditional accounts as may have been known by Moses were quite incidental.

History. A large portion of the Old Testament conforms to the pattern of history. In such sections, the writer is speaking about events known to many and concerning which other documents not inspired may have been written. In many cases, the writer is dealing with contemporary events in which the element of revelation is practically absent. How may inspiration be said to operate in such Scripture? As in all Scripture, inspiration is not concerned with the source of the facts but only with their accurate statement. In the record of history, the Holy Spirit guided the writers in the selection of events to be noted, the proper statement of the history of these events, and the omission of all that should not be included. The result is an infallibly accurate account of what happened with the emphasis on the events important to the mind of God.

Law. Certain portions of the Old Testament consist in laws governing various phases of individual and national life. This kind of Scriptures is found chiefly in the Pentateuch, where the law is revealed in three major divisions: the commandments, governing the moral life of the people; the ordinances, governing the religious life of the people; and the judgments, dealing with the social life of the people. In some cases, the law consisted in commandments given by means of dictation, the laws retaining in every particular the character of being spoken by God. In other cases, Moses charges the people as God's prophet and gives commandments which can hardly be construed to have been committed to him by way of dictation; yet the commandments have equal force with other commandments. Inspiration operates in the writing of all law in the Scriptures to the end that the laws perfectly express the mind of God for the people to whom they are given; the laws are kept from error and include all that God desires to command at that time; the laws are authoritative and are a proper basis for all matters to which they pertain.

Dictation. As previously intimated, some portions of God's Word consist in direct quotation of God's commands and revelation. How does inspiration operate under these circumstances? Inspiration guarantees that commands and revelation received from God are properly recorded in the exact way in which God wills. On His part, God speaks in the language of the one writing, using his vocabulary and speaking His message in such a way that naturally or supernaturally the writer can receive and record the message from God. In such portions, the writer's peculiarities are probably noticed least. Dictation, however, should not be regarded as more authoritative than other portions of Scripture. Inspiration extends freely and equally to all portions of Scripture, even in the faithful record of human sin and the repetition of human speech which may be untruth. Inspiration adds to the account the stamp of an infallible record, justifying the reader in accepting the Scriptures in all confidence.

Devotional literature. One of the intricate problems of inspiration is to relate its operation to the writing of the devotional literature of the Old Testament, of which the Psalms are the major portion. Does inspiration merely guarantee an accurate picture of what the writers felt and thought, or does it do more than this? In the case of the recording of human speech, inspiration does not necessarily vouch for the truth of what is said. For instance, in the record of the temptation, Satan is recorded to have said, "Ye shall not surely die" (Gen. 3:4). Inspiration guarantees the accuracy of this quotation of the words of Satan, but does not make these words true. In the case of the Psalmists, then, who were men subject to sin and mistake, whose experiences and thoughts were not necessarily accurate, does inspiration do more than merely give a faithful record?

The answer to the problem is found in the Psalms themselves.

An examination of their content will reveal that God not only caused an inspired record of their thoughts to be written, but worked in their thoughts and their experiences with the result that they revealed God, portrayed the true worship of the heart, the hearing ear of God to prayer, the joy of the Spirit, the burden of sin, and even prophesied of future events. Thus David in his own experience, realizing the preservation of God, speaks of the goodness of God, his praise transcending the bounds of his own experience to that of Christ's, the greater David. He exults, "Therefore my heart is glad, and my glory rejoiceth: my flesh also shall dwell in safety. For thou wilt not leave my soul to Sheol; neither wilt thou suffer thy holy one to see corruption" (Ps. 16:9-10). Much that David said would apply to himself. David could say that his heart was glad, that his flesh rested in hope. David knew that his soul would not remain forever in Sheol. But when David said that his body would not see corruption, he was clearly beyond his own experience and was revealing that of Christ. Peter states this fact in his sermon at Pentecost (Acts 2:25-31), and points out the difference between David and Christ.

Inspiration can, therefore, be said to result in more than a record of devotional thoughts. While the process is inscrutable, inspiration so wrought that an accurate record was made of the thoughts of the writers, these thoughts being prepared by the providence of God. All that the writers experienced was not incorporated in Scripture. Inspiration was selective. As Warfield describes it, "Or consider how a psalmist would be prepared to put into moving verse a piece of normative religious experience: how he would be born with just the right quality of religious sensibility, of parents through whom he should receive just the right hereditary bent, and from whom he should get precisely the right religious example and training, in circumstances of life in which his religious tendencies should be developed precisely on right lines; how he would be brought through just the right experiences to quicken in him the precise emotions he would be called upon to express, and finally would be placed in precisely the exigencies which would call out their expression."[9] While providential preparation should not be confused with inspiration, it can be seen that *with* providential preparation, inspiration of the devotional literature of the Old Testament takes on the nature of the recording of revelation, not revelation by the voice of God, but revelation by the workings of God in the human heart.

---

[9]Warfield, *op. cit.*, p. 1481.

The contemporary prophetic message. Much that is recorded as a message from a prophet concerned the immediate needs of his own generation. To them he would bring God's messages of warning; he would exhort; he would direct their armies; he would choose their leaders; in the manifold needs of the people for the wisdom of God, the prophet would be God's instrument of revelation. In this aspect of prophetic ministry, the Scriptures doubtless record only a small portion. The record is given for the sake of its historic importance and to constitute a living example to later generations. How is inspiration related to this aspect of Scripture?

As in the case of other types of Scripture, inspiration is first of all selective. In the writing of the Scripture, the writer is guided to include and exclude according to the mind of God. Inspiration assures that the record is an accurate one, giving the message of the prophet the character of infallibility. This was true even in the case of the few ungodly men who gave voice to prophecy and were guided in it by God. The work of inspiration in this particular type of Scripture is similar to that operative in recording history in the larger sense, in the writing of history, guiding in the selection and statement of the history, and in the case of prophecy, guiding in the selection and statement of the message and deeds of God through His prophets.

Prophecy of the future. In the nature of prophecy, it frequently took the aspect of predicting future events. It would warn of impending judgment, and in the midst of chastening experiences, it would portray the glory and deliverance that would come with the Messiah. Approximately a fourth of the Old Testament is in the form of prediction. Does inspiration have a peculiar relation to this form of prophecy?

Most of the Old Testament Scripture was comprehended by the writers. They could understand to a large degree the events of history. They could appreciate much of the Psalms. What they wrote was in a large measure passing through their own thoughts and was subject to their understanding. The introduction of predictive prophecy, however, brings to the foreground the statements of future events which were not understood. The prophets themselves confessed that they did not always understand what they wrote. As Peter writes, "Concerning which salvation the prophets sought and searched diligently, who prophesied of the grace that should come unto you: searching what time or what manner of time the Spirit of Christ which was in them did point unto, when it testified beforehand the sufferings of Christ, and the glories that should follow them" (1 Pet. 1:10-11).

The work of inspiration in predictive prophecy is probably more evident than in the other types of Scripture. Here indeed human wisdom was of no avail, and accuracy of the finest kind was demanded. Here inspiration can be tested more severely than in any other field, and the testimony of fulfilled prophecy gives its conclusive voice to the work of the Holy Spirit which caused it to be written. Predictive prophecy required revelation from God in such form that inspiration could cause it to be written revealing the eternal purposes and sovereign will of God. Visions and trances play an important part in some revelation of future events, and the power of God through the Holy Spirit was especially evident.

While distinctive aspects of the operation of the Holy Spirit may be seen, corresponding to the various types of Scripture, in the main inspiration bears the same characteristics in all kinds of Old Testament Scripture. In it all the Spirit guided, excluding the false, including all that the mind of God directed, giving to revelation accurate statement, to history purposeful selection and authentic facts, to providentially guided experience its intimate record of God dealing with the hearts of His servants, to prophecy, whether a contemporary message or predictive, the unfailing accuracy that made it the proper standard for faith to apprehend. The work of inspiration was not accomplished by an impersonal force, by a law of nature, or by providence alone; but the immanent Holy Spirit, working in the hearts and affairs of men, not only revealed the truth of God, but caused the Old Testament to be written, the most amazing document ever to see the light of day, bearing in its pages the unmistakable evidences that the hands which inscribed them were guided by the unwavering, infinitely wise, unfailing Holy Spirit.

V. Inspiration in the New Testament

Inspiration of both Testaments the same. The general facts of inspiration as found in the Old Testament may be applied to the New Testament with equal felicity. The inspiration of the New Testament, like that of the Old, is supernatural, extending to the very words of Scripture without destroying the human element and without losing infallible accuracy. The writings of the New Testament have the same authority, divine origin, and infallibility as the Scriptures of the Old Testament. Each book of the New Testament has its own supporting evidence testifying to its canonicity and inspiration, the details of which cannot be examined here.

The same types of operation of inspiration observed in the Old Testament are found in the New Testament. In the New Testament also the work of inspiration may be seen in the treatment of the unknown past, in the accuracy of historical references, in its moral standards, in its quotation of the words of Christ, in the occasional passages of a devotional or autobiographical nature, in the messages dealing with contemporary problems, and in the accurate prophecies of future events. As in the Old Testament, inspiration selects only what God directed, excludes all that should be omitted, and issues in statement which bears the authority of God however spoken through human medium. The Scriptures of the Old and New Testament are one in authority and in inspiration. Certain peculiarities of the New Testament aspect of inspiration may be noted, however.

The New Testament authenticated by Jesus Christ. It has already been demonstrated that the Old Testament Scriptures are authenticated by the various statements of Christ attributing to them the accuracy and authority of inspired Scripture. A similar authentication may be observed in the New Testament though on a somewhat different basis. Before Christ left His disciples, He promised them the ministry of the Holy Spirit who would guide them in the truth and reveal new truth to them (John 16:12-15). C. I. Scofield has given a concise analysis of this aspect of the truth: "Christ's pre-authentication of the New Testament: (1) He expressly declared that He would leave 'many things' unrevealed (v. 12). (2) He promised that this revelation should be completed ('all things') after the Spirit should come, and that such additional revelation should include new prophecies (v. 13). (3) He chose certain persons to receive such additional revelations, and to be His witnesses to them (Mt. 28:19; John 15:27; 16:13; Acts 1:8; 9:15-17). (4) He gave to their words when speaking for Him in the Spirit precisely the same authority as His own (Mt. 10:14, 15; Lk. 10:16; John 13:20; 17:20; see e. g., 1 Cor. 14:37, and 'Inspiration,' Ex. 4:15; Rev. 22:19)."[10] The apostles, then, spoke and wrote with the authentication and authority of Christ, and the inspiration of the New Testament Scriptures partakes of the peculiar quality of being a work of the Holy Spirit as the person of the Godhead sent into the world at Pentecost. While the work of inspiration in the Old Testament proceeded from the Holy Spirit as immanent in the world, inspiration in the New Testament issues from the Holy Spirit as resident in the church.

The inspiration of the New Testament claimed by the apostles.

---

[10]*Scofield Reference Bible,* Note, p. 1138.

A study of the writings of the New Testament reveal unmistakable evidence that the writers were conscious of inspiration and that they claimed the authority of God not only for their own writings but for the other writings of the New Testament. That the various writers claimed authority for their own teachings is clear enough from Scripture as Warfield, for instance, notes (1 Cor. 2:13; 14:37; Gal. 1:7-8; 1 Thess. 4:2, 15; 2 Thess. 3:6, 12, 14).[11] The interesting and conclusive feature of their testimony, however, is that they declare the inspiration of each other's writings. Warfield cites 1 Timothy 5:18, as an instance of quotation from Deuteronomy ("For the scripture saith, Thou shalt not muzzle the ox when he treadeth out the corn"), and from Luke ("And, The laborer is worthy of his hire"), in one sentence as being both "scripture."[12] Peter, while declaring his own inability to understand all that Paul had written, declares *all* Paul's epistles to be a part of the Scriptures (2 Pet. 3:16). Peter further declares that those who "wrest" Paul's epistles treat other Scriptures with the same unbelief.

Warfield accordingly concludes, "It is no pressure of the writers of the NT to the inspiration of the Scripture, therefore, to look upon it as covering the entire body of 'Scriptures,' the new books which they were themselves adding to this aggregate, as well as the old books, which they had received as Scripture from the fathers."[13]

Method of quotation of the Old Testament a proof of inspiration. It has been commonly argued that the writers of the New Testament claim inspiration for the Old Testament as shown in the method and character of their quotations from the Old Testament. This has already been pointed out in the consideration of inspiration in the Old Testament. There is conversely a testimony to the inspiration of the New Testament in the character of the quotation of the Old Testament. Many writers have discussed the fact that numerous quotations of the New Testament are taken from the LXX, a Greek translation of the Old Testament, which as a translation is that much removed from the accuracy of the original. The quotation of the LXX has been taken by some to indicate that inspiration is not accurate as witnessed by the loose quotations. An analysis of these quotations will demonstrate, however, that the text of the LXX is followed only where it presents the full truth, that the LXX rendering is *changed* freely when correction is necessary, and that quotation of the Old Testament is sometimes rendered in a paraphrase when this is neces-

---

[11]Warfield, *op. cit.*, p. 1483.
[12]*Loc. cit.*
[13]*Loc. cit.*

sary to bring out the meaning. The important fact remaining is that the Holy Spirit evidently guided the whole process of quotation.

Gaussen quotes the findings of Horne as follows: "That learned author reckons eighty-eight verbal quotations that agree with the Alexandrine translations; sixty-four more that are borrowed from them, but with variations; thirty-seven that adopt the same meaning with them without employing their words; sixteen that differ from them in order to agree more nearly with the Hebrew; and, finally, twenty that differ from both the Hebrew and the Septuagint, but in which the sacred authors have paraphrased the Old Testament, in order that the sense in which they quote it may be better understood."[14] The problem instead of being a hindrance to the doctrine of inspiration constitutes an interesting example that the treatment of Old Testament quotations has the authority and accuracy of the Holy Spirit, who is the divine author of both Testaments.

The acceptance of the New Testament by the Apostolic Church. One important fact remains to be noted in the doctrine of inspiration in the New Testament. The testimony of the early church is that the New Testament Scriptures were accepted immediately, book by book, as they were written. Much has been written concerning the date at which the New Testament canon was closed, but the record of the Scriptures themselves indicates it was closed the first moment any portion of the church received all the New Testament books.

Warfield has summed up the matter briefly as follows: "The Canon of the New Testament was completed when the last authoritative book was given to any church by the apostles, and that was when John wrote the Apocalypse, about A. D. 98. . . . The early churches, in short, received, as we receive, into their New Testament all the books historically evinced to them as given by the apostles to the churches as their code of law; and we must not mistake the historical evidences of the slow circulation and authentication of these books over the widely-extended church, for evidence of slowness of 'canonization' of books by the authority of the taste of the church itself."[15]

The New Testament doctrine of inspiration is therefore at one with that of the Old Testament. The problem of apologetics does not change the character of the work of inspiration. The doctrine of the inspiration of the Old Testament is, to all practical purposes, the doctrine of the inspiration of the New Testament.

---

[14]Gaussen, *Theopneustia*, pp. 163-64.
[15]B. B. Warfield, *Revelation and Inspiration*, pp. 455-56.

Chapter VIII

THE OLD TESTAMENT MINISTRY
OF THE HOLY SPIRIT TO MAN

I. Ministry to All Creation

IT IS fundamental to an understanding of the work of the Holy Spirit in the Old Testament to realize that His ministry extends in one way or another to every creature. To some, of course, are given the more general ministries of providence and creation, but the larger work of the Holy Spirit in fallen man has been frequently overlooked. While seldom noted in works on the Holy Spirit, the work of the Holy Spirit in man in the Old Testament is on a large scale and of equal importance to His work in the New Testament, though it is of different character.

Kuyper has summarized the general characteristics of the work of the Holy Spirit in two important propositions: "First, *The work of the Holy Spirit is not confined to the elect and does not begin with their regeneration; but it touches every creature, animate and inanimate, and begins its operations in the elect at the very moment of their origin.* Second, *The proper work of the Holy Spirit in every creature consists in the quickening and sustaining of life with reference to his being and talents, and, in its highest sense, with reference to eternal life, which is his salvation."*[1]

The general nature of the work of the Holy Spirit as Kuyper states it has frequent illustration in the Old Testament as well as in the New Testament. Consideration has already been given to the work of the Spirit in creation, revelation, and inspiration. All of these are illustrations of the general proposition that the work of the Holy Spirit *"touches every creature."* The further consideration of the work of the Holy Spirit in man gives many explicit examples of this ministry which enables one to realize that behind all the history of the Old Testament is the unseen Holy Spirit, touching every phase of the life of man.

---

[1] Abraham Kuyper, *The Work of the Holy Spirit*, p. 46.

II. The Sovereign Indwelling of the Holy Spirit

The Old Testament in contrast to the present age. In the dispensation of grace the Holy Spirit undertakes to indwell every Christian from the moment of regeneration. It is one of the testimonies to God's grace that the Holy Spirit thus makes the bodies of saved men His holy temple. Throughout the entire Old Testament period up to the Day of Pentecost no such universal indwelling of the Holy Spirit is observed. While it was not in the program of God for this feature of the ministry of the Holy Spirit to become universal among believers prior to the age of grace, nevertheless God in His sovereign will and according to His own purposes selected individuals in the Old Testament to whom was given the abiding presence of the Holy Spirit.

Old Testament references to indwelling. The first reference to this doctrine is found in Genesis 41:38, where Pharaoh asks the question concerning Joseph, "Can we find such a one as this, a man in whom the spirit of God is?" Both the Authorized Version and the Revised Standard Version capitalize "spirit" indicating deity, though the American Revision does not. It would seem that the divine Spirit was the intended meaning. While, of course, it may be held that Pharaoh was mistaken, and Joseph was not indwelt by the Holy Spirit, in view of what Joseph had already accomplished and the later revelation of the doctrine of indwelling in the Old Testament, it may be concluded that Pharaoh unwittingly gave voice to the first specific instance of a great doctrine, and the Scriptures include his testimony.

Further references to this same operation of the Spirit are not difficult to find. The tailors who made the garments for the priests are said to have been "filled with the spirit of wisdom" (Ex. 28:3). Of Bezaleel and Aholiab, fine craftsmen who helped build the Tabernacle, it is said, "I have filled him with the Spirit of God, in wisdom, and in understanding, and in knowledge, and in all manner of workmanship" (Ex. 31:3; cf. 35:30-35). The seventy elders who assisted Moses were indwelt by the Holy Spirit (Num. 11:17, 25). Joshua is described as "a man in whom is the Spirit" (Num. 27:18). In the times of the judges, some of the leaders raised up to deliver Israel were filled with the Spirit: Othniel (Judg. 3:10), Gideon (Judg. 6:34), Jephthah (Judg. 11:29), and Samson (Judg. 13:25; 14:6, 19; 15:14). A. B. Simpson would add Deborah to the list, an illustration of a woman leader no doubt indwelt by the Holy Spirit (cf. Judg. 4:4 ff.).[2] The Holy Spirit indwelt both Saul and David (1 Sam. 10:9-10; 16:13). The prophet Daniel was indwelt by the Holy Spirit

[2] A. B. Simpson, *The Holy Spirit or Power From on High*, I, 148-50.

(Dan. 4:8; 5:11-14; 6:3). No doubt all the prophets were indwelt by the Holy Spirit, though this was not necessarily essential to their ministry. From these specific instances and inferences which may be fairly drawn in other cases, the fact that the Holy Spirit indwelt some saints in the Old Testament can be conclusively established.

Important features of indwelling in the Old Testament. Several features of the indwelling of the Holy Spirit in the Old Testament are quite distinctive from the same ministry in the age of grace. It will be noted, first, that the coming of the Spirit to indwell individuals has no apparent relation to spiritual qualities. No record is found of regeneration in these cases as necessarily antecedent to the indwelling of the Holy Spirit. Saul, it is true, received another heart (1 Sam. 10:9), but this is not the normal experience judging by other instances.

A second important factor quite distinct from indwelling as known in the New Testament Church is that indwelling was a sovereign gift usually associated with a special call to service, and it had in view enablement for a specific task. Indwelling was not a universal privilege. Only a few were indwelt by the Holy Spirit, and these were known for their distinctive gift, were sought out as leaders and prophets, and were usually marked men.

A third important distinction found in the Old Testament doctrine of indwelling was that it was in many cases temporary. While the New Testament saint need never fear loss of the indwelling presence of the Holy Spirit, however He may be hindered in His ministry by sin, the Old Testament saint knew the presence of the Spirit was a special privilege which could be withdrawn at will even as it was given. Thus, of Saul, it is revealed that the Holy Spirit left him (1 Sam. 16:14), and David prayed earnestly after his sin, "Cast me not away from thy presence; and take not thy holy Spirit from me" (Ps. 51:11). No Christian need ever pray the prayer of David, but under the Old Testament order there was great danger of losing the presence of the Spirit.

The contrast between the Old Testament and New Testament order is brought out clearly by the teachings of Christ in the Gospels. When Christ predicted: "He that believeth on me, as the scripture hath said, from within him shall flow rivers of living water" (John 7:38), He was speaking of the future fullness of the Spirit which would begin at Pentecost. John adds the explanation, "But this spake he of the Spirit, which they that believed on him were to receive: for the Spirit was not yet given; because Jesus was not yet glorified" (John 7:39). In John 14:17, the same contrast between the Old Testament order obtaining up to Pentecost and the present age is made. Christ said of the Spirit, "for he abideth with you, and shall be in you" (John 14:17). The permanent indwelling was still a future expectation. In John 16:13 Christ again speaks of the Spirit as one who is to come: "Howbeit when he, the Spirit of truth, is come. . . ." The presence of the indwelling Spirit in the Old Testament must, therefore, be regarded as sovereign, a rare rather than a usual gift, and often associated with some specific task for which enablement was necessary.

III. The Work of the Holy Spirit in Restraining Sin

From the very nature of the Holy Spirit, one could anticipate that He would be engaged in a ministry designed to restrain sin not only in the life of the saint but also in the life of the unsaved. A study of the various ministries of the Holy Spirit will reveal that many of them tended to restrain from sin though comparatively few direct references to this ministry are found.

References in Scripture. In connection with the antediluvian civilization, God said, "My Spirit shall not strive with man for ever, for that he also is flesh: yet shall his days be a hundred and twenty years" (Gen. 6:3). The pronouncement that the work of striving with man would cease is sufficient evidence that this ministry had been given to the world prior to the flood. The Holy Spirit undertook to restrain the power of Satan and the display of sin of the human heart.

From the New Testament, we gather that the work of the Holy Spirit in restraining men from sin continues throughout the dispensation of grace. According to 2 Thessalonians 2:7, the Holy Spirit restrains from sin, "For the mystery of lawlessness doth already work: only there is one that restraineth now, until he be taken out of the way." Isaiah 59:19 in the Authorized Version indicates that it is the customary work of the Holy Spirit to lift up a standard against sin now and in the millennium.

Works related to restraining sin. While the work of the Holy Spirit in restraining sin is sustained by relatively few explicit references, a survey of His other ministries reveals several which have a direct bearing on restraint of sin. His work in oral revelation, revealing the will of God and warning against judgment, tended to restrain sin. A similar effect resulted from the inspiration of the written Word. Further confirmation of the doctrine is found in reference to the Third Person as the *Holy Spirit* (Ps. 51:11; Isa. 63:10-11) and as the *Good Spirit* (Neh. 9:20; Ps. 143:10), the titles not only speaking of His person, but of His work. In the Isaiah passage, particularly, it is noted that the judgment came because they had rebelled against the Holy Spirit. This rebellion was not only a rejection of His person, but a rejection of His restraint and striving with them. From these several indications, then, it may be concluded that the Holy Spirit had a most vital relationship to the moral character of men in the Old Testament, a ministry which resulted in the restraint of sin, comparable to that observed in a general way throughout every dispensation. It may be noted that there is prediction of a great future work of the Holy Spirit in the millennium in which the Holy Spirit effects a great restraint of sin and inspires holy character (Isa. 32:15 ff.; 44:3-5; Ezek. 36:26 ff.; Zech. 12:10).

IV. Illumination and Enablement for Service

The most frequent mention of the Holy Spirit in the Old Testament is in connection with enablement for various kinds of service, including illumination and bestowal of wisdom. A wide variety of this type of ministry can be observed. While the extent of this enablement is in sharp contrast to the abundant grace evident in the life of the Christian, it was suited for the Old Testament period and in harmony with the covenant relation of God and Israel.

Gift of wisdom. First to be noted in the Scripture is the work of the Holy Spirit in giving wisdom for leadership and administration. Illustrations are frequently found throughout the Old Testament, beginning with Joseph, who was recognized by Pharaoh as possessing more than human attainments (Gen. 41:38-40). Joshua possessed a work of the Holy Spirit in enabling him (Num. 27:18), and in the times of the judges, Othniel (Judg. 3:10), Gideon (Judg. 6:34), and Jephthah (Judg. 11:29) were given enablement for their tasks. The bestowal of the Holy Spirit upon Saul (1 Sam. 10:10), and upon David (1 Sam. 16:13), was in anticipation of their future work as kings of Israel. It will be noted that enablement was objective. Rather than a universal enablement available for all who were yielded to the Holy Spirit, the enablement granted was sovereign, paralleling to some degree the sovereign bestowal of spiritual gifts in the New Testament period.

Gifts of special skills. A second aspect of the work of the Holy Spirit in enablement is found in imparting special skill in various arts. The cases of the tailors for the priestly garments (Ex. 28:3), and the workmen of the Tabernacle (Ex. 31:3; cf. 35:30-35) have already been noted in another connection. The few instances which are given specific mention probably are only illustrations of a far more widespread ministry by the Holy Spirit. It is possible that such instances as the mention of Hiram of Tyre (1 Kings 7:14) as one "filled with wisdom and understanding and skill, to work all works in brass," may be taken to indicate a work of the Holy Spirit in enablement, as E. Y. Mullins holds.[3] The thought of spiritual enablement in such cases does not exclude the idea of natural ability, but indicates both an act of providence in the bestowal of the natural ability latent in the individual and a special quickening to accomplish the task. While the natural is not excluded, the resultant is clearly supernatural and impossible without the enablement of the Holy Spirit.

Gifts of unusual physical strength. A third aspect of the work of the Holy Spirit in this connection is found in occasional instances where physical strength is bestowed on certain individuals in such measure as to exceed the possible strength of the human body. The outstanding illustration, of course, is Samson, who during his life gave frequent illustrations of superhuman feats when the power of the Holy Spirit was upon him (Judg. 13:25; 14:6, 19; 15:14). Because of persistent sin, his power was lost for a time, only to be regained in the final act of his life. Without doubt many of the feats of the Old Testament heroes were accomplished in the power of the Holy Spirit, though explicit reference is lacking.

The most important work of the Holy Spirit on behalf of man has already been discussed at length in the consideration of the work of the Holy Spirit in oral revelation and in prophecy, to which can be added the work of inspiration of the Scriptures. In all these important fields of ministry, the powers of the human mind were exceeded by far in the enablement given by the Holy Spirit. The supernatural revelation, the prophetic gift, the spiritual wisdom displayed in the interpretation of dreams, the infallible guidance of the Holy Spirit in the writings of the Scriptures are each severally most vital undertakings by the Holy Spirit. As in the other ministries of the Holy Spirit, these also were sovereign in their bestowal, by no means being available to all who sought them. While there are some indications of a universal ministry of the Holy Spirit (cf. Neh. 9:20), and the invitation of Proverbs 1:23 to pour out the Holy Spirit on those who turn to God seems general, a close study of the Old Testament will reveal that these ministries were never universal, the benefits accruing from their operation being known only through the prophets and those who were chosen of God. Reserved for the New Testament are the peculiar benefits of grace in the universal indwelling of the Holy Spirit and the possibility of all spiritual fruit.

---

[3]*International Standard Bible Encyclopaedia,* "Holy Spirit," p. 1407.

V. Old Testament Miracles

Extent of Old Testament miracles. A survey of the Old Testament reveals an abundance of miracles of all descriptions accomplished by the power of God. As in the New Testament, no occasion is found where miracles are subject to explanation, their power being explained by the immediate agency of God. Two of the three great periods of miraculous works are found in the Old Testament: the period of Moses, and the period of Elisha and Elijah. The third belongs to the lifetime of Christ and the apostles. The question is not directly answered whether the miracles of the Old Testament are to be ascribed to the Godhead without personal distinction, or whether the Scriptures give sufficient testimony to attribute miracles in the Old Testament to the ministry of a distinct person.

Relation of the Holy Spirit to Old Testament miracles. A clear reference to miracles as being generally accomplished by the work of the Holy Spirit is not found in the Old Testament. The power which effects miracles is usually said to be Jehovah, without distinction as to the persons of the Godhead. The work of miracles seems to be the prerogative of each person of the Trinity severally as well as the work of the one God. Specific reference, however, is found to some ministries of the Holy Spirit which would lead us to believe that the Third Person was the agent of miracles in many instances. From the work of the Holy Spirit in creation and providence, it is clear that He is engaged in a vital work in the material world. The immanence of the Holy Spirit is more prominent than the immanence of the other persons, though the attribute, of course, is equal in all three persons. His work in men both in prophetic ministry and enablement for all service indicates His intimate relation to events. From these general arguments, it may be inferred that it would be in harmony with all we know for the Holy Spirit to effect miracles, but the conclusion remains an inference.

Owen comes to this conclusion, even though the specific arguments are less definite then we might wish: "The third sort of the immediate extraordinary operations of the Holy Ghost are miracles; such as were frequently wrought under the Old Testament, by Moses, Joshua, Elijah, Elisha, and others; those by Moses exceeding, if the Jews mistake not, all the rest. Now these were all the immediate effects of the Divine power of the Holy Ghost; for by miracles we mean such effects as are really beyond and above the power of natural causes, however applied."[4]

An examination of men who were filled with the Holy Spirit

---

[4] *A Discourse Concerning the Holy Spirit,* p. 79.

under the Old Testament economy will reveal many miraculous works accomplished by them. Samson, for instance, did the humanly impossible through the power of the Holy Spirit. Obadiah expressed the fear that the Holy Spirit would catch Elijah away when he would try to find him (1 Kings 18:12). Ezekiel was caught up by the Holy Spirit (Ezek. 3:12 ff.). These operations of the Holy Spirit connote a work very similar to the work of God in effecting miracles.

Relation of the Holy Spirit to New Testament miracles. The Gospel records reveal an extended ministry by Christ in the form of miracles. These were the prophesied emblems to be displayed when the Messiah came. In two instances, the miracles of Christ are attributed to the power of the Holy Spirit. In Matthew 12:28, Christ states that He casts out demons by the Holy Spirit, and in Luke 4:14-18, the work of Christ in healing the sick is said to result from His anointing by the Holy Spirit. If Christ in the flesh wrought miracles by the power of the Holy Spirit, even though His human nature was joined to the divine nature of the Second Person of the Trinity, how much more would it be necessary for men who are subject to sin to be dependent on the same Holy Spirit to effect their miracles! The fact that the Holy Spirit accomplished miracles on the behalf of Christ is a strong argument for assuming that a similar ministry was given to men in the Old Testament whom God had appointed His prophets.

While revelation on the agency of miracles in the Old Testament lacks the definite proof afforded in other phases of the doctrine of the Holy Spirit, it may be safely assumed that the Holy Spirit as the Third Person was the divine agency in many miraculous works in the Old Testament, without excluding the possibility that the other persons of the Trinity had a similar ministry.

The work of the Holy Spirit in the Old Testament taken as a whole is an important sphere of doctrine, not because it forms the pattern of His present undertaking, but because it reveals the need for His ministry in every age, and serves to indicate some of the principles which abide amidst all the dispensational distinctions revealed in the Scripture. In contrast, the age of grace shines with all the more brilliant luster, the exceeding abundance of all the ministries of the Spirit to all saints constituting a display of the grace of God such as the world has never seen before. As we contemplate the noble lives of so many of the Old Testament saints in spite of their more limited privilege, what a challenge arises to the Christian basking in all the fullness of spiritual privilege to yield himself utterly to the control of the Holy Spirit that in his life may be found all the full-orbed fruit of the Spirit!

PART THREE

THE HOLY SPIRIT IN RELATION TO CHRIST

CHAPTER IX

THE HOLY SPIRIT IN RELATION TO THE BIRTH OF CHRIST

I. THE CHARACTER OF THE GOSPELS

TO THE careful interpreter of the Scriptures, no portion of the Word of God requires more careful exegesis than the Gospel narratives. The combination of the elements of three dispensations, Law, Grace, and Kingdom, multiply the problems of interpretation, yet the accounts are so simple in statement that a child may read with profit.

Christ lived in the days of the setting sun of Mosaic law. Its provisions had ruled Israel for fifteen hundred years, more frequently disobeyed than obeyed, equally misinterpreted by the literal Pharisee and the liberal Sadducee. It had been intended as a schoolmaster to bring Israel to Christ (Gal. 3:24), but its pupils had not learned their lessons.

Christ came to fulfill the law, not only in His death on the cross, but in His own life to demonstrate perfect obedience. He was "made under the law" (Gal. 4:4). Repeatedly in His messages, Christ referred to and interpreted the law, correcting the interpretations which had abused it and adding new concepts of God and truth. Even as Christ had a backward look at times to the law, so also His prophetic message anticipated the coming glorious kingdom. He taught the people the principles of the kingdom, warned of the danger of exclusion, raised a lofty standard which pierced through the outward forms of religion to matters of the heart. His Messianic message was presented with all the clarity and revelation which could be expected from His lips. As the growing unbelief of the people indicated their rejection and brought the shadow of the cross nearer, Christ turned to truth concerning the present age, the kingdom not in its outward display, but in its mystery form. The fulfillment of the promise of God to David was postponed, and into the foreground came the undeclared purpose of God to call out from every nation a new company, composed of both Jew and Gentile, independent of all His promises to Israel, having its own calling and destiny. Only by bearing in mind that Christ lived in His prophetic ministry in the three dispensations of law, grace, and kingdom is it possible to interpret with accuracy and profit the Gospel narratives which contain extended reference to all three systems of truth.

The incarnation. Aside from the intricate nature of the prophetic truth revealed by Christ, a further amazing event was enacted by God becoming incarnate, assuming human form, and living for a time within the limitations of the human frame. Culminating in the death and resurrection of Christ, the pages of the Gospels portray the most magnificent revelation, have reference to every important line of truth, and furnish a field of study which has been explored rather than mined for its treasures. It is not without point that the Old Testament so largely anticipates and looks forward to the coming of the Messiah, and the New Testament, beginning with Acts, looks back to the work of Christ and gives itself to the task of interpreting what He did and what He is yet to do.

Mosaic law continues to the cross. The period of time spanned by the Gospels is largely in the dispensation of the law, at least up to the death of Christ, and after this event fulfilling the law, the period of transition properly begins. Of primary interest in the Gospels is the relation of the Holy Spirit to Christ during His life on earth. Little that is new is found in the relation of the Holy Spirit to other men.

II. The Work of the Spirit in the Gospels

The work of the Spirit Messianic. The period of the Gospels is of special interest in the study of the doctrine of the Holy Spirit because the work of the Spirit is Messianic in every dispensation to a large degree. In the Old Testament, prophecy abounds on the theme of the Messiah and of the work of the Holy Spirit in relation to Him. Much of this is in reference to the millennium, but some is more general. Notable passages are Isaiah 11:2-3, speaking of the fact that the Spirit would rest on Christ; Isaiah 42:1-4, quoted as fulfilled in His person and work (Luke 4:17-21). Not only in relation to His person, but also in relation to Messianic times the Holy Spirit is revealed to undertake for man. It is clear that the work of the Holy Spirit is inseparably related to all the Messianic purpose (Isa. 32:15 ff.; 44:3-5; Ezek. 36:26 ff.; Zech. 12:10).

The work of the Spirit in the Gospels follows the Old Testament pattern. As in the Old Testament, the work of the Holy Spirit in relation to men other than Christ is individual and sovereign throughout the period of the Gospels. As in the Old Testament, some saints were filled with the Spirit, but this ministry was limited to a few, only four people being mentioned in addition to Christ: John the Baptist

(Luke 1:15). Elizabeth (Luke 1:41), Zacharias (Luke 1:67), and Simeon (Luke 2:25). It was predicted that the disciples would be told by the Spirit what to say in persecution (Matt. 10:20; Mark 13:11; Luke 12:12). In John 20:22, apparently a temporary filling of the Spirit was given to provide for their spiritual needs prior to Pentecost. These Gospel passages were not intended to be a norm for the present age, but in general continue the ministry of the Spirit as it had been in the Old Testament.

The matter of greatest importance in the study of the Holy Spirit in the Gospels is the consideration of His ministry to Christ, to be considered here, and the predictions of His ministry through this age which will be subject to later discussion.

III. The Virgin Birth

There are few supernatural acts of God which present a more inscrutable mystery than the birth of Christ. All the elements of the miraculous are present, defying the reason of man and the normal course of nature; but whereas other miracles seem out of harmony with known natural law, the birth of Christ seems to require a change in the nature of God Himself. While the difficulties present no problem to faith, the statement of the factors that entered into the birth of Christ and their meaning are a most serious problem to the theologian. The doctrine of the virgin birth has been attacked vigorously because of its central importance to the Christian faith, and it has been defended with the best of scholarship and sustained by a mass of argument. If one comes to the Scriptures in simple faith, building on the foundation of their inspiration and infallibility, the problem is to fathom and state in accurate terms what actually occurred. While all the questions which might arise cannot be answered, certain truths are made clear in the Scripture.

The Holy Spirit the agent of conception. The Scriptures bear a clear testimony to the work of the Holy Spirit which resulted in the conception of Christ. Matthew reveals that Mary "was found with child of the Holy Spirit," and quotes the angel, "Joseph, thou son of David, fear not to take unto thee Mary thy wife: for that which is conceived in her is of the Holy Spirit. And she shall bring forth a son, and thou shalt call his name JESUS; for it is he that shall save his people from their sins" (Matt. 1:18, 20-21). Luke is even more specific. "And the angel answered and said unto her, The Holy Spirit shall come upon thee, and the power of the Most High shall overshadow thee: wherefore also the holy thing which is begotten shall be called the Son of God" (Luke 1:35). These passages should settle beyond doubt that Christ had no human father. The conception of Christ is definitely attributed to the Holy Spirit.

As in other operations of the Holy Spirit, however, the First Person and the Second Person are vitally related to His work. According to Hebrews 10:5, quoting Psalm 40:6, Christ said, "Sacrifice and offering thou wouldest not, but a body didst thou prepare for me." The preparation of the body of Christ is related to a work of the Father. Hebrews 2:14, on the other hand, indicates that Christ took flesh and blood by an act of His own will. The life which was joined to the humanity of Christ was none other than the Second Person, who had existed from eternity. The inscrutable mystery can be stated, then, that Christ was begotten of the Holy Spirit; the life which was joined to humanity was that of the Second Person, and the First Person became the Father of the humanity of Christ. The Scriptures never refer to the Holy Spirit as the Father of Christ.

Mary the mother of Christ. The Scriptures considered are unequivocal in tracing the origin of the humanity of Christ to normal birth to Mary, the wife of Joseph. While the conception was supernatural, the birth of Christ seems to follow the natural pattern. The prophecies of the Old Testament are explicit that the Messiah should be born of a woman, a virgin, and Mary is said to fulfill these prophecies (Gen. 3:15; Isa. 7:14; Matt. 1:18, 20-23; 2:11, 13, 20-21; 12:48; 13:55; Mark 3:31; 6:3; Luke 1:35, 43; 2:5-7, 16, 34, 48, 51; 8:19-20; John 19:25-27; Acts 1:14; Gal. 4:4). The evidence is so abundant for the motherhood of Mary that no serious attempts have been made to deny it even on the part of modern liberal scholarship. In the ancient church only heretics questioned it. The Cerinthian heresy denied that the conception was miraculous and held that human Jesus was possessed only for a time with a heavenly spirit,[1] but this did not deny a normal birth. The Docetics, however, held that His body was unreal, which implies that Jesus was not actually born.

IV. The Nature of the Conception of Christ

An investigation into the nature of the conception of Christ has its chief difficulty in solving the problem of the origin of the humanity of Christ. It is clear that Christ was born of Mary, yet certain features of His person are quite distinct from the human race. The problem of deity becoming part of humanity is a great miracle, but the origin of a sinless humanity is a theological problem of the first magnitude. Many questions could be asked. Did the humanity

---

[1]George Park Fisher, *History of Christian Doctrine*, p. 56.

of Christ proceed from Mary alone? Was the humanity a product of generation or creation? Why was the imputation of sin upon the whole human race apparently nonoperative in the case of Christ? Was His human nature sinless or merely sanctified? Such questions naturally arise in the course of the study of the conception of Christ. To a large extent we are shut up to reason, without explicit revelation, but to the degree a solution can be found a defense of the conception of Christ from serious errors is furnished. A proper examination of this field of truth would refute such doctrines as that of the immaculate conception of Mary and heresies in the statement of the hypostatic union.

Was the humanity of Christ a product of generation or creation? The language of the Scriptures seems to portray the birth of Christ as proceeding from generation. It is therefore said that Christ was *born* (Matt. 2:1), *conceived* (Matt. 1:20), *brought forth* (Luke 2:7), *made of a woman* (Gal. 4:4). It is equally clear that the generation of Christ is quite distinct from all other cases; He was born of a virgin. The language of Scripture in speaking of the birth of Christ does not, then, finally settle the question. It is not a problem of the nature of His birth, but of the nature of His conception.

The problem of transmission of life is by no means limited to the birth of Christ. The opposing theories of traducianism and creationism in respect to the origin of the soul of man have some of the same problems. Traducianism as far as the race as a whole is concerned has the advantage in explaining the transmission of sin from generation to generation, whereas creationism must postulate the creation of each soul, with the attendant dilemma of God either creating an impure soul, or creating a pure soul with immediate defilement following. The creationist, in regard to the conception of Christ, could say that His soul was created sinless and that in His case it was not subsequently defiled, while the traducianist must find some other explanation. The creation theory, however, applies only to the immaterial part of man, and does not take into account the human body, which ordinarily in the race has in it the sinful desires which are observed in everyone. In the case of Christ, He was not only born with a sinless soul and spirit, but He had with it an undefiled body. The creation theory, then, does not really solve the problem, as Charles Hodge would argue.[2]

No solution has ever been offered which solved all the problems in the case. All must confess that the unknown factors are far greater

---

[2]Charles Hodge, *Systematic Theology*, II, 72.

in number than the known and that we are dealing with an effect for which no explanation is given in Scripture aside from the agency of the Holy Spirit and the known attributes of God. The truth probably is that the conception of Christ is both generation and creation, generation in the sense that He was born of a woman who conceived by the Holy Spirit, creation in the sense that a Second Adam was the product, a member of the race and yet the Federal Head of a new race. By analogy, Abraham was at once a Gentile and the first of the Israelite fathers. Christ was at once a member of the race and the Head of a new people.

Owen advances the argument that the conception of Christ can be thought of as creation more accurately than generation: "This act of the Spirit was a creating act; not indeed like the first creating act, which produced the matter of all things out of nothing; but like those subsequent acts of creation, whereby out of matter already prepared, things were made what they were not before, and which they had not active disposition to, nor concurrence in. So man was formed of the dust of the earth, and woman of a rib taken from man. Thus in forming the body of Christ; though it was effected by an act of infinite creating power, yet it was made of the substance of the blessed Virgin."[3] Dorner seems to hold much the same view: "And the soul itself is not given by Mary nor by the race, but by a Divine creative act."[4] The viewpoint of Owen and Dorner, including as it does the necessary connection with the race, presents less difficulties than the other view. Those holding the traducian view of the origin of the soul generally avoid the use of the word *creation* in connection with the humanity of Christ, but this is not at all necessary. The natural method as used in the race might be traducian, while the supernatural method used in Christ might be likened to creation. If the word *creation* is used in regard to Christ, it must be severely limited as Owen does to avoid any thought of creation *ex nihilo*. It partakes of the idea of both creation and generation.

Was the humanity of Christ sinless or merely sanctified? One of the chief difficulties in avoiding the idea of generation of the humanity of Christ is that one is faced with the problem of producing through a sinful medium a holy child. The fact that the child born to Mary is sinless is conceded by all who accept the Scriptures. How can Mary become the mother of a holy and sinless child?

Modern Roman Catholics attempt to solve the problem of the sinlessness of Christ by declaring the immaculate conception of Mary.

---

[3]John Owen, *A Discourse Concerning the Holy Spirit*, pp. 91-92.
[4]I. A. Dorner, *A System of Christian Doctrine*, III, 341.

Moran writes: ". . . because she was to be the Mother of Our Saviour, she was in view of His merits preserved free from the stain of original sin from the very first instant of her conception. This glorious prerogative of Mary was revealed by God and solemnly defined by His Church."[5] Protestant objection to this doctrine is that it is not sustained in Scripture and does not solve this problem at all. It removes it from Christ to Mary, who had both human parents, which would make the problem even greater. The difficulty is that Mary, though partaking of the sin of the race, yet gave birth to a holy child. The problem is related to the human nature of Christ.

If the humanity is the object of an act described as creative, the problem is much relieved, but if the humanity is transmitted in the act of conception, some explanation must be found. Shedd's answer is that the humanity is sanctified before it is joined to deity: "The human nature assumed in union with the Logos was miraculously sanctified, so as to be sinless and perfect."[6] In support of this argument he quotes various Scriptures to the point that Christ is holy and sinless. Shedd concludes: "With these statements of the symbols, the theologians agree. They assert the sinfulness of the Virgin Mary, the consequent sinfulness of human nature as transmitted by her, and the necessity of its being redeemed and sanctified, in order to be fitted for a personal union with the Logos."[7] What Shedd apparently overlooks is the tremendous difference between being sanctified and being holy. Every saint in heaven is sanctified and free from all sin, and as such is a token of God's grace through eternity. The case would be quite different, however, if any saint could be found who had never known sin. Of Christ, however, it is said specifically that He "knew no sin" (2 Cor. 5:21).

One must choose, then, between the view that the humanity of Christ came into existence creatively, and the view that it was transmitted in its natural sinful state and sanctified before being joined to deity. Augustine who advanced and supported the idea of traducianism in respect to the race as a whole sums up the dilemma in these words: "If the soul of Christ be derived from Adam's soul, he, in assuming it to himself, cleansed it so that when he came into this world he was born of the Virgin perfectly free from sin either actual or transmitted. If, however, the souls of men are not derived from that one soul, and it is only by the flesh that original sin is

---

[5]Kieran P. Moran, *Discourses on the Holy Ghost*, edited by Lester M. Dooley, p. 134.
[6]W. G. T. Shedd, *Dogmatic Theology*, II, 296.
[7]*Ibid.*, p. 297.

transmitted from Adam, the Son of God created a soul for himself, as he creates souls for all other men, but he united it not to sinful flesh, but to the 'likeness of sinful flesh,' Rom. 8:3."[8]

There is a sense, however, in which both views demand sanctification. Owen who insists on the creative idea also affirms the idea of sanctification: "The human nature of Christ being thus miraculously formed, was sanctified from the instant of its conception, and filled with grace according to its capacity. Being not begotten by natural generation, it desired no taint of original sin from Adam; it was obnoxious to no charge of sin, but was absolutely innocent and spotless, as Adam was in the day he was created."[9] Owen, however, uses the thought of sanctification in a different sense than Shedd does. To Owen, sanctification is merely setting aside to holy use with a positive endowment of grace, while Shedd includes in the idea the thought of cleansing from defilement.

The question of whether the humanity of Christ was sinless or merely sanctified must be answered by the positive assertion that it was ever sinless.

Was Adam's sin imputed to Christ? The doctrine of imputation, while not a popular subject of study by Christians generally, lies at the heart of the whole program of salvation. The Epistle to the Romans has as its central theme the doctrine of imputation. When Christ died on the cross, all sin was imputed to Him, with the result that all the righteousness of God can be imputed to the believer in Christ. While the imputation of Adam's sin to Christ on the cross is commonly accepted, what can be said of the imputation of sin to Christ at His conception? A study of Romans 5:12-21 will reveal the whole race under the condemnation of Adam in that Adam's sin, while not theirs experimentally, by imputation becomes the burden of his seed. Entirely apart from the sin nature of man which may be transmitted mediately, imputation of sin is immediate.[10] If the problem of the mediate transmission of a sin nature to Christ may be solved by accepting the theory of creation as Owen defines it, the problem of imputation remains. It is clear from Scripture that Adam's sin was not imputed to Christ until the cross. How can this be explained?

Very little attention has been given to this theme by theological writers, and this not without cause. The Scriptures make it clear

---

[8]Augustine, Letter 164, quoted by Shedd, *loc. cit.*
[9]Owen, *op. cit.*, p. 95.
[10]Charles Hodge, *Systematic Theology*, II, 192-203.

that Adam's sin was not imputed to Christ until the cross, but do not explain why. While the problem cannot be finally solved, certain observations can be made.

First, it is in the nature of imputation that it is related to judgment rather than to experience. Imputation has in view our standing before God as our Judge. Imputation in itself does not influence men to sin or have any real effect upon man's will or experience, though it may result in a difference in divine blessings. Thus in the case of Christ, imputation of sin does not become an issue until Christ takes our place of judgment on the cross. Then imputation becomes a reality.

Second, in the nature of His position as the Second Adam, Christ was the Head of a new people. While it was necessary for the purpose of incarnation for Christ to become truly human, it was not necessary in His conception to partake of Adam's sin. The imputation of sin to Christ at birth is contrary to the evident purpose of God and out of harmony with the program of His life and ministry prior to the cross. Christ is never said to be *in Adam,* while everyone else at birth is so regarded in Scripture. To be *in Christ* is to sever our connection *in Adam.* The two ideas and two positions are at opposite poles.

Third, it was essential to redemptive purpose that the Savior be able to save and be willing to save. All those in Adam fail to meet either of these conditions. If sin had been imputed to Christ at His conception, it would not only have made impossible the union of God and man, but it would have made impossible His substitutionary sacrifice. He would, therefore, be dying for His own sins justly His because of imputation, rather than dying willingly as the sinless One who voluntarily took unto Himself the judgment of sin. It may be concluded, therefore, that the imputation of Adam's sin to Christ did not take place at the conception and that this is in harmony with all we know of Christ.

V. The Humanity of Christ

More important from a practical standpoint than the inquiry as to the nature of the conception of Christ are the conclusions relative to the nature of His humanity. Here we deal not with speculation but with revelation, and the conclusions reached are of great importance in determining the doctrine of His person. While it is not possible to discuss the intricacies of the doctrine of the hypostatic union, attention may be directed to the humanity of Christ resulting from the work of the Holy Spirit, that humanity which was joined inseparably without confusion or loss of its true humanity to the Second Person of the Trinity.

The elements of the humanity of Christ. The Scriptures make it clear that the humanity of Christ included all the essential elements. Christ possessed a true body, composed of flesh and blood and all the normal human functions (Heb. 2:14). The immaterial factors of soul (Matt. 26:38; Mark 14:34; John 12:27; Acts 2:27) and spirit (Mark 2:8; 8:12; Luke 23:46; John 11:33; 13:21) are included in His humanity. It may be conceded that some of the characteristics of His body were temporary and were abandoned after His death in the glory of His resurrection, but this argument has no bearing on the validity and completeness of His humanity. Only the characteristics of the body were subject to change, and this also followed the pattern of all flesh in that Christ died and in resurrection received a spiritual body, the pattern of those who will be raised in Him. The Scriptures make it clear, then, that Christ did not take to Himself in the incarnation a human body which was indwelt by deity, but that rather He took to Himself a human nature *and* body. He did not simply possess a human body, but He possessed a human nature. Yet, in the incarnation, Christ did not take possession of a human person, else He would have had dual personality. As Charles Hodge says, "The Son of God did not unite Himself with a human person, but with a human nature. The proof of this is that Christ is but one person."[11] It may be concluded that the Scriptures demand that the humanity of Christ be complete, and any other viewpoint is a serious departure from revealed truth.

The human nature without sin. In contrast to all other human beings, Christ was without sin both in His immaterial and His material being. This was essential to the hypostatic union as it is inconceivable that deity could be united with humanity in one person if this would involve sin. While the attributes of the divine nature do not transfer to the human nature, the attributes of either nature may be attributed to the person of Christ. Therefore, if the human nature were sinful, the person of Christ would have this characteristic. It is essential to every important doctrine that the person of Christ be sinless and to this the Scriptures give abundant testimony (Isa. 53:9; John 8:46; 2 Cor. 5:21; Heb. 4:15; 7:26; 1 Pet. 1:19; 2:22; 1 John 3:5). The sinlessness of the human nature is a result of the work of the Holy Spirit in conception, as we have seen, the humanity being kept from all sin.

---

[11]*Ibid.,* II, 391.

The human nature partook of unmoral limitations. While guarded from every taint of sin, the human nature of Christ partook of the limitations true of humanity. This involved on the part of the human nature that it was temptable and peccable, even though the person of Christ was impeccable. The human nature lacked omniscience, omnipotence, omnipresence, and infinity which, of course, characterized the divine nature. The body of Christ had all the normal feelings and emotions which are natural to humanity except those arising in a sin nature. There was nothing lacking in His humanity which was essential to it, and there was nothing added to His humanity which was unusual, apart from the divine nature itself. The human nature of Christ was very similar to that of Adam's before the fall, the great difference being found in its union with the divine nature.

Christ was the seed of David. While the birth and conception of Christ involved many unusual factors, and while we do not understand how all these elements were produced, the fact is clear that Christ was born of the seed of David as Mary's true son. His was the lineage of David as to His humanity, and probably the racial characteristics of Israel were evident in the body of Christ apart from sin. Christ was never accused of not being a true Israelite as far as His race was concerned. It is essential to all the purpose of God in fulfilling His promises to David that Christ should be of his seed. On this hangs the fulfillment of the prophecies relating to the millennial kingdom and God's purpose relative to the earth. The viewpoint that the humanity of Christ was effected creatively does not exclude this aspect, but rather includes all the natural features related to His conception and birth.

The record of Scripture does not satisfy in every respect the natural curiosity of an inquiring mind into the various factors of the conception and birth of Christ. Sufficient is revealed, however, to satisfy both faith and reason. However inscrutable the process, the birth of Christ is clearly revealed to have resulted from conception by the Holy Spirit. The eternal Second Person was forever united to a complete and sinless humanity, providing in His birth the provision of God for revelation and salvation.

CHAPTER X

THE HOLY SPIRIT IN THE LIFE OF CHRIST

I. THE HOLY SPIRIT IN CHRIST AS A CHILD

CONCERNING the period of the life of Christ from His birth to the beginning of His public ministry, comparatively little is known, only the events surrounding His birth and the incident in the temple at the age of twelve being revealed. The relation of the Holy Spirit to Christ during this period is not the subject of extended revelation, but a number of important conclusions may be reached.

Christ filled with the Holy Spirit from the moment of conception. In the Old Testament predictions of Christ, it is expressly revealed that Christ should have the fullness of the Holy Spirit. Such passages as Isaiah 11:2-3, 42:1-4 and 61:1-2 are explicit. The Gospels speak frequently of the fulfillment of these passages, and particularly after His baptism reveal Christ as filled with the Holy Spirit (Luke 4:1). While it is not possible to produce evidence beyond question, it is a matter of reasonable inference that Christ was filled with the Holy Spirit from the very moment of conception. A number of reasons present themselves for holding this opinion.

From the doctrine of the Trinity, it may be inferred that the persons of the Trinity are inseparable. For this reason, the person of Christ even when in the womb of the Virgin Mary was attended and filled by the Father and the Holy Spirit.

In the case of John the Baptist, it is revealed that he was filled with the Holy Spirit from his mother's womb (Luke 1:15). If this blessing should attend the birth of the forerunner of Christ, it is inconceivable that the blessedness of Christ Himself should be less in degree.

According to John 3:34, the Holy Spirit is not given by measure unto Christ, His ministry to Christ and His presence being abundant in every particular. As the verb is in the present tense, it would indicate that this is characteristic and continual.

Not a single reason can be found why the Holy Spirit should not have filled Christ from the moment of conception. As the person of Christ was ever holy and without sin there was nothing to hinder the full ministry of the Spirit. The purposes of God being so great in Christ, and the filling of the Holy Spirit being so evidently in keeping with His person, the reasonable conclusion may be reached that Christ always possessed the fullness of the Holy Spirit.

The human nature of Christ possessed all spiritual gifts. As a result of being filled with the Holy Spirit, the human nature of Christ may be said to have possessed all spiritual gifts. It is clear that in the case of the average Christian being filled with the Spirit does not necessarily mean that all spiritual gifts have been bestowed, but merely that all the human faculties are under the control of the Holy Spirit. In the person of Christ, however, the human nature was perfect and possessed every spiritual gift. Careful distinction must be made between the excellencies of the human nature and the attributes of the divine nature. While both are true of the same person, the work of the Holy Spirit was in relation to the gifts of the human nature. The gifts of teaching, ministering, administering rulership, evangelism, shepherding the flock, exhortation, and giving as found in the church are all eminently fulfilled in the person and work of Christ, in addition to some of the gifts which were temporary in nature as far as ordinary men are concerned such as the gifts of prophecy, miracles, healing, and discerning of spirits. In Christ was a manifestation of the fullness of the Holy Spirit as this could be revealed in no other (John 3:34). These gifts did not arise from the divine nature, nor were they subject to acquirement in time, but Christ possessed every spiritual gift from the moment of conception. In Christ, then, we have a supreme illustration of one not only filled with the Spirit but possessing every gift of the Holy Spirit.

The human nature of Christ subject to development. The person of Christ is revealed in Hebrews 13:8 to be eternally unchanged, "Jesus Christ is the same yesterday and to-day, yea and for ever." This must be interpreted as meaning that the attributes of the divine nature are unchanged from eternity to eternity, but that while unchanged in His attributes, His person may have the quality of a human nature added to it. While the divine nature must, therefore, remain immutable, the human nature is subject to change as the Scriptures bear testimony.

One of the obvious facts about the earthly life of Christ is that He was subject to physical growth. Without possibility for argument, the Scriptures make clear that Christ in His physical development followed the general pattern of all flesh. He was a normal baby when born, and during the ensuing years grew physically into manhood. This is expressly stated in Luke 2:40, 52, where we learn that he "grew," and "advanced in wisdom and stature." Without departing from the natural aspects and characteristics of physical growth, it is entirely possible that the body of Christ, being devoid of sin, developed more rapidly and manifested perfection of body which could not be true in sinful men. In contrast to the picture often drawn of Christ, His body was probably unusually strong and graceful, devoid of the hereditary effects of sin as manifested in the race. The account in the temple of Christ at the age of twelve, while chiefly in reference to His mental powers, indicated that He was developed beyond His years in every way. While the omniscience of deity was present then, as always, it is not clear that His divine attributes are manifested in this instance.

In the Gospel narratives it is revealed that Christ advanced in wisdom as well as in physical growth. While it will always be an inscrutable mystery how in one person, Christ can be said at the same time to be ignorant and omniscient, weak and omnipotent, these apparent contradictions are dissolved when the characteristics are traced to their respective natures, human and divine. Without detracting from any of the attributes of the divine nature, it may be said of the human nature that it was capable of growing in knowledge and mental ability. This is expressly claimed in Luke 2:40, 52 where Christ is said to be "filled with wisdom," and to have "advanced in wisdom." Christ Himself referred to the limitations of wisdom in His human nature (Matt. 24:36; Mark 13:32; John 14:10). How can this process of increase in wisdom with its attendant factor of lack of knowledge be defined?

It is clear first of all that the human nature is not omniscient. However wise its own mental powers may have been, unaided by deity it lacked the attribute of omniscience which is a quality only God possesses. The human nature of Christ was undoubtedly the seat of the most brilliant human mind ever found in the world. Whatever lack of knowledge may be found in it is likewise evident in every other human mind apart from revelation. The limitations of humanity must be acknowledged, but not overstressed. It is evident that the ministry of the Holy Spirit to the humanity of Christ supplied knowledge of every fact necessary to duty, to avoid sin, or to do the will of God. The lack of knowledge consisted in some cases in the contrast of theory to experience. Hence, Christ learned obedience by suffering (Heb. 5:8), and the nature of trial and temptation was experienced by actual contact (Heb. 2:18). In it all, Christ reached a perfection in development through His experiences (Heb. 2:10). All of these elements applied only to the human nature and through the human nature became the properties of the person of Christ.

II. THE HOLY SPIRIT IN RELATION TO THE BAPTISM OF CHRIST

The baptism of Christ by John has been the subject of considerable discussion. All agree that the incident was the induction of Christ into His Messianic ministry proper, although the interpretation of the meaning of baptism in the case of Christ varies. All the Gospels record that Christ was baptized by John and that on that occasion the Holy Spirit descended from heaven in the form of a dove and abode on Christ. What is the meaning of this unique ministry of the Holy Spirit?

Baptism not the beginning of the Holy Spirit's ministry to Christ. It has been demonstrated already that Christ was filled with the Holy Spirit from the moment of conception. The coming of the Holy Spirit in the form of a dove must not be interpreted, then, as meaning the beginning of the ministry of the Holy Spirit to Christ.

A new phase of the ministry of the Holy Spirit. The filling of the Holy Spirit is ordinarily associated with some outward manifestation, but it is not necessarily so at all times. During the years of preparation, Christ was in relative obscurity, though filled with the Holy Spirit. The descent of the Holy Spirit upon Christ at His baptism does not make any essential change in His relationship, but it does mark the beginning of a new phase of His ministry. From now on, the Holy Spirit will effect the outward signs of Messiahship, the miracles and the prophetic ministry of Christ being its major evidence. As the coming of the Spirit in the form of a dove was visible and outward, so the ministry of the Spirit would be visible and outward.

A renewed declaration of the unity of the Trinity. The baptism of Christ was the occasion for a notable illustration of the doctrine of the Trinity. After Christ had been baptized, the Father spoke from heaven, "This is my beloved Son, in whom I am well pleased" (Matt. 3:17). The Holy Spirit descended in the form of a dove, and Christ was coming up from the Jordan. No better instance of revelation of the Trinity could be desired. At the same time, however, the occasion was one for declaration of unity. Christ is proclaimed as the Son of God, and the Holy Spirit is declared to be permanently resident in Christ. While Three Persons are revealed, it is clear that there is One God.

III. THE HOLY SPIRIT IN RELATION TO THE PROPHETIC OFFICE OF CHRIST

Christ during His earthly life lived and taught as a prophet. His office was attested by miracles, and His unusual teachings led many to recognize His prophetic gift. In the sphere of limitation which Christ voluntarily assumed in the incarnation, He was dependent on the Holy Spirit for the exercise of His prophetic office. This conclusion is sustained by an examination of Christ's own teachings.

The Holy Spirit the normal source of the prophetic gift. The work of the Holy Spirit in revelation in the Old Testament has already been considered at length. The New Testament is equally explicit in referring the work of revealing truth to the Holy Spirit. Christ in particular gave extended teaching on the subject. He told His disciples that when they were brought before rulers in judgment for preaching the gospel the Holy Spirit would give them what they should speak (Matt. 10:19; Mark 13:11; Luke 12:12). Concerning the need of the apostles for spiritual revelation, Christ promised that they would receive the teaching of the Holy Spirit which would enable them to give their prophetic message (John 16:13-14). The Epistles frequently allude to the same truth. It is therefore a normal operation of the Holy Spirit to sustain the prophetic gift.

Christ anointed of the Holy Spirit to preach. At least two references point to the special work of the Holy Spirit in relation to the prophetic office of Christ. According to Matthew 12:18-21, Christ claimed fulfillment of Isaiah's prophecy (Isa. 42:1-4) that the Messiah would have the Spirit upon Him in His prophetic work. Even more explicit are the words of Christ in the synagogue at Nazareth where He quoted Isaiah 61:1-2 and said, "This day is this Scripture fulfilled in your ears" (Luke 4:21). The anointing of the Holy Spirit in preparation for His preaching ministry as prophesied by Isaiah is fulfilled in Christ. While there was resident in the person of Christ all the attributes of deity, in the limitations of His earthly walk Christ chose to be dependent on the Holy Spirit for the exercise of His prophetic gift. By the Spirit He was "anointed" to preach, and His prophetic office is sustained by the constant ministry of the Holy Spirit.

IV. THE HOLY SPIRIT IN RELATION TO THE MIRACLES OF CHRIST

The period of the lifetime of Christ and the apostles affords one of the great displays of miraculous works performed by the power of God to authenticate the testimony of His witnesses. In the study of the work of the Holy Spirit on behalf of Christ, the question arises concerning the relation of the Holy Spirit to the many miracles performed by Christ. While there are no extended passages explaining this relation, sufficient is revealed to form certain conclusions.

Miraculous works of Christ performed in the power of the Holy Spirit. Two specific instances are found in the Gospels wherein the power of Christ to perform miracles is traced to a ministry of the Holy Spirit. The first is found in Matthew 12:28 where Christ indicates that He casts out demons in the power of the Spirit, "But if I by the Spirit of God cast out demons, then is the kingdom of God come upon you." While in most instances, Christ does not mention the Holy Spirit when casting out demons, this passage seems to take for granted that other cases follow the same pattern. Luke 11:20 is a companion passage.

A second passage relating miracles to the Holy Spirit is found in Luke 4:14-15, 18. In this quotation of Isaiah 61:1-2, to which we have had previous reference, it is revealed concerning Christ, "The Spirit of the Lord is upon me, because he anointed me to preach good tidings to the poor; he hath sent to proclaim release to the captives, and recovering of sight to the blind, to set at liberty them that are bruised, to proclaim the acceptable year of the Lord" (Luke 4:18-19). While the major burden of the passage is to sustain the prophetic ministry of Christ by the power of the Holy Spirit, the healing of the blind and the deliverance of the bruised probably have reference to the miracles which attended the prophetic ministry of Christ. If so, a clear proof that miracles are performed by the power of the Spirit is afforded. It may be noted that Luke 4:14, preceding the passage, reveals that Jesus had returned from His temptation "in the power of the Spirit into Galilee." The display of divine power in various forms apparently resulted from the work of the Holy Spirit on His behalf.

Did Christ perform miracles in His own power? From the Scriptures considered it is evident that at least some miracles of Christ were performed in the power of the Holy Spirit. The question is often raised whether some of the miracles of Christ were performed in the power of His divine nature. The incarnation and the self-limitation which this involved did not strip Christ of a single attribute; it only denied their independent use where this would conflict with His purpose to live among men as a man. Even in the limitations of the flesh, before the cross, Christ possessed omnipotence. In effecting miracles was the power that of the Second Person or that of the Third Person? The same question could be raised in some of the other works of Christ, such as His work as Prophet.

While the problem is beyond final solution, there are some clear instances in Scripture which point to a conclusion that the power of the Second Person was not entirely inoperative and could be used at will. It seems that Christ *chose* to perform miracles in the power of the Spirit rather than that He had no alternative. Frequently in reference to the miracles of Christ the word *power (dunamis)* is used (Mark 5:30; Luke 5:17; 6:19; 8:46). The power in point is often said to have proceeded from Christ. In connection with the healing of the woman who touched Christ in the throng, Christ perceived that "power proceeding from him had gone forth" (Mark 5:30; cf. Luke 8:46). Again in Luke 5:17, the power to perform healing is referred to Christ Himself: "The power of the Lord was with him to heal." According to Luke 6:19, power came forth from Christ in performing the miracles of healing. From the language of these passages, a conclusion might be reached that Christ in some instances acted in His own power. The final solution to the problem cannot be reached except to state that Christ performed His miracles in the power of the Spirit, and that He could if He wished and probably did exercise His own power as well. In the unity of will and action of the Trinity, the cooperation of the Second and Third Persons in doing mighty works should be expected.

CHAPTER XI

THE HOLY SPIRIT IN THE SUFFERINGS AND GLORIFICATION OF CHRIST

I. THE HOLY SPIRIT
IN RELATION TO THE SUFFERINGS OF CHRIST

THE SUFFERINGS of Christ are an inexhaustible theme for meditation and study. From them flow many precious truths and foundational doctrines. The relation of the Holy Spirit to these is seldom mentioned, though the Holy Spirit admittedly has an important ministry to Christians in their times of sufferings. From all we know of the Holy Spirit and His relation to Christ, it would seem most natural that Christ should be sustained by Him in His sufferings. As revealed in the Scripture, though there are few passages, it is clear that the Holy Spirit did have this ministry.

The relation of the Holy Spirit to the sufferings of Christ in life. Fulfilling the prophecy of Isaiah, Christ on earth was "a man of sorrows, and acquainted with grief" (Isa. 53:3). It was the ministry of the Holy Spirit to sustain and strengthen Him. In connection with the temptation of Christ, we note that Mark records that He was driven by the Spirit into the wilderness: "And straightway the Spirit driveth him forth into the wilderness" (Mark 1:12). While in the wilderness, angels were His ministers, but immediately after this trial, Luke records that Christ "returned in the power of the Spirit into Galilee" (Luke 4:14). While there are no direct statements, it would be reasonable to assume that the Holy Spirit ministered to Him during this time of suffering and trial.

A twofold inference aids in establishing this fact. First, from the unity of the Trinity, it must be concluded that their relationship involves mutual support. While this concept is hardly necessary when all Three Persons are free to exercise omnipotence, when the Second Person denies Himself the use of some of His attributes for a time, it would be proper for the other persons to minister to Him.

A second inference may be drawn from the abundant ministry of the Comforter to Christians while they are in this world. The Holy Spirit is ever ready to strengthen and comfort the saints in distress (John 14:26; 15:26), and teach them the truth of God.

It may be concluded that the Holy Spirit continually ministered to Christ. As Owen writes: "By him he was directed, strengthened, and comforted in his whole course, in all his temptations, troubles, and sufferings from first to last; for there was a confluence of them upon him in his whole way and work; a great part of his humiliation for our sakes consisting in these things. This God promised to him, and this he expected, Isa. l. 7, 8, xlii. 4, 6, xlix. 5, 8."[1]

The relation of the Holy Spirit to the sufferings of Christ in death. According to Hebrews 9:14, Christ offered Himself to God in death by the Holy Spirit: "How much more shall the blood of Christ, who through the eternal Spirit offered himself without blemish unto God, cleanse your conscience from dead works to serve the living God?" There has been opposition, of course, to this interpretation, Westcott, for instance, arguing that the absence of the article before "Spirit" (*pneumatos*) indicates that the reference is to Christ's spirit.[2] Others have taken the view referring it to the Holy Spirit. Moule, for instance, disagrees with Westcott,[3] and Smeaton writes plainly, "The expression: 'eternal Spirit,' can only mean the Holy Spirit according to the usual acceptation of the term,—not the divine nature of Christ, as too many expositors have understood it."[4] While in the last analysis the Greek would admit either interpretation, the matter must be settled on theological grounds. The question is whether Christ offered up His whole person as a sacrifice, or whether merely the human nature was the sacrifice. As Smeaton puts it: "To explain the text as if it described the divine nature as priest and the human nature as the sacrifice, is inadmissable. The WHOLE PERSON is priest and victim; for all done by either nature belongs to the Person: He offered HIMSELF, says the apostle."[5]

If the reference to the Spirit is a reference to the Holy Spirit, in what sense did Christ offer Himself to God through the Holy Spirit? The context does not give us any specific light on the subject, but the general content of Scripture points to the inclusion of all the ministry of the Holy Spirit to Christ as being antecedent to His act in dying. There is implication that the whole process of the incarnation leading to the cross was related to the work of the Holy Spirit. As Christ was sustained in life, so also in death the Holy Spirit sustained Christ. In the difficult hours of Gethsemane and all the

---

[1]John Owen, *A Discourse Concerning the Holy Spirit*, p. 99.
[2]B. F. Westcott, *The Epistle to the Hebrews*, pp. 263-64.
[3]H. C. G. Moule, *Veni Creator*, p. 32.
[4]George Smeaton, *The Doctrine of the Holy Spirit*, p. 132.
[5]*Ibid.*, pp. 132-33.

decisive moments leading to the cross, the Holy Spirit faithfully ministered to Christ.

While on the cross, Christ, in fulfillment of Psalm 22:1, cried, "My God, my God, why hast thou forsaken me?" (Matt. 27:46). It is possible that there was a cessation of the Spirit's ministry during this period without altering the fact that Christ offered Himself by the Spirit of God. While the Holy Spirit could succor Christ in making His decision and in fulfilling the eternal purpose of God in taking the path which led to the cross, only Christ could bear the load of sin. In this the Holy Spirit could not avail.

The work of the Holy Spirit in relation to the sufferings of Christ on the cross consisted, then, in sustaining the human nature in its love of God, in submission to the will of God and obedience to His commands, and in encouraging and strengthening Christ in the path of duty which led to the cross. In it all the ministry was to the human nature, and through it to the person of Christ. The inquiring mind must ever confess that this truth is infinite and beyond our complete comprehension.

II. The Holy Spirit in Relation to the Resurrection and Glorification of Christ

The Holy Spirit who had sustained Christ through the period of His humiliation might be expected to have part also in His resurrection and glorification. The Scriptures on these points are either not entirely clear or are silent, however.

The Trinity in relation to the resurrection of Christ. The Scriptures frequently refer the resurrection of Christ to God without distinction as to persons. In Acts 2:24, for instance, Peter in reference to Christ said, "whom God hath raised up." Christ before His death had revealed His own power in resurrection. To Martha He had said, "I am the resurrection, and the life" (John 11:25). In John 10:17-18, Christ announced: "Therefore doth the Father love me, because I lay down my life, that I may take it again. No one taketh it away from me, but I lay it down of myself. I have power to lay it down, and I have power to take it again." In contrast to these passages which attribute the resurrection of Christ to His own power, Ephesians 1:17-20 indicates that the Father "raised him from the dead." If the Father and the Son both had part in the resurrection of Christ, what can be said of the Spirit?

The Holy Spirit in relation to the resurrection of Christ. Three principal passages are suggested as indicating the part of the Spirit in the resurrection of Christ. Romans 8:11 reads: "But if the Spirit of him that raised up Jesus from the dead dwelleth in you, he that raised up Christ Jesus from the dead shall give life also to your mortal bodies through his Spirit that dwelleth in you." The expression "through his Spirit that dwelleth in you" attributes the giving of life to our mortal bodies to a work of the Spirit. While a textual problem exists, this seems to be the correct reading and translation.[6] By "life" is probably meant "resurrection life" such as will be given in the future resurrection of saints.[7] Calvin, however, interpreted it as spiritual life such as we have now—which is refuted by Hodge.[8] The best interpretation assigns to the Holy Spirit a part in the resurrection of the saints. The earlier part of the verse as it refers to the resurrection of Christ is less clear, however. It does not say that the Spirit raised Christ, but that "the Spirit of him that raised up Jesus from the dead dwelleth in you." While the "Spirit" is probably a reference to the Holy Spirit, the "him" seems to refer to the Father as does also the "he" in the expression "he that raised up Christ from the dead." The argument is rather that if the Holy Spirit is from the Father who raised Christ, then we are assured resurrection ourselves by virtue of the power and indwelling presence of the Spirit. At most, it is only implied that the Holy Spirit is related to the resurrection of Christ.

A second passage found in 1 Peter 3:18 is translated in the Authorized Version "quickened by the Spirit," but in the American Revised and Revised Standard Versions, "made alive in the spirit." The issue hangs on whether "spirit" (Greek, *pneumati*) is locative (in the spirit) or instrumental (by the Spirit). Because of the expression "in the flesh" which is clearly locative, the revisers have taken "in the spirit" to be the antithesis and have so translated it. Their position has been strengthened by the omission of the article before "spirit" in some texts. On the other hand, if the writer intended to say "by the Spirit," the form would have been exactly the same. From an orthodox theological point of view, the passage is best explained as referring to a work of the Holy Spirit. The thought implied by the revisers that Christ was "made alive in spirit," meaning alive in His essential spiritual being, is not the orthodox doctrine. Christ needed no restoration to spiritual life, but He did need a physical resurrection which is in contrast to "being put to death in the flesh." The expression "by the Spirit" enhances and

---

[6]Charles Hodge, *Commentary on the Epistle to the Romans,* pp. 409-10.
[7]Hodge, *loc. cit.*
[8]*Loc. cit.*

makes more pointed the fact of bodily resurrection. This conclusion also helps in solving the exegesis of the verse which follows as a reference to the work of the Holy Spirit, rather than to Christ as a spirit without a body, as Hart teaches on this passage.[9] While expositors are divided, and liberals particularly tend to eliminate the Holy Spirit as the instrument of the resurrection of Christ, the passage remains as evidence in support of this doctrine.

A third passage, Romans 1:4, referring to the "spirit of holiness" may be a reference to the holy nature of Christ rather than to the Third Person. While Calvin referred this expression to the Holy Spirit, Hodge is probably right that it does not.[10] The entire testimony of Scripture on the relation of the Holy Spirit to the resurrection of Christ hangs on two disputed passages, only one of which, 1 Peter 3:18, has any substantial weight.

The exact nature of the work of the Holy Spirit in the resurrection of Christ is not revealed. Owen feels it included rendering the dead body of Christ holy and free from all natural process of corruption during the time it was in the tomb.[11] While this seems in harmony with the predictions of Psalm 16:10 that His body would not see corruption, this idea must be left in the realm of opinion. More sure is the fact that the resurrection of Christ involved the production of a spiritual body, embodying the characteristics of immateriality and spirituality along with its physical aspects. The realm of creation and resurrection is in the proper office of the Holy Spirit, and the reunion of the soul and body of Christ seems to fit into the sphere of ministry of the Spirit. In any event, the act of resurrection displays the power and glory of God as few other events.

The Holy Spirit in relation to the glorification of Christ. From the evidence that the Holy Spirit had part in the resurrection of Christ, it may be assumed that He also had part in the glorification of Christ. On this subject, however, the Scriptures are silent. As Kuyper says, "The work of the Holy Spirit in the *exaltation* of Christ is not so easily defined. The Scripture never speaks of it in connection with His ascension, His sitting at the right hand of the Father, nor with the Lord's second coming."[12] From the nature of the Holy Spirit we may assume that He would be related to the blessed estate of our Savior. From His work in us, we would

---

[9] J. H. A. Hart, *Expositor's Greek Testament,* V, 68.
[10] Hodge, *op. cit.,* p. 28.
[11] Owen, *op. cit.,* pp. 102-3.
[12] Abraham Kuyper, *The Work of the Holy Spirit,* p. 110.

assume a most intimate relation between the glorified Savior and the indwelling Spirit. Of the Spirit we learn not only of His sufferings and death, but we are also taught the power of the resurrection of Christ and the riches of the glory of His grace. Even as the Holy Spirit was infinitely faithful in every ministry to Christ, so in the experience of the Christian whether in the flesh or in glory the ministrations of the Spirit are infinitely wonderful.

Part Four

THE WORK OF THE HOLY SPIRIT IN SALVATION

CHAPTER XII

COMMON GRACE

I. DIVINE PROVIDENCE AND SOVEREIGNTY

THE DOCTRINES of providence and of the sovereignty of God demand that the power of God be effective not only in the saved but also in the unsaved world. While the ministry of the Holy Spirit is ever primarily directed toward the Christian, it is evident that He is working in the world as well, bringing to pass the will of the Father and the Son. The Scriptures reveal that it is characteristic of the Holy Spirit to minister in scenes of disorder and sin. The chaos of the primeval earth as described in Genesis 1:2 was not without His presence. The wicked generation of Noah's day was opposed in its mad course by the striving of the Spirit (Gen. 6:3). The degeneracy of the period of the judges had its Samson who was empowered by the Holy Spirit. The prophets of the period of Israel's decadence before the captivities were living examples of the power of the Holy Spirit to minister in the midst of sin and unbelief. We are reminded in the New Testament that God is "not willing that any should perish, but that all should come to repentance" (2 Pet. 3:9). It should therefore be expected that the Holy Spirit should have a special ministry to the unsaved world in every age, particularly in the age of grace during which the Holy Spirit is resident in the world in the church.

II. THE MAGNITUDE OF COMMON GRACE

The entire work of the Holy Spirit on behalf of the unsaved world is sometimes given the terminology *common grace,* including in its scope the restraining work of the Holy Spirit in addition to the work of revealing the gospel. Charles Hodge, for instance, states in reference to common grace, "The Bible therefore teaches that the Holy Spirit as the Spirit of truth, of holiness, and of life in all its forms, is present with every human mind, enforcing truth, restraining from evil, exciting to good, and imparting wisdom or strength, when, where, and in what measure seemeth good. . . . This is what in theology is called common grace."[1]

[1]Charles Hodge, *Systematic Theology,* II, 667.

107

The extensive work of the Spirit in common grace is described by John Calvin as follows: "Yet let us not forget that these are most excellent gifts of the Divine Spirit, which for the common benefit of mankind he dispenses to whomsoever he pleases. For if it was necessary that the Spirit of God should infuse into Bezaleel and Aholiab the understanding and skill requisite for the construction of the tabernacle, (a) we need not wonder if the knowledge of those things, which are most excellent in human life, is said to be communicated to us by the Spirit of God. Nor is there any reason for inquiring what intercourse with the Spirit is enjoyed by the impious who are entirely alienated from God. For when the Spirit of God is said to dwell only in the faithful, that is to be understood of the Spirit of sanctification, by whom we are consecrated as temples to God Himself. Yet it is equally by the energy of the same Spirit that God replenishes, actuates, and quickens all creatures, and that, according to the property of each species which he has given it by the law of creation. Now, if it has pleased the Lord that we should be assisted in physics, logic, mathematics, and other arts and science, by the labour and ministry of the impious, let us make use of them; lest, if we neglect to use the blessings therein freely offered to us by God, we suffer the just punishment of our negligence."[2]

III. The Importance of Common Grace

The work of the Holy Spirit revealing the gospel to the unsaved is an important aspect of a larger program of God in dealing with the need of a lost world. It is founded on a desperate need for enablement to understand the gospel. It is designed to articulate the preaching of the gospel and the plan of God to give a universal call to faith in Christ. It is antecedent to the effectual call of God to the elect. The doctrine of the work of the Holy Spirit in revealing the gospel to the world is most important not only in its relation to the plan of God but also in carrying out effectively the preaching of the gospel. The Christian desiring to win souls for Christ should study this subject carefully, for in it lie the principles which God has revealed concerning His methods of dealing with the lost.

The ministry of the Holy Spirit in common grace falls into two important categories which are not necessarily independent. The Holy Spirit is related to divine providence in general in which He resists sin and restrains the world in its manifestation, directing

---

[2]John Calvin, *Institutes of the Christian Religion* (Philadelphia: Presbyterian Board of Publication, 1936), I, 297 (Book II, Chapter II, XVI).

human history in its consummation of God's purposes. To the Holy Spirit, also, is committed the task of revelation, of making known the way of salvation to a race which has no natural capacity to receive it with understanding. Most of the attention of theologians during the Christian centuries has been directed to the latter ministry, that of revealing the message of salvation to the lost and providing enablement for saving faith. The ministry of the Holy Spirit in restraining sin in the world is most important, however, though few direct references are found in Scripture.

The work of the Holy Spirit in relation to the world is most important for a number of reasons. In view of the power of Satan and his evident hatred of Christians and the truth, the work of the Holy Spirit in restraining sin is required to explain the relative freedom allowed the Christian in the world and the preservation of those conditions which make possible the preaching of the gospel and the maintenance of some order in the sinful world. The work of the Holy Spirit in revealing the gospel to the lost is essential to the whole program of completing the purpose of God to call out the church in this age. It provides for the inability of man and makes possible the salvation of souls. The doctrine is, therefore, important in its significance and necessary to a full appreciation of proper gospel preaching.

IV. Man's Need of Grace

The fall of Adam was full of tremendous consequences. Because of it, sin was imputed to the race; men are spiritually dead apart from Christ; men possess a fallen nature which issues in manifestation; and, important to our present study, men are unable to comprehend the truth of God. The Scriptures bear constant witness to the inability of man. It is stated flatly in 1 Corinthians 2:14, "Now the natural man receiveth not the things of the Spirit of God: for they are foolishness unto him." Again in 1 Corinthians 1:18, the gospel is declared to be foolishness to the lost, "For the word of the cross is to them that perish foolishness; but unto us who are saved it is the power of God." The unsaved Gentiles are declared to walk in spiritual darkness, "Being darkened in their understanding, alienated from the life of God, because of the ignorance that is in them, because of the hardening of their heart" (Eph. 4:18). According to Romans 8:7, the natural mind is not capable of being subject to the law of God: "because the mind of the flesh is enmity against God; for it is not subject to the law of God, neither indeed can it be." Christ bore witness to the inability of natural man to come to God when He said, "No man can come to me, except the Father that sent me draw him" (John 6:44). In addition to natural inability is the work of Satan blinding the hearts of the lost to the light of the gospel (2 Cor. 4:4). The condition of man is hopeless apart from divine intervention.

Inability on the part of man has its rise in ignorance of God and His grace due to corruption of man's whole being, perversion of his sensations, feeling, and tastes, and blinding of his understanding. In the fall, man did not lose his moral determination. He is still accountable and relatively remains a free agent. He retains ability to understand and may rise in this realm to unusual heights. Even his aversion to the good and inclination to the evil, while springing from his fallen nature, has its origin in his utter inability to appreciate the person of God and the inherent loveliness of righteousness. The real reason for man's hatred of God is his ignorance of what God is. The will of man, however, in itself has no power to transcend its natural ability as found after the fall any more than it had power to transcend its natural ability before the fall. Man in himself is utterly unable to understand the truth of God. The answer to the problem, therefore, is not found in any development of the natural man or cultivation of latent abilities, but is disclosed in the power of God as manifested in the work of the Holy Spirit. Apart from this work of the Holy Spirit, God would continue to be unrevealed to a lost race; the death of Christ would be inapplicable to men; and the purpose of God to save the elect would be impossible of fulfillment. The importance of this doctrine, therefore, justifies a careful study.

V. THE NATURE OF COMMON GRACE

The term *common grace* is a general one, as previously indicated, and has reference to the influence of the Holy Spirit upon the world. It has a special application, however, to the problem of the inability of man to receive the things of God. In this sense, common grace is a ministry of the Holy Spirit which reveals the truth of God to man whenever given in any form. Arminian theologians use a similar term, *sufficient grace*, by which they mean common grace of such character and extent as is sufficient to give adequate revelation for intelligent saving faith. Another term, *efficacious grace* or *irresistible grace*, is in the same field of truth, but it is quite distinct in its character and operation. Efficacious grace is the ministry of the Holy Spirit which is certainly effectual in revealing the gospel and in leading to saving faith. This aspect of grace will be considered under the work of the Holy Spirit in efficacious grace discussed in the next chapter.

Relation to the Word of God. The Scriptures affirm constantly the necessity of preaching the Word of God in reaching the lost. It is the gospel which is "the power of God unto salvation" (Rom. 1:16), and men are urged to preach the gospel to every creature. Accordingly, Paul raises the question, "How shall they believe in him whom they have not heard?" (Rom. 10:14), and comes to the conclusion, "So belief cometh of hearing, and hearing by the word of Christ" (Rom. 10:17). The Word of God, referred to here as the word of Christ, is the divine means used to reveal God and His grace to the world, and it is the Word of God which is the sword of the Spirit. While God could, if He desired, reveal Himself through other channels, the way of salvation is made known to us through the Bible as it is read and preached. Where the Scriptures have not been made known in one form or another, salvation is not found. It is significant, then, that those who desire to lead men to Christ must preach the Word of God.

The sacraments of baptism and the Lord's Supper have their place in bearing witness to the gospel. While the importance of this means of revelation has undoubtedly been overemphasized by the church, these sacraments reveal in symbol the gospel message, and the Lord's Supper in particular is to be observed because it shows "the Lord's death till he come" (1 Cor. 11:26).

In relating the Word of God to the doctrine of common grace, two extremes in doctrine may be observed. Lutheran theologians tend to overemphasize the living character of the Word of God (Heb. 4:12) to the point where it is claimed that the Bible has power in itself, and no attendant work of the Holy Spirit is necessary to make it effective. While the Lutheran church has fully supported the immanence and power of the Holy Spirit, they regard His work as being limited in some sense to the Word itself. As Charles Hodge summarizes the Lutheran position, "This divine efficacy is inherent in, and inseparable from the Word."[3] The chief difficulty with this view is the obvious fact that many unsaved men are completely unaffected by hearing or reading the Bible. Lutherans explain this by conditioning its power on faith, but it is difficult to see how one can believe who does not know what to believe. The fact is that the Spirit of God brings conviction and understanding to many who never believe, who turn from the gospel even after the way of salvation is made plain to them. The work of the Holy Spirit in revealing the gospel to the unsaved is rather a sovereign operation of God, not

---

[3]Hodge, *op. cit.*, II, 656.

conditioned upon the receptivity of man. The experience of many Christians bears witness to the possibility of understanding the issues of saving faith and at the same time being rebellious against God and unwilling to accept Christ for some time before the decision for Christ is finally made.

Another extreme in the doctrine of common grace is found in the viewpoint that the Word of God is unnecessary. While the Word of God is not necessarily related to the general works of God in restraining sin, in providence, and in acts of sovereignty, the revelation of the truth of the gospel comes only through the Word of God. The extreme position which makes the Word of God unnecessary to common grace is supported by two opposite schools of theology, the rational and the mystic. The deists, of course, assume that God is not immanent in the world, and trace all spiritual experience to a normal process of human mind. To them the realm of common grace is purely a discovery of the human intelligence proceeding from natural causes. Less extreme than the deists is the Pelagian viewpoint, holding that man is inherently able to understand the truth and make his own decisions in relation to it. The rationalistic approach to the subject is diametrically opposed to the Scriptural revelation, and is not seriously considered by Reformed theologians.

The view of the mystics is quite the opposite of the rationalist. The mystic assumes that God gives direct revelation to all who will receive it, and that truth so given can be understood properly by the recipient. The view partakes of all the errors of false mysticism, going far beyond the relation of false mysticism to the Christian, and attributes even to the unsaved the power to receive special revelation and understand it. Genuine salvation is never found except among those who have heard the Word of God. Missionaries entering unevangelized fields never come upon a Christian community, or even an individual Christian won by direct revelation. The view of the mystics is based on speculation rather than Scripture or experience, and must therefore be dismissed.

The work of the Holy Spirit in revealing the gospel to the unsaved is peculiarly a ministry of enablement to understand the way of salvation. As the Word is preached, the Holy Spirit attends with power to make it known to those who naturally are blind to the truth and unable to comprehend it. The importance of this ministry of the Spirit must be recognized before the necessity of prayer for the lost can be realized.

The extent of revelation to the world. The work of the Holy Spirit in revealing truth to the world is specified as one of the primary reasons why the Holy Spirit is making His residence in the world in this age. According to the words of Christ, "And he, when he is come, will convict the world in respect of sin, and of righteousness, and of judgment" (John 16:8). This threefold work of the Spirit is further defined in the passage which follows. The work of convicting or convincing the world of sin is given the specific character of revealing the one sin of unbelief as being the issue between the unsaved and God, as verse nine indicates, "Of sin, because they believe not on me." Because of the death of Christ it is no longer a question of being condemned simply because of sin. The death of Christ is seen to satisfy all the righteous demands of God. To the unsaved, the determining factor in his destiny is whether he believes in Christ. Far removed from a character building program, or merely an encouragement to live more righteously, the Holy Spirit reveals that it is necessary to believe in Christ to be saved.

A second revelation of the Holy Spirit to the world is that of making known the righteousness of God. According to verse ten, this revelation is necessary because Christ is no longer bodily present in the earth, "Of righteousness, because I go to the Father, and ye behold me no more." While Christ was on earth, His presence and His teaching were a demonstration of the righteousness of God. When Christ ascended into heaven, it was necessary for the Holy Spirit to undertake this ministry. As a work for the unsaved, the Holy Spirit reveals the righteousness of God in two distinct aspects. First, the Holy Spirit reveals that we are dealing with a righteous God. It is not a question of conformity to any earthly standard or comparison. Our life is seen measured by the righteousness of the person of God. Second, the Holy Spirit reveals to the unsaved that there is available through Christ an imputed righteousness which God gives the believer. It is no doubt true that many come to Christ in faith and are saved who comprehend very imperfectly the nature of this imputed righteousness. It is possible that many only understand vaguely that God through Christ provides for their lack of righteousness without realizing all the wonders of justification. It is essential to intelligent faith, however, that the unsaved understand that through Christ it is possible for God to deal with them as those who are righteous. This revelation is inseparable from the gospel.

A third revelation is given the unsaved by the Holy Spirit concerning the relation of the cross to judgment and Satan. Christ said the Holy Spirit would convict the world "Of judgment, because the prince of this world hath been judged" (John 16:11). The Holy Spirit presses upon the heart of the unsaved the fact of God's judgment. The unsaved need to know that sin was judged in the cross, and for those who trust in Christ there is deliverance from judgment upon sin and deliverance from condemnation. The unsaved must see Christ as judged and executed for them, and their judgment for sin as already past. As a token of this, Satan, as the "prince of this world," is mentioned as already condemned. In the cross Satan met his defeat. The cross is the power of God over Satan. Satan stands already convicted, doomed, and waiting the executing of the sentence. While in the providence of God, Satan is allowed freedom and great power in this age, his end is sure, and those who reject Christ will share his destiny.

The ministry of the Holy Spirit to the unsaved follows three specific lines, then. First, the unsaved must understand that salvation depends upon faith in Christ. Second, the unsaved must understand the righteousness of God as belonging to the person of God and as made available for the sinner through Christ. Third, the unsaved must face the fact of judgment and find in Christ one who was judged and executed as their substitute. While these elements may not be always seen clearly, they form the principles which combine to bring the unsaved into the knowledge necessary to place saving faith in Christ. Needless to say, the subjects included in the ministry of the Holy Spirit to the unsaved should constitute an important part of effective gospel preaching.

VI. THE RESTRAINT OF SIN

The restraining work of the Holy Spirit in the Old Testament. The work of the Holy Spirit in restraining the world from sin is found in every age, except during the period of unprecedented sinfulness predicted for the great tribulation when it is God's purpose to demonstrate the character of unrestrained sin. The nature of the restraint varies in different ages, however.

The principal Old Testament passage is found in Genesis 6:3, "And Jehovah said, My Spirit shall not strive with man for ever, for that he is also flesh." This text gives us a broad view of the work of the Spirit in Noah's time restraining the course of sin. Some have found the same doctrine inferred in the Authorized Version of Isaiah 59:19, but the text is not clear. An outstanding illustration of the restraining hand of God on sin is found in the book of Job, where Job is presented as protected by God. The sorrows of Job, while permitted by God, are within the permissive will of God beyond which Satan could not go. While not expressly related to a work of the Spirit of God, it nevertheless confirms the doctrine.

Most of the restraining works of the Spirit are revealed as accomplished through various means. The work of the Spirit in revealing truth through the prophets, particularly the warning of judgment to come, and the work of the inspiration of the Scriptures with their power helped to restrain sin. The judgments which followed rejection of His striving against sin (Isa. 63:10-11) had their effect. The presence and power of the Holy Spirit by virtue of His holy character was conducive to restraint of sin. Throughout the Old Testament, then, the power of the Holy Spirit guided human events into the path of divine providence.

The restraining work of the Holy Spirit in the present age. The work of the Holy Spirit in restraining sin as found in the Old Testament continues in the present age. Further confirmation of His ministry is found in 2 Thessalonians 2:7, "For the mystery of lawlessness doth already work: only there is one that restraineth now, until he be taken out of the way." The subject of the passage is the coming day of the Lord in which the man of sin will be revealed (2 Thess. 2:3). According to the passage, the man of sin will not be revealed until the one who restrains is removed. The present age enjoys the ministry of this restrainer whose presence and ministry make impossible the manifestation of the man of sin. The question concerning the identity of this one who restrains sin, in the light of the Old Testament, is answered by referring it to the Holy Spirit.

Interpreters of Scripture have not all agreed on the identity of the one restraining lawlessness. A popular view of this passage is that human government is this restraining force. Human government, however, continues during the period of tribulation in which the man of sin is revealed. While all forces of law and order tend to restrain sin, they are not such in their own character, but rather as they are used and empowered to accomplish this end by God. It would seem a preferable interpretation to view all restraint of sin, regardless of means, as proceeding from God as a ministry of the Holy Spirit. As Thiessen writes: "But who is the one that restraineth? Denney, Findlay, Alford, Moffatt, hold this refers to law and order, especially as embodied in the Roman Empire. But while human governments may be agencies in the restraining work of the Spirit, we believe that they in turn are influenced by the Church. And again, back of human government is God Who instituted it (Gen. 9:5, 6; Rom. 13:1-7) and controls it (Ps. 75:5-7). So it is God by His Spirit that restrains the development of lawlessness."[4]

---

[4]H. C. Thiessen, "Will the Church Pass Through the Tribulation?" *Bibliotheca Sacra*, 92:301, July-September, 1935.

Some have advanced another view which contends that Satan himself is restraining sin lest it manifest its true character. This idea is hardly compatible with the revelation of Satan in the Scriptures. Satan is nowhere given universal power over the world, though his influence is inestimable. A study of 2 Thessalonians 2:3-10 indicates that the one who restrains is removed from the scene before the man of sin is revealed. This could hardly be said of Satan. The period of tribulation on the contrary is one in which Satan's work is most evident. The Scriptures represent him as being cast into the earth and venting his fury during those tragic days (Rev. 12:9). The theory that Satan is the great restrainer of lawlessness is, accordingly, untenable.

If it be conceded that the Holy Spirit undertook to strive with men to restrain sin in the Old Testament, it is even more evident that a similar ministry will be found in the present age in which the Spirit is present in the church. While it is not in the purpose of God to deal finally with the world while the church is in the world, the sovereignty of God overrules the wickedness of men and the power of Satan to make possible the accomplishment of His purpose to call out a people to His name. While the restraining hand of the Holy Spirit is little realized by the church at large, His protection and power shield the Christian from the impossible task of living in a world in which sin is unrestrained.

Contributing factors in the work of restraining sin. The Scriptures do not enlarge upon the ministry of the Holy Spirit in restraining sin. Reason would point, however, to a number of contributing factors all of which are used of God to check the course of sin. The presence of the individual Christian, indwelt by the Holy Spirit, constitutes a force to hinder the world in its sin. The church corporately has done much to influence the world, even though it has failed to measure up to Biblical standards itself. The Bible, wherever it has gone, has produced its attendant effect not only on those who believed it but also indirectly has influenced the thought and action of the unsaved world. Human governments, ordained of God, are a means to divine ends. While these many factors in themselves are not the work of the Holy Spirit in restraining, they are means used by the Holy Spirit in accomplishing His purpose. The work of the Holy Spirit in restraining sin is seen, therefore, to be an important work of God, essential to divine providence, and a part of the work of God in common grace.

VII. The Limitations of Common Grace

From preceding discussion it is evident that common grace falls far short of efficacious grace. While the unsaved may be led to understand the gospel sufficiently to act intelligently upon it, common grace does not have any certain effect upon the will and does not issue certainly into salvation. Two unsaved men may understand the gospel equally, and yet one never comes to the point of saving faith while the other trusts in Christ and is saved. Common grace must be sharply distinguished from any work of God which is efficacious in bringing the unsaved to salvation.

Common grace also falls far short of the Christian's experience of illumination. The indwelling Holy Spirit opens to the yielded Christian the storehouses of truth in the Word of God. Common grace is related almost entirely to revelation on the one subject of salvation with a view to providing an intelligent basis for faith. The revelation of common grace can never rise higher than the plane of the natural man even in the realm of salvation truth. It is closely parallel to the idea of moral and intellectual persuasion, constituting an influence, but in itself not resulting in decision.

Common grace provides none of the normal experiences of the Christian such as are produced by the unhindered indwelling Holy Spirit. The love, joy, peace, and other fruit of the Spirit are never found in those who have merely experienced common grace. While unsaved men may be able to imitate some of the outward manifestations of Christian conduct, there is never the reality of inward experience, though in some cases it may be difficult to determine whether some individuals are unsaved or saved.

While common grace is greatly limited in its character and its results, it cannot be said to be without certain phenomena. Religious instinct and fear of God are no doubt related to common grace, though they may not be connected definitely with the Scriptures. This phase of common grace is never sufficient to provide understanding of the issues of the gospel. Common grace in its broader sense may have the effect of restraining sin, and it is often regarded as including this aspect. Outward profession of faith in Christ and conformity to moral standards without being saved may be a result of common grace. Charles Hodge writes, for instance, "Unrenewed men in the Bible are said to repent, to believe, to be partakers of the Holy Ghost, and to taste the good Word of God, and the powers of the world to come."[5] There are no doubt stages in the work of common grace from religious instinct and a fear of God which is almost universal to the experience of those who understand clearly the condition of salvation. In it all the Holy Spirit is working, striving to bring men to the knowledge

---

[5]*Hodge, op. cit.,* II, 673.

of Christ. Without this preliminary ministry, the work of efficacious
grace would be impossible.

The work of the Holy Spirit for the unsaved world constitutes
another proof that God is a God of infinite grace and condescension,
working in those who are the objects of His righteous judgment,
striving to bring them to the knowledge of Christ as Savior. Without
this ministry, the world would be an impossible situation for the
Christian, and gospel preaching would be fruitless. The trophies of
the grace of God which some day will stand complete before God
in glory will bear witness to the power of the Spirit in effectively
accomplishing the task given to Him by Christ.

CHAPTER XIII

EFFICACIOUS GRACE

I. THE IMPORTANCE OF THE DOCTRINE

EFFICACIOUS grace is a theological term having in view the work of the Holy Spirit in moving men to effective faith in Jesus Christ as Savior. After common grace which is antecedent, efficacious grace is the first aspect chronologically and logically in the work of the Spirit in man's salvation. It is a theme of Scripture greatly misunderstood and misrepresented, but few doctrines are more determinate in their bearing on theology as a whole. It involves the whole point of view of the sovereign and effective direction of God of all events to fulfill God's purposes. It affects the most important work of God in saving men, and is vital to a proper doctrine of the work of the Holy Spirit.

From a practical standpoint, there are few subjects more worthy of careful study than the work of the Holy Spirit in the salvation of the believer. For the one who believes in Christ, it is a glorious revelation of the working of God in his own heart, the foundation of his spiritual experience and the ground of his hope of glory. Much of the confusion on the subject of assurance of salvation would be eliminated if the work of the Holy Spirit in salvation were made clear. It would destroy the philosophy of salvation by works. It would deliver the assurance of our salvation from the realm of emotional experience. It would give the baptism of the Holy Spirit its proper place and wrest the doctrine from its erroneous expositors in the holiness movements. It would provide the basis for understanding how God is working in His own in this age.

To the preacher of the gospel, the doctrine of the work of the Holy Spirit in salvation, rightly understood, is a necessary background to accurate gospel preaching. The necessary work of God, the human factors, and the evident need for the power of God in winning any souls for Christ are seen in their proper relation. The preacher is delivered from dependence on self or homiletical skill, and without diminishing the effort to preach the gospel in power he is led into conscious dependence upon God and the power of prayer for fruitfulness in ministry. His own relation to the Holy Spirit who alone can save is made a matter of paramount importance.

Any writer familiar with the many attempts at expounding these doctrines must approach the task with humility. The doctrines are so vast in their implications. The possibilities of intrusion of human wisdom where only the divine will suffice are ever present. The discussion which follows here seeks only to interpret accurately the Scriptures.

II. Efficacious Grace a Biblical Doctrine

The doctrine of efficacious grace is pre-eminently a doctrine of the Scriptures though its title is theological. The Scriptures speak frequently of a divine call to salvation which results in certain salvation (Rom. 1:1, 6, 7; 8:28, 30; 9:11, 24; 11:29; 1 Cor. 1:1, 2, 9, 24, 26; 7:15, 17, 18, 20, 21, 22, 24; Gal. 1:6, 15; 5:8, 13; Eph. 1:18; 4:1, 4; Col. 3:15; 1 Thess. 2:12; 4:7; 5:24; 2 Thess. 2:14; 1 Tim. 6:12; 2 Tim. 1:9; Heb. 3:1; 9:15; 1 Pet. 1:15; 2:9, 21; 3:9; 5:10; 2 Pet. 1:3, 10). This divine call which results in salvation is called *efficacious grace* because it is certainly effectual in revealing the gospel and in leading to saving faith. In contrast to this work of God is the general call to salvation given to all who hear the gospel. In this sense, Christ said, "I come not to call the righteous, but sinners" (Matt. 9:13).

The call to repentance and faith was not always heeded, as demonstrated by the fact that Christ also said, "For many are called, but few chosen" (Matt. 22:14). An examination of the many references to calling in the New Testament will reveal, however, that in most instances, they refer to the efficacious call. Efficacious grace, then, stands in contrast to common grace as the effectual call stands in contrast to the general call. For practical purposes, the grace provided is involved in the call given, and divine calling and the grace which is inherent in it are the same subject.

A study of the many passages dealing with the effectual call brings out several important aspects of the truth. The first of these is that the doctrine is unmistakably Biblical. Salvation and the divine calling are seen to be inseparable, one without the other being impossible. Christians are "called to be saints" (Rom. 1:7; 1 Cor. 1:2); called to "eternal life" (1 Tim. 6:12); called "out of darkness into his marvellous light" (1 Pet. 2:9); and called "by his own glory and virtue" (2 Pet. 1:3). Paul was "called to be an apostle" (Rom. 1:1; 1 Cor. 1:1). "Whom he foreordained, them he also called: and whom he called, them he also justified" (Rom. 8:30). Christians are referred to as "called to be Jesus Christ's" (Rom. 1:6), and "them that are called according to his purpose" (Rom. 8:28). A significant reference is found in 1 Corinthians 1:23-24, "But we preach Christ crucified, unto Jews a stumblingblock, and unto Greeks foolishness; but unto them which are called, both Jews and Greeks, Christ the power of God, and the wisdom of God." To those not called, the gospel remains foolishness, but to the called it is the power of God. We may conclude from these many passages that the work of the Holy Spirit in calling effectually to salvation is revealed abundantly in Scripture, and that the ministry is very important.

III. EFFICACIOUS GRACE AN ACT OF GOD

While the nature of efficacious grace in its operation is inscrutable, as presented in Scripture it is an act of God dependent solely upon God for its execution. Reformed theologians are in substantial agreement upon this point, and the Scriptures bear a consistent testimony. Events of all classes may be distinguished by certain inherent characteristics which it is most important to discern. This is particularly true of efficacious grace. As Charles Hodge writes: "There are, as has been before remarked, three classes into which all events of which we have any knowledge may be arranged. First, those which are produced by the ordinary operations of second causes as guided and controlled by the providential agency of God. Secondly, those events in the external world which are produced by the simple volition, or immediate agency of God, without the cooperation of second causes. To this class all miracles, properly so called, belong. Thirdly, those effects produced on the mind, heart, and soul, by the volition, or immediate agency of the omnipotence of God. To this class belong inward revelation, inspiration, miraculous powers, as the gift of tongues, gift of healing, etc., and regeneration."[1] To this third class belongs the work of efficacious grace.

The Scriptures bear faithful testimony to the fact that efficacious grace is an act of God. Every reference to divine calling presumes or states that it is an act of God. It is specifically linked with the sovereignty of God as opposed to human choices. Hence Paul speaks of being "called to be an apostle" (Rom. 1:1) etc. Never in the Scriptures is divine calling attributed to human choice. It is rather an act of God proceeding from omnipotence and sovereignty.

In keeping with their doctrine of total depravity and total inability, Reformed theologians have insisted that efficacious grace is an immediate act of God accomplished without human assistance. While

---

[1]Charles Hodge, *Systematic Theology*, II, 683.

they freely admit the necessity of the work of common grace as antecedent in which the individual hears and understands the gospel and sees his own need of salvation, efficacious grace is defined as the instantaneous work of God empowering the human will and inclining the human heart to faith in Christ. Efficacious grace immediately results in salvation in all cases because it is accomplished by the omnipotence of God. The Westminster Confession of Faith states it as follows:

"I. All those whom God hath predestinated unto life, and those only, he is pleased, in his appointed and accepted time, effectually to call, by his Word and Spirit, out of that state of sin and death, in which they are by nature, to grace and salvation by Jesus Christ; enlightening their minds spiritually and savingly, to understand the things of God; taking away their heart of stone, and giving unto them an heart of flesh; renewing their wills, and by his almighty power determining them to that which is good; and effectually drawing them to Jesus Christ, yet so as they come most freely, being made willing by his grace.

"II. This effectual call is of God's free and special grace alone, not from any thing at all foreseen in man, who is altogether passive therein, until, being quickened and renewed by the Holy Spirit, he is thereby enabled to answer this call, and to embrace the grace offered and conveyed in it."[2]

Efficacious grace because of its nature is not to be considered a process, but rather an instantaneous act of God. Whatever preparation precedes this belongs to common grace which cannot by its nature bring to salvation. Many a Christian can bear witness to the work of God in common grace leading to salvation, but the work of efficacious grace is distinct and decisive. In a moment the soul passes from a state of spiritual death to spiritual life. As an act of God, the work is inscrutable. As the human mind does not inquire how God could make man a living soul though composed of the dust of the earth, so the human mind need not inquire how God works in efficacious grace.

IV. Efficacious Grace Certainly Effectual

Efficacious grace by its very title signifies that it is always effectual in bringing the soul to salvation. In this it is sharply contrasted to common grace. Common grace may be successfully resisted, and

---

[2]*The Constitution of the Presbyterian Church in the United States of America* (1946 edition), pp. 49-52.

even if considered sufficient to bring to salvation, as Arminians hold, it is not efficacious. It is not that efficacious grace is greater in extent and power than common grace, and therefore efficacious, but rather that in its nature, proceeding from the omnipotence of God, it is certainly effective. It may be admitted that some of the acts of God may be successfully resisted. The pleading of the Spirit grieved by sin in the life of the Christian may be resisted and go unheeded. The work of common grace does not require a willingness to receive the truth, but efficacious grace is an immediate act of God which by its nature cannot be resisted. As Charles Hodge writes: "According to the Augustinian doctrine the efficacy of divine grace in regeneration depends neither upon its congruity nor upon the active cooperation, nor upon the passive non-resistance of its subject, but upon its nature and the purpose of God. It is the exercise of 'the mighty power of God,' who speaks and it is done. This is admitted to be the doctrine of Augustine himself."[3]

Efficacious grace is irresistible not in the sense that it is resisted and all such resistance is overcome, but it is irresistible in the sense that it is never resisted. Its nature forbids it. It is irresistible in that it is certainly effectual. A. H. Strong, accordingly, prefers not to use the term irresistible: "We prefer to say that this special call is efficacious,— that is, that it infallibly accomplished its purpose of leading the sinner to the acceptance of salvation. This implies two things: (a) That the operation of God is not an outward constraint upon the human will, but that it accords with the laws of our mental constitution. We reject the term 'irresistible,' as implying a coercion and compulsion which is foreign to the nature of God's working in the soul. (b) That the operation of God is the originating cause of that new disposition of the affections, and that new activity of the will, by which the sinner accepts Christ. The cause is not in the response of the will to the presentation of motives by God, nor in any mere cooperation of the will of man with the will of God, but is an almighty act of God in the will of man, by which its freedom to choose God as its end is restored and rightly exercised (John 1:12-13)."[4]

A proper view of efficacious grace, then, fully recognizes its certain result in the salvation of its beneficiary. In every case, the one who receives efficacious grace is instantly saved. While in the experience of the individual, faith in Christ is a result of choice and act of the

---

[3]Hodge, *op. cit.,* II, 680.
[4]A. H. Strong, *Systematic Theology,* pp. 792-93. John Dick uses the term, "invincible" and "effectual" for efficacious grace rejecting "irresistible." Cf. his *Lectures on Theology,* Lecture LXVI, p. 157.

human will, it is nevertheless a work of efficacious grace. Efficacious grace never operates in a heart that is still rebellious, and no one is ever saved against his will. It is rather in keeping with the principle that "it is God who worketh in you both to will and to work, for his good pleasure" (Phil. 2:13).

V. Defense of Efficacious Grace

An act of God must be effectual. At least four arguments may be advanced in support of the assertion that efficacious grace is bestowed and that it is certainly effectual. Efficacious grace is certainly effectual by its nature as an act of God. As has been shown, this act, proceeding from the omnipotence of God, and being independent of human volition, is certainly effectual by its nature. God's persuasion may be resisted as evinced in the operation of common grace, but God's acts cannot be resisted in that they are supported by omnipotence and the sovereignty of His will. As Charles Hodge says, "If this one point be determined, namely, that efficacious grace is the almighty power of God, it decides all questions in controversy on this subject. . . . Volumes have been written on the contrary hypothesis; which volumes lose all their value if it be once admitted that regeneration, or effectual calling, is the work of omnipotence."[5]

The doctrine of efficacious grace is vital to predestination. It is essential to the plan of God that all the elect be saved. It is therefore necessary that more than common grace be given to the elect. Grace must be effectual in bringing the elect to salvation. Predestination and effectual calling are definitely linked in Scripture. God calls according to His purpose (Rom. 8:28), and it is further revealed: "Whom he foreordained, them he also called: and whom he called, them he also justified: and whom he justified, them he also glorified" (Rom. 8:30). It is manifest that the calling herein mentioned is the efficacious call. All who are foreordained are called, and all who are called are justified and glorified. A distinction is clearly made here between the general call of the gospel and the particular call which is effectual. Whatever may be the mysteries of the relation of this efficacious call to the operations of the human will, the fact of a certainly effectual call remains. It is necessary that the elect come to Christ to fulfill the purpose of redemption (John 6:37, 39; 17:12).

Total depravity and spiritual death require efficacious grace. The work of efficacious grace is necessary in view of the absence of spiritual

---

[5]Hodge, *op. cit.* II, 683.

life before regeneration. Herein lies the foundation of the doctrine of efficacious grace. A man spiritually dead cannot do a spiritual work. Total depravity demands as its corollary the doctrine of efficacious grace. According to Ephesians 2:8, "For by grace have ye been saved through faith; and that not of yourselves; it is the gift of God." While there are diverse interpretations of this passage, the implication clearly is that grace, salvation, and faith all proceed from God, and do not rise in the heart of the unsaved apart from an act of God. Charles Hodge writes on this point, "All who hold that original sin involves spiritual death and consequent utter inability to any spiritual good, do also hold that his recovery from that state is not effected by any process of moral suasion, human or divine, but by the immediate exercise of God's almighty power."[6] If one accepts the Biblical revelation of man's state of spiritual death and total inability, he must accept the doctrine of efficacious grace as the solution to the problem. Common grace does not provide life nor does it renew the human will. It consists chiefly in enablement in understanding the gospel and its issues, and understanding itself does not bring the ability to act upon that new knowledge.

Analogy from regeneration. The work of efficacious grace as wholly an act of God is supported by analogy from the doctrine of regeneration. Like efficacious grace, regeneration is an act of God, not a process, matter of persuasion, or rational change. If regeneration is wholly an act of God, instantaneous, and independent of human assistance, efficacious grace may well be in the same category. Both are inscrutable, and both are essential to salvation.

VI. OBJECTIONS TO THE DOCTRINE OF EFFICACIOUS GRACE

Contrary to human effort. It is natural that a doctrine which depends in large measure on faith rather than reason should be opposed on various grounds. A common objection is that this doctrine is contrary to all human effort to believe. The Scriptures, however, give adequate witness both to the fact of the effectual call and to the human responsibility to believe in Christ. The problem of the relation of human effort to divine undertakings is always real, and the solution cannot be reached apart from faith. The fact of divine undertaking in efficacious grace should not discourage human effort to believe, however, except that men should not seek to do what only God can do. In the realm of salvation, men should seek to be saved, but not to save themselves. The secret of salvation remains in trusting God to save us.

---

[6]*Ibid.*, II, 705-6.

The fact that we need a work of grace before we can believe should make us recognize all the more the inability of the natural man, and should make men cast themselves on God for the work which He alone can do. 'The blind man who besought Christ to heal him was not hindered in his plea by his own total inability to heal himself. Rather, his own need drove him to Christ who alone could help him. The doctrine of total depravity instead of discouraging human effort to turn to God should magnify the power of God and reveal our utter need of salvation. We are reminded in Scripture, "All that which the Father giveth me shall come unto me; and him that cometh to me I will in no wise cast out" (John 6:37). On the one hand, the certainty of the call of God is seen—all the elect shall come to Christ. On the other hand, everyone who comes shall not be cast out. The human responsibility of coming to Christ remains.

Contrary to human responsibility. A second objection to the doctrine of efficacious grace is made on the ground that it is contrary to human responsibility. It is argued that if God alone can do it, we cannot be held responsible for unbelief. The Bible, however, does not remove responsibility because of inability. Men are judged because they follow actions natural to a sin nature. The fact remains that "He that believeth not hath been judged already, because he hath not believed on the name of the only begotten Son of God" (John 3:18). Even the factor of inability is lessened by the presence of common grace. While common grace is not sufficient to renew the will or bring to salvation, it can and does reveal the terms of the gospel, the need of salvation, the judgment of God upon sin, and the responsibility of accepting Christ. It is clear that God does not oppose anyone who might will to believe. *In every case where efficacious grace is not given, common grace has been spurned.* While all difficulties of human responsibility in relation to the sovereignty of God cannot be solved by human minds, the Christian can accept by faith the revelation of the Word of God even when there is seeming incongruity.

Is sufficient grace given to all? The third objection to the doctrine of efficacious grace is based on the false premise that sufficient grace is given to all men to believe. On this ground, it is argued that efficacious grace is in fact only sufficient grace which in some cases is successful and in others is not. This, in brief, is the position of the Semi-Pelagian school of theology, the Roman Catholic position, and that held by Arminians, though their particular interpretations vary in details. The weakness of this objection is found in its faulty premise, namely, that sufficient grace is given to all to believe. This the Scriptures do not teach, and experience contradicts. The very fact that some resist successfully the work of grace attending the gospel is proof sufficient that it is not efficacious in its nature. As has been previously shown, the call of God to salvation extended to the elect is certainly effectual, in that all who are called are saved. The Arminian view is wholly lacking in an adequate explanation of this certainty.

The doctrine of efficacious grace must remain essentially inscrutable to human minds. All the problems cannot be solved, but the difficulty lies in our lack of knowledge of the supernatural work of grace which results in salvation and our faulty comprehension of the working of our own wills rather than in any disharmony with revealed truth. The fact of the effectual call is supported by such abundant Scripture reference as to forbid denial. A rejection of this doctrine removes from salvation the divine certainty which it most assuredly possesses.

CHAPTER XIV

REGENERATION

I. IMPORTANCE OF REGENERATION

F EW DOCTRINES are more fundamental to effective preaching than the doctrine of regeneration. Failure to comprehend its nature and to understand clearly its necessity will cripple the efficacy of gospel preaching. Both for the Bible teacher and the evangelist an accurate knowledge of the doctrine of regeneration is indispensable. The Biblical concept of regeneration is comparatively simple, and a study of its theological history is not entirely necessary to accurate preaching. The history of the doctrine, however, reveals its natural pitfalls and may warn the unwary of the dangers of a shallow understanding of regeneration. The doctrine of regeneration offers a rich reward to those who contemplate its treasures and live in the light of its reality.

II. THE MEANING OF REGENERATION

Definition. The word *regeneration* is found only twice in the New Testament (Matt. 19:28; Titus 3:5), but it has been appropriated as the general term designating the impartation of eternal life. Only one of the two instances in the New Testament is used in this sense (Titus 3:5), where reference is made to "the washing of regeneration and renewing of the Holy Spirit." The Greek word *palingenesias* is properly translated *"new birth, reproduction, renewal, re-creation"* (Thayer). It is applied not only to human beings but also to the renewed heaven and earth of the millennium (Matt. 19:28). In relation to the nature of man, it includes the various expressions used for eternal life such as *new life, new birth, spiritual resurrection, new creation, new mind, "made alive," sons of God,* and *translation into the kingdom.* In simple language, regeneration consists of all that is represented by eternal life in a human being.

Theological usage. The word *regeneration* as used by theologians has confused the Biblical meaning. Other words such as *conversion, sanctification,* and *justification* have been either identified or included in the concept of regeneration. Roman Catholic theologians have regarded regeneration as including all that is embraced in salvation,

128

not only justification and sanctification, but even glorification. Regeneration is taken to include the means, the act, the process, and the ultimate conclusion of salvation.

Protestant theologians have been more cautious in extending the meaning of regeneration. The early Lutheran theologians used regeneration to include the whole process by which a sinner passed from his lost estate into salvation, including justification. Later Lutherans attempted a clarification of the doctrine by holding that justification did not include a transformation of life, thereby excluding sanctification from the doctrine of regeneration. The Lutheran Church continues to hold that infants are regenerated at the moment of water baptism, however, at the same time affirming that this regeneration signifies only their entrance into the visible church, not their certain salvation. Regeneration becomes then merely a preparatory work of salvation.

On the subject of infant regeneration, the Lutheran theologian Valentine writes: "May the child be said to be regenerated by the act of Baptism? We may properly answer, Yes; but only in the sense that the established vital and grace-conveying relation, under imputed righteousness and the Holy Spirit, may be said to hold, in its provisions and forces, the final covenanted development."[1] Valentine objects, however, to the statement that baptism regenerates children. Elsewhere, Valentine writes, "Justification *precedes* regeneration and sanctification."[2] It is clear that Lutheran theology does not use the term in the Biblical sense of impartation of eternal life. The Lutheran theology does, however, exclude sanctification from the doctrine of regeneration.

Reformed theologians have failed to be consistent in usage also, and have shared to some extent the errors embraced by others. During the seventeenth century, conversion was used commonly as a synonym for regeneration. This usage ignored a most important fact, however, that conversion is the human act and regeneration is an act of God. Further, conversion, while usually related to regeneration, is not always so, as demonstrated by its use in connection with Peter's repentance and restoration (Luke 22:32), as prophesied by Christ. Even Calvin failed to make a proper distinction between regeneration and conversion. Charles Hodge, however, argues effectively for the necessary distinction in the meaning of these terms.[3] Shedd agrees with Hodge and cites the following contrasts: "Regeneration, accordingly, is an act;

---

[1]Milton Valentine, *Christian Theology*, II, 329-30.
[2]*Ibid.*, II, 237.
[3]Charles Hodge, *Systematic Theology*, III, 3-5.

conversion is an activity, or a process. Regeneration is the origination of life; conversion is the evolution and manifestation of life. Regeneration is wholly an act of God; conversion is wholly an activity of man. Regeneration is a cause; conversion is an effect. Regeneration is instantaneous; conversion is continuous."[4]

For the last century, Reformed theologians have agreed that regeneration properly designates the act of impartation of eternal life. As Charles Hodge states it: "By a consent almost universal the word regeneration is now used to designate, not the whole work of sanctification, nor the first stages of that work comprehended in conversion, much less justification or any mere external change of state, but the instantaneous change from spiritual death to spiritual life."[5] In a study of the doctrine of regeneration, then, the inquirer is concerned only with the aspect of salvation related to the impartation of eternal life. Other important works which may attend it, be antecedent to it, or immediately follow it must be considered as distinct works of God.

III. REGENERATION AN ACT OF THE HOLY SPIRIT

A work of God. Regeneration by its nature is solely a work of God. While sometimes considered as a result, every instance presumes or states that the act of regeneration was an act of God. A number of important Scriptures bear on the subject of regeneration (John 1:13; 3:3-7; 5:21; Rom. 6:13; 2 Cor. 5:17; Eph. 2:5, 10; 4:24; Titus 3:5; James 1:18; 1 Pet. 2:9). It is explicitly stated that the one regenerated is "born, not of blood, nor of the will of the flesh, nor of the will of man, but of God" (John 1:13). Regeneration is likened unto resurrection, which by its nature is wholly of God (John 5:21; Rom. 6:13; Eph. 2:5). In other instances regeneration is declared to be a creative act, the nature of which assumes it to be the act of God (Eph. 2:10; 4:24; 2 Cor. 5:17). It may be seen clearly, then, that regeneration is always revealed as an act of God accomplished by His own supernatural power apart from all other agencies.

Ascribed to the Holy Spirit. The work of regeneration is properly ascribed to the Holy Spirit. Like the work of efficacious grace, regeneration is often ascribed to God without distinction as to persons, and in several instances is ascribed to the Father, to the Son, and to the Holy Spirit severally. The First Person is declared to be the source of regeneration in at least one instance (James 1:17-18). Christ Himself is linked with regeneration several times in Scripture (John

---

[4]W. G. T. Shedd, *Dogmatic Theology*, II, 494.
[5]Hodge, *op. cit.*, III, 5.

5:21; 2 Cor. 5:17; 1 John 5:12). Again, the Holy Spirit is declared the agent of regeneration (John 3:3-7; Titus 3:5). As in other great undertakings of the Godhead, each person has an important part, in keeping with their one essence. As in the birth of Christ, where all the persons of the Godhead were related to the conception of Christ, so in the new birth of the Christian the First Person becomes the Father of the believer, the Second Person imparts His own eternal life (1 John 5:12), and the Holy Spirit, the Third Person, acts as the efficient agent of regeneration. The work of regeneration can be assigned to the Holy Spirit as definitely as the work of salvation can be assigned to Christ.

IV. REGENERATION THE IMPARTATION OF ETERNAL LIFE

Eternal life central to regeneration. As the word itself implies, the central thought in the doctrine of regeneration is that eternal life is imparted. Regeneration meets the need created by the presence of spiritual death. The method of impartation is, of course, inscrutable. There is no visible method or process discernible. By its nature it is supernatural and therefore its explanation is beyond human understanding. The Scriptures in presenting the impartation of eternal life use three figures to describe it.

New birth. Regeneration is sometimes presented in the figure of new birth. As Christ told Nicodemus, "Ye must be born anew" (John 3:7). In contrast to human birth of human parentage, one must be born "of God" (John 1:13) in order to become a child of God. According to James 1:18, "Of his own will he brought us forth by the word of truth, that we should be a kind of firstfruits of his creatures." The figure is eloquent in portraying the intimate relation of the child of God to his heavenly Father and in relating the kind of life the believer in Christ receives to the eternal life which is in God.

Spiritual resurrection. Frequently in Scripture, regeneration is portrayed as spiritual resurrection. The Christian is revealed to be "alive from the dead" (Rom. 6:13), and God "even when we were dead through our trespasses made us alive together with Christ" (Eph. 2:5). Christ Himself said, "Verily, verily, I say unto you, The hour cometh, and now is, when the dead shall hear the voice of the Son of God; and they that hear shall live" (John 5:25). The fact of our resurrection is made the basis for frequent exhortation to live as those raised from the dead (Rom. 6:13; Eph. 2:5-6; Col. 2:12; 3:1-2).

New creation. Regeneration is also presented in the figure of creation or recreation. We are "created in Christ Jesus for good works" (Eph. 2:10), and exhorted to "put on the new man, that after God hath been created in righteousness and holiness of truth" (Eph. 4:24). The revelation of 2 Corinthians 5:17 is explicit, "Wherefore if any man is in Christ, he is a new creature: the old things are passed away; behold, they are become new." The figure of creation indicates that regeneration is creative in its nature and results in a fundamental change in the individual, a new nature being added with its new capacities. The individual becomes a part of the new creation which includes all the regenerated ones of this dispensation and Christ its Head. The new life given to the Christian is manifested in the new capacities and activities found only in those regenerated, forming the source and foundation of all other divine ministry to the saved.

Eternal life received by faith. The important fact, never to be forgotten in the doctrine of regeneration, is that the believer in Christ has received eternal life. This fact must be kept free from all confusion of thought arising from the concept of regeneration which makes it merely an antecedent of salvation, or a preliminary quickening to enable the soul to believe. It is rather the very heart of salvation. It reaches the essential problem of the lack of eternal life without which no soul can spend eternity in the presence of God. Regeneration supplies eternal life as justification and sanctification deal with the problem of sin specifically. It is a smashing blow to all philosophies which hold that man has inherent capacities of saving himself. Regeneration is wholly of God. No possible human effort however noble can supply eternal life. The proper doctrine of regeneration gives to God all glory and power due His name, and at the same time it displays His abundant provision for a race dead in sin.

V. Regeneration Not Accomplished by Means

Reformed theology opposed to means. Reformed theology has definitely opposed the introduction of any means in accomplishing the divine act of regeneration. The question of whether means are used to effect regeneration is determined largely by the attitude taken toward efficacious grace. Pelagian and Arminian theologians, holding as they do to the cooperation of the human will and the partial ability of the will through common grace or natural powers, recognize to some extent the presence of means in the work of regeneration. If the total inability of man be recognized, and the doctrine of efficacious grace believed, it naturally follows that regeneration is accomplished apart from means.

The human will ineffectual. Reformed theology in keeping with its doctrine of efficacious grace has held that the human will in itself is ineffectual in bringing about any of the changes incident to salvation of the soul. As related to faith, the human will can act by means of efficacious grace. The human will can act even apart from efficacious grace in hearing the gospel. In the act of regeneration, however, the human will is entirely passive. There is no cooperation possible. The nature of the work of regeneration forbids any possible human assistance. As a child in natural birth is conceived and born without any volition on his part, so the child of God receives the new birth apart from any volition on his part. In the new birth, of course, the human will is not opposed to regeneration and wills by divine grace to believe, but this act in itself does not produce new birth. As in the resurrection of the human body from physical death, the body in no way assists the work of resurrection, so in the work of regeneration, the human will is entirely passive. It is not that the human will is ruled aside, nor does it waive the human responsibility to believe. It is rather that regeneration is wholly a work of God in a believing heart.

Other means excluded. All other means are likewise excluded in the work of regeneration. While regeneration is often preceded by various antecedents such as the work of common grace and accompanying influences, these must be sharply distinguished from regeneration. Even the work of efficacious grace, though simultaneous with regeneration, and indispensable to it, does not in itself effect regeneration. Efficacious grace only makes regeneration possible and certain. Regeneration in its very nature is instantaneous, an immediate act of God, and in the nature of an instantaneous act, no means are possible. The fact that regeneration is consistently revealed as an act of God and the Scriptural revelation of the doctrine of efficacious grace are sufficient evidence for excluding the possibility of the use of means in effecting regeneration.

VI. Regeneration Not Experimental

Experience follows regeneration. In Christian testimony, much has been said of the experience of regeneration. If regeneration is instantaneous and an act of divine will, it follows that regeneration in itself is not experimental. It may be conceded freely that abundant experimental phenomena follow the act of new birth. The experiences of a normal Spirit-filled Christian may immediately ensue upon the new birth. This fact does not alter the nonexperimental character of regeneration. If it be admitted that regeneration is an instantaneous act of God, it is logically impossible for it to be experimental, in that

The Holy Spirit

experience involves time and sequence of experience. It may be concluded, therefore, that no sensation attends the act of new birth, all experience proceeding rather from the accomplished regeneration and springing from the new life as its source. In the nature of the case, we cannot experience what is not true, and regeneration must be entirely wrought before experience can be found. While the regenerated soul may become immediately conscious of new life, the act of regeneration itself is not subject to experience or analysis, being the supernatural instantaneous act of God. The new life may be a source of experience, but the act of regeneration itself is not experienced.

Regeneration not dependent upon experience. The nonexperimental nature of regeneration if comprehended would do much to deliver the unsaved from the notion that an experience of some sort is antecedent to salvation, and in turn, it would prevent those seeking to win souls of expecting in partial form the fruits of salvation before regeneration takes place. The popular notion that one must *feel* different *before* being saved has prevented many from the simplicity of faith in Christ and the genuine regeneration that God alone can effect.

Regeneration inseparable from salvation. The nonexperimental nature of regeneration has also, unfortunately, opened the door for the teaching of infant regeneration as held by the Lutheran Church. It is argued that, if regeneration is not experimental, there is no valid reason why infants cannot be regenerated. Shedd surprisingly approves the idea of infant regeneration on the ground that regeneration is not experimental in the following statement: "Regeneration is a work of God in the human soul that is below consciousness. There is no internal sensation caused by it. No man was ever conscious of that instantaneous act of the Holy Spirit by which he was made a new creature in Christ Jesus. And since the work is that of God alone, there is no necessity that man should be conscious of it. This fact places the infant and the adult upon the same footing, and makes infant regeneration as possible as that of adults. Infant regeneration is taught in Scripture. Luke 1:15, 'He shall be filled with the Holy Spirit, even from his mother's womb.' Luke 18:15, 16, 'Suffer little children to come unto me; for of such is the kingdom of God.' Acts 2:39, 'The promise is unto your children.' 1 Corinthians 7:14, 'Now are your children holy.' Infant regeneration is also taught symbolically. (*a*) By infant circumcision in the Old Testament; (*b*) By infant baptism in the New Testament."[6]

---

[6]Shedd, *op. cit.*, II, 505-6.

None of the proof texts offered by Shedd proves infant regeneration. While it is true that many Christians never know a crisis experience to which the act of new birth may be traced, there is no certain Scripture warrant for affirming infant regeneration. The normal pattern for regeneration is that it occurs at the moment of saving faith. No appeal is ever addressed to men that they should believe because they are already regenerated. It is rather that they should believe and receive eternal life. Christians are definitely told that before they accepted Christ they were "dead in trespasses and sins" (Eph. 2:1, A.V.).

The case of those who die before reaching the age of responsibility is a different problem. The proper doctrine seems to be that infants are regenerated at the moment of their death, not before, and if they live to maturity, they are regenerated at the moment they accept Christ. Infant baptism, certainly, is not efficacious in effecting regeneration, and the Reformed position is in contrast to the Lutheran on this point. The doctrine of infant regeneration, if believed, so confuses the doctrine as to rob it of all its decisive character. No one should be declared regenerated who cannot be declared saved for all eternity.

VII. THE EFFECT OF REGENERATION

The work of regeneration is tremendous in its implications. A soul once dead has received the eternal life which characterizes the being of God. The effect of regeneration is summed up in the fact of possession of eternal life. All other results of regeneration are actually an enlargement of the fact of eternal life. While life itself is difficult to define, and eternal life is immaterial, certain qualities belong to anyone who is regenerated in virtue of the fact that eternal life abides in him.

A new nature. Eternal life involves first of all the creation of a divine nature in the regenerated person. Without eradicating the old nature with its capacity and will for sin, the new nature has in it the longing for God and His will that we could expect would ensue from eternal life. The presence of the new nature constitutes a fundamental change in the person which is denominated "creation" (2 Cor. 5:17; Gal. 6:15) and "new man" (Eph. 4:24). A drastic change in manner of life, attitude toward God and to the things of God, and in the desires of the human heart may be expected in one receiving the new nature.

The new nature which is a part of regeneration should not be confused with the sinless nature of Adam before the fall. Adam's nature was a human nature untried and innocent of sin. It did not have as its source and determining its nature the eternal life which is bestowed in a regenerated person. The human nature of Adam was open to sin and temptation and was peccable. It is doubtful whether the divine nature bestowed in connection with regeneration is ever involved directly in sin. While the Scriptures are clear that a regenerated person can sin, and does sin, the lapse is traced to the sin nature, even though the act is that of the whole person. This must not be confused with various statements to the effect that a Christian can be sinless or unable to sin. The state of sinless perfection can never be reached until the sin nature is cast out, and this is accomplished only through the death of the physical body or the transformation of the body without death at the rapture.

Even the new nature, though never the origin of sin, does not have the ability sufficient to conquer the old nature. The power for victory lies in the indwelling presence of God. The new nature provides a will to do the will of God, and the power of God provides the enablement to accomplish this end in spite of the innate sinfulness of the sin nature. The state of being in the will of God is reached when the will of the new nature is fully realized. Eternal life and the new nature are inseparably united, the nature corresponding to the life which brings it into being.

A new experience. While regeneration in itself is not experimental, it is the fountain of experience. The act of impartation of eternal life being instantaneous cannot be experienced, but the presence of eternal life after regeneration is the source of the new spiritual experience which might be expected. New life brings with it new capacity. The person who before regeneration was dead spiritually and blind to spiritual truth now becomes alive to a new world of reality. As a blind man for the first time contemplates the beauties of color and perspective when sight is restored, so the newborn soul contemplates new revelation of spiritual truth. For the first time he is able to understand the teaching ministry of the Holy Spirit. He is able now to enjoy the intimacies of fellowship with God and freedom in prayer. As his life is under the control of the Holy Spirit, he is able to manifest the fruit of the Spirit, utterly foreign to the natural man. His whole being has new capacities for joy and sorrow, love, peace, guidance, and all the host of realities in the spiritual world. While regeneration is not an experience, it is the foundation for all Christian experience. This at once demands that regeneration be inseparable from salvation, and that regeneration manifest itself in the normal experiences of a yielded Christian life.

Regeneration that does not issue into Christian experience may be questioned.

Eternal security. One of the many reasons for confusion in the doctrine of regeneration is the attempt to avoid the inevitable conclusion that a soul once genuinely regenerated is saved forever. The bestowal of eternal life cannot be revoked. It declares the unchangeable purpose of God to bring the regenerated person to glory. Never in the Scriptures do we find anyone regenerated a second time. While Christians may lose much of a normal spiritual experience through sin, and desperately need confession and restoration, the fact of regeneration does not change. In the last analysis, the experiences of this life are only antecedent to the larger experiences the regenerated person will have after deliverance from the presence and temptation of sin. Regeneration will have its ultimate display when the person regenerated is completely sanctified and glorified. Our present experiences, limited as they are by the presence of a sinful nature and sinful body, are only a partial portrayal of the glories of eternal life. Through the experiences of life, however, the fact of regeneration should be a source of constant hope and abiding confidence "that he who began a good work . . . will perfect it until the day of Jesus Christ" (Phil. 1:6).

CHAPTER XV

THE BAPTISM OF THE HOLY SPIRIT

I. PREVAILING CONFUSION OF OPINION

OF THE various works of the Holy Spirit related to the salvation of the believer, the work of baptism is most difficult to present. While in its nature it is far more simple than the work of efficacious grace, it has been given such divergent interpretation that its essential character is widely misunderstood. The difference of opinion which exists on this doctrine is often found among writers who are essentially agreed on the doctrine of the Holy Spirit as a whole, and at the same time, the attitude of any writer on the doctrine of the baptism of the Holy Spirit may well be considered a definite basis of classifying his whole position. The recent work by Merrill F. Unger, *The Baptizing Work of the Holy Spirit,* has done much to correct the prevailing misunderstanding.

The confusion prevailing in the treatment of this doctrine has its rise in many factors. The principal cause of disagreement is found in the common failure to apprehend the distinctive nature of the church. Many theologians regard the church as a universal group of saints of all ages, some extending even these boundaries to include in the conception all who outwardly belong to it, even if not saved. If this concept of the nature of the church is held, the baptism of the Holy Spirit has no relation to it. As this ministry is not found in the Old Testament and is not included in any prophecies regarding the millennium, it is peculiarly the work of the Holy Spirit for the present age, beginning with Pentecost and ending at the resurrection of the righteous when the living church is translated. If, however, the church be defined as the saints of this age only, the work of the Holy Spirit in baptizing all true believers into the body of Christ takes on a new meaning. It becomes the distinguishing mark of the saints of the present age, the secret of the peculiar intimacy and relationship of Christians to the Lord Jesus Christ. It is, therefore, essential to a proper doctrine of the baptism of the Holy Spirit that it be recognized as the distinguishing characteristic of the church, the body of Christ.

Other sources of confusion in this doctrine are manifold. Baptism is improperly linked with other ministries of the Spirit such as the indwelling of the Spirit or regeneration. These works are simultaneous in point of time with the work of baptism, but are to be distinguished sharply in their nature. Baptism is often identified with the filling of the Holy Spirit. Particularly older writers such as D. H. Dolman[1] use the expression *baptism* as a synonym for *filling*. While their teaching may be most helpful as in the case of Dolman, the terminology is confusing and in the case of some writers results in the end in unscriptural teaching.

A serious departure from the truth is found in the attempt by some of the holiness movements to link the baptism of the Spirit with certain temporary spiritual gifts and their exercise. The special acts of revelation which occurred in the early church and the phenomenon of speaking in tongues are not to be confused with the baptism of the Holy Spirit. While these special ministrations of the Spirit occurred only to the saved, they are not to be expected as the usual signs accompanying baptism of the Holy Spirit. Particularly objectionable is the teaching that baptism is a work of the Spirit subsequent to salvation and involving special sanctification.

Because of the maze of conflicting opinions on the doctrine of the baptism of the Holy Spirit, the student of the subject must remain close to the Scriptures, particularly avoiding assumptions which the Scriptures do not warrant. The Scriptures present the doctrine in sufficient passages to permit the careful student to arrive at an accurate understanding of the truth. In all, there are eleven specific references to spiritual baptism in the New Testament (Matt. 3:11; Mark 1:8; Luke 3:16; John 1:33; Acts 1:5; 11:16; Rom. 6:1-4; 1 Cor. 12:13; Gal. 3:27; Eph. 4:5; Col. 2:12). All references prior to Pentecost are prophetic. All the references after Pentecost treat the baptism of the Holy Spirit as an existing reality. The major passage, which may be taken as the basis of interpretation of the other passages, is 1 Corinthians 12:13.

II. BAPTISM OF THE HOLY SPIRIT UNIVERSAL AMONG CHRISTIANS

Salvation and baptism coextensive. One of the prevailing misconceptions of the baptism of the Holy Spirit is the notion that it is a special ministration enjoyed by only a few Christians. On the contrary, the Scriptures make it plain that every Christian is baptized by the Holy Spirit at the moment of salvation. Salvation and baptism are therefore coextensive, and it is impossible to be saved without this work of the Holy Spirit. This is expressly stated in the central passage on the doctrine, "For by one Spirit are we all baptized into

---

[1] D. H. Dolman, *Simple Talks on the Holy Spirit*.

one body, whether we be Jews or Gentiles, whether we be bond or free; and have been all made to drink into one Spirit" (1 Cor. 12:13).

All Christians baptized by the Spirit. It is evident from this passage that *all* Christians are baptized by the Holy Spirit, and that all who enter the number of the body of Christ do so because they are baptized by the Spirit. It may be noted that this passage is found in an epistle addressed to a church which is guilty of gross sins, of factions, and defection from the faith. Yet they are reminded that they are baptized by the Spirit. This work of the Spirit is not directed toward those who are free from guilt, nor is it held as an objective or height to reach. It is rather stated to be the universal work of the Spirit in every believer.

One baptism. This thought is confirmed by Ephesians 4:5, "One Lord, one faith, one baptism." While this passage has been given various interpretations, it is clear that it refers to the things which are universal among Christians. All have the same Lord; all have the same faith or essential doctrine; and all have one baptism. It is patent that this passage could not refer to water baptism, as the sacrament of baptism is observed in various forms and with different interpretations by Christians, and by some few is not observed at all. Instead of the symbol, the reality is in view here, the baptism of the Holy Spirit. This passage serves to confirm the teaching that the baptism of the Spirit is universal among Christians. All other references to baptism of the Holy Spirit are in harmony with this viewpoint.

No exhortation to be baptized by the Spirit. It is significant that Christians are never exhorted to seek the baptism of the Spirit. While there is every exhortation to seek a proper adjustment to the Holy Spirit, this is never called by the term *baptism*. Never in Scripture is baptism by the Spirit recorded as occurring subsequent to salvation. It is rather an inseparable part of it, so essential that it is impossible to be saved in this age without it. From these considerations, and from the nature of the truth itself as considered in all its aspects, it may be concluded that the baptism of the Holy Spirit is universal among Christians.

III. Baptism into the Body of Christ

Union of the body. One of the important results of the baptism of the Holy Spirit is the union which is effected of believers in the body of Christ. According to 1 Corinthians 12:13, baptism of believers is "into one body." Using the figure of the human body as representing the church, individual believers are revealed to be joined to this living church by the baptism of the Holy Spirit. Baptism is, then, the work of the Holy Spirit forming and adding to the living unity of the church.

The body of Christ an important doctrine. Frequent reference is made in the Scriptures to the church as the body of Christ. Its formation and increase is often mentioned (Acts 2:47; 1 Cor. 6:15; 12:12-14; Eph. 2:16; 4:4-5, 16; 5:30-32; Col. 1:24; 2:19). Christ is revealed as Head of His body (1 Cor. 11:3; Eph. 1:22-23; 5:23-24; Col. 1:18). The work of Christ nurturing His body is mentioned in at least three passages (Eph. 5:29; Phil. 4:13; Col. 2:19). The sanctification of the body of Christ is revealed in Ephesians 5:25-27, and indirectly is implied in many other passages. Extended Scriptures are also found on the doctrine of the gifts of Christ to His body (Rom. 12:3-8; 1 Cor. 12:27-28; Eph. 4:7-16). The doctrine of the church as the body of Christ is a major doctrine of the New Testament.

Place in the body. The work of baptism assures the unity of the various members of the body. Without regard to race or culture, all true believers are united in a living union in the body of Christ. Frequent mention is made of this fact in Scripture, and its basis is the baptism of the Spirit. The union effected, however, is not one in which individuals are lost in the mass. It is rather a sovereign assignment of God, in which every believer is given his distinct place in the body of Christ. Every believer is essential to the harmony and perfection of the whole. The body is "fitly joined together" (Eph. 4:16, A.V.). An understanding of the basic doctrine of the baptism of the Holy Spirit is necessary, then, to comprehend not only the origin of the church, but also its working and sovereign arrangement.

IV. Baptism Into Christ

A new position. Intimately connected with the fact that baptism by the Spirit brings the believer into the body of Christ is the inseparable truth that baptism also places the believer in Christ Himself. This truth was anticipated by Christ when He pronounced the words, "In that day ye shall know that I am in my Father, and ye in me, and I in you" (John 14:20). The "ye in me" relationship was accomplished through the baptism of the Spirit. The importance of this position and the extent of its implications can hardly be overemphasized. Before salvation, the individual was in Adam, partaking of Adam's nature, sin, and destiny. In salvation, the believer is removed from his position in Adam, and he is placed in Christ. All the details of his salvation spring from this new position. His justification, sanctification, deliverance, access to God, inheritance, and glorification are actual and possible because of the believer's position in Christ. Failure to recognize the importance and significance of this doctrine has issued in many false teachings and has denied to many Christians the joy of their salvation.

Identification with Christ. Baptism into Christ is primarily identification. The believer is identified with Christ in His righteousness, His death, His resurrection, and His glorification. The much disputed passage of Romans 6:1-4, if approached with these doctrines in mind, becomes a plain declaration of the identification of the believer with Christ in His supreme work of death and resurrection: "Or are ye ignorant that all we who were baptized into Christ Jesus were baptized into his death? We were buried therefore with him through baptism into death: that like as Christ was raised from the dead through the glory of the Father, so we also might walk in newness of life" (Rom. 6:3-4). Before water baptism could be administered to converts, the glorious reality of identification with Christ was already a fact, made real the moment of saving faith. Having been joined to Christ by the baptism of the Spirit, the believer is identified with the work of Christ on the cross and His triumph in resurrection. Water baptism is the symbol of the baptism of the Spirit which effected the identification, but it is not the portrayal of the result of this identification, nor of the process of salvation. It is a sad reflection on the church's spiritual discernment to observe the historic emphasis upon the sacrament without the recognition of the baptism of the Holy Spirit which it should represent. In human hands the sacrament has become a divisive force in the church instead of the portrayal of the unity of the body of Christ and its identification with Christ. How important and how precious is the truth that the believer is in Christ Himself with all that this position entails.

A companion passage to Romans 6:3-4 is that of Colossians 2:12, "Having been buried with him in baptism, wherein ye were also raised with him through faith in the working of God, who raised him from the dead." The revelation in Colossians is complementary to that of Romans. Here is added the thought that we are identified with Christ in His burial. The aspect of burial is included in the essential gospel (1 Cor. 15:4). Its significance is that of finality. The burial of Christ makes clear the certainty of His death and the completion of His sacrifice. The believer goes with Christ to the grave and there becomes dead to sin and in resurrection becomes alive to God.

A new union of life. Baptism into Christ is not identification alone; it is also a union of life. Through regeneration the believer partakes of eternal life. He is united to Christ not alone by divine reckoning, but also in the reality of common life. It is the living unity of the Head and the body, sharing one vital and eternal life. From this reality spring many wonderful truths. It is the foundation of fellowship, fruit-bearing, strength for victory, and direction by the Head of the body. The two aspects of baptism into Christ are inseparable and blend into one entity. Christ becomes the sphere in which the believer lives. As Lewis Sperry Chafer has written: "A sphere is that which surrounds an object on every side and may even penetrate that object. To be within a sphere is to partake of all that it is and all that it imparts. Thus the bird is in the air, and the air is in the bird; the fish is in the water and the water is in the fish; the iron is in the fire and the fire is in the iron. Likewise, in the spiritual realm, Christ is the sphere of the believer's position. He encompasses, surrounds, encloses, and indwells the believer. The believer is *in Christ,* and Christ is *in the believer.* Through the baptism with the Spirit, the Christian has become as much an organic part of Christ as the branch is a part of the vine, or the member is a part of the body. Being thus conjoined to Christ, the Father sees the saved one only *in Christ,* or as a living part of His own Son, and loves him as He loves His Son (Eph. 1:6; John 17:23)."[2]

V. Baptism of the Holy Spirit Only in This Dispensation

Baptism of the Spirit important to dispensationalism. Theologians generally have failed to realize the importance of the baptism of the Holy Spirit. This springs from many causes. The distinctive purpose of God for the church is often not given its proper place. The contrasting spheres of law, grace, and kingdom are often confused. The work of the Holy Spirit in baptism, if properly understood, would do much to correct these errors. It is the one work of the Holy Spirit which is found only in the present dispensation. Other ministries are duplicated in either past or future ages. The work of baptism is, therefore, of great significance. By the act of the baptism of the Holy Spirit, the present age began at Pentecost. By an act of the Holy Spirit, some future day the church will receive its last addition, and Christ will come to receive her to Himself. These facts are made clear in the testimony of the Acts.

References in Acts. Only two references to baptism by the Holy Spirit are found in Acts (1:5; 11:16), and these passages are complementary. In Acts 1:5, Christ in His parting words to His disciples

---

[2]L. S. Chafer, *Grace,* pp. 307-8.

said, "For John indeed baptized with water; but ye shall be baptized in the Holy Spirit not many days hence." Two important facts appear in this statement: (1) Up to this time the Holy Spirit had not baptized them; (2) they would receive the baptism in or with the Holy Spirit in a few days—"not many days hence." They were told to wait in Jerusalem until they were baptized by the Holy Spirit (Acts 1:4). The indications are unmistakable that this prophecy was fulfilled on the Day of Pentecost. The power to witness, while not connected with the baptism of the Spirit, was present on the Day of Pentecost, and the disciples immediately began the work Christ specified as their program in Acts 1:8, and they no longer felt any necessity of remaining in Jerusalem awaiting a work of the Spirit. According to Acts 2:4, on the Day of Pentecost, the disciples were filled with the Holy Spirit. As this is a work limited to the saved in this age, and as all the saved are baptized by the Holy Spirit (1 Cor. 12:13), it follows that the believers were baptized at the same instant the other important ministries of the Holy Spirit began in them.

The second passage in Acts (11:16) confirms the testimony of Acts 1:5. In reciting the incident of the conversion of Cornelius, Peter said, "And as I began to speak, the Holy Spirit fell on them, even as on us at the beginning. And I remembered the word of the Lord, how he said, John indeed baptized with water; but ye shall be baptized in the Holy Spirit. If then God gave unto them the like gift as he did also unto us, when we believed on the Lord Jesus Christ, who was I, that I could withstand God?" (Acts 11:15-17). In making this statement, Peter is clearly stating that Acts 1:5 had already been fulfilled "at the beginning," no doubt a reference to Pentecost. The proof that Cornelius and his household had been baptized by the Holy Spirit is found in the fact that they spake with tongues (Acts 10:46). This has been misunderstood by many who have concluded from this fact that there is a direct relation between the baptism of the Holy Spirit and speaking with tongues.

Relation to tongues. On the Day of Pentecost a number of ministries of the Holy Spirit began simultaneously. No doubt the new converts in the house of Cornelius, like the converts on the Day of Pentecost, including the apostles, were regenerated, indwelt, sealed, and filled with the Spirit at the same moment they were baptized with the Spirit. The evidence that any part of the work of salvation had been accomplished in an individual can be taken as evidence that the other universal ministries of the Spirit are also present. Accordingly, any outward sign of salvation can be taken as evidence of the baptism of the Holy Spirit, even though there is no direct connection. It is clear that only Christians spoke in tongues, and the presence of this phenomenon was sufficient to justify Peter in concluding that the house of Cornelius was saved and therefore baptized by the Spirit. It is significant that speaking in tongues is found in Acts particularly where strong assurance of the reality of salvation and the truth of the gospel was needed. Thus, on the Day of Pentecost, this phenomenon is present, and again in the case of Cornelius where the gospel is extended freely to Gentiles. Speaking in tongues is properly numbered with the temporary spiritual gifts bestowed in the apostolic period. It sprang from the ministry of the Spirit in filling the believer, rather than from any of the universal ministries to the saved. There is actually no more connection between the baptism of the Spirit and speaking with tongues than there is between speaking in tongues and regeneration or justification. All are within the sphere of ministry to the saved.

Baptism at the moment of saving faith. From the two references to the baptism of the Holy Spirit in the Acts, it may be safely concluded that this ministry is never found before Pentecost and that it occurs simultaneously with the other ministries of the Spirit given to all who believe the moment they place saving faith in Christ. It is also clear that baptism did not occur once and for all on the Day of Pentecost as some writers have inferred. James Gray, for instance, states in his introduction to *Simple Talks on the Holy Spirit* by D. H. Dolman, "In my opinion, the baptism of the Holy Ghost came upon the disciples on the day of Pentecost (Acts 2) once and forever, and it is of that baptism that all believers partake as soon as they come to Christ by faith."[3]

It is true that the work of Christ was accomplished once and for all upon the cross, becoming effective for individuals when they become saved, even though the act of sacrifice was accomplished once and for all. The work of the Holy Spirit in baptism is different, however. It is the active joining of a soul to the body of Christ in a point of time. While it can be said that Christ died for all, even before they are saved, it cannot be said that individuals are baptized into the body of Christ until they come to the moment of saving faith.

Baptism never repeated. The work of baptism wrought in any individual is accomplished once and for all, however, and it is never repeated, involves no subsequent process in itself, and is never improved. The position and union effected are perfect from the moment of baptism. Throughout the present age, everyone who turns to

---

[3]*Simple Talks on the Holy Spirit*, p. 6.

Christ in faith is baptized by the Holy Spirit. No reference to this is ever found in the Old Testament. In the Gospels all references are prophetic. Again, in all prophecies of the future kingdom there is no reference to baptism by the Spirit. It may be concluded that it is, therefore, a work of the Holy Spirit found only in the present dispensation, a work peculiar to the church, and constituting the work of the Spirit by which the church is formed and joined to Christ forever.

VI. Baptism Not Experimental

Spiritual experience related to the filling of the Spirit. A careful study of the various ministries of the Holy Spirit will reveal that only the work of the Holy Spirit in filling is experimental. The work of the Holy Spirit in regeneration, indwelling, sealing, and baptism, while the ground for the filling of the Spirit and all subsequent experience, is not experimental in itself. As no one ever experienced a process in regeneration, so no one ever experienced a process in the baptism of the Spirit. A number of considerations point to this conclusion.

Baptism universal among believers. Baptism is not experimental because of the fact that it is universal among Christians. It is not a question of spiritual maturity, yieldedness, or indoctrination. Every believer, while totally unconscious of the reality of the truth until taught, is baptized by the Spirit as soon as faith is placed in Christ. It is a patent fact that most Christians know little concerning the baptism of the Holy Spirit. The great realities of union with Christ and our position in Him are known only as they are taught by the Spirit in a heart yielded to Him. While experience may play its part in bringing assurance of salvation, and thereby confidence in the fact of baptism by the Spirit, the act of the Spirit in itself is not experienced.

Baptism related to positional truth. Baptism is not experimental because it is positional truth. While our position in Christ is the ground of our experience when we are yielded to the Spirit, our position in itself does not produce experience. All Christians have the same position in Christ, but many have little spiritual experience. While experience may vary and be far from static in any individual, the position of the believer in Christ remains unalterably the same. It is particularly evident that the original act of the Spirit, placing us in Christ, produced no sensation. The new life which entered our souls may have brought a flood of the joy of salvation. The consciousness of forgiveness and justification may have relieved the heart under conviction. The act of being placed in the body of Christ, however, was not experienced in itself.

Baptism an instantaneous act of God. The very nature of the baptism of the Holy Spirit forbids that it be experimental. As an act of God, it is clearly instantaneous. There is no period of transition. The believer is brought from his position in Adam to his position in Christ instantly. In the nature of any instantaneous act, there can be no experience of process. Whatever may have been felt after the baptism of the Holy Spirit was complete, the act itself did not produce any experimental phenomena.

If the baptism of the Holy Spirit is properly seen in its character as an instantaneous act of God, it removes the doctrine from all its erroneous expositors who anticipate an unusual or phenomenal experience in connection with it. It becomes instead a sovereign act of God in which the soul is taken to Himself.

VII. Baptism an Act of the Holy Spirit

The Holy Spirit has been recognized as the agent of baptism by most students of the doctrine. Objection is found sometimes, however, to this thought. A study of the various passages speaking of baptism by the Spirit reveals that the customary Greek preposition used is *en*. From this it has been induced that we are baptized not *by* the Spirit, but *in* the Spirit. Christ is regarded as the actor, inasmuch as He is said to be the one baptizing, and the Holy Spirit is merely the sphere into which we come. A strict interpretation of the preposition would lead to this locative idea. The same preposition is used, however, in an instrumental sense with sufficient frequency in Scripture to free the translator from any artificial interpretation (cf. Matt. 12:24; Luke 22:49; Heb. 11:37; Rev. 2:16; 6:8; 13:10). When the Pharisees said, "This fellow doth not cast out devils, but by Beelzebub the prince of the devils" (Matt. 12:24), it is clear that they regarded the "prince of the devils" as the one performing the miracle. Likewise when the disciples asked, "Lord, shall we smite with the sword?" (Luke 22:49), they had in mind the use of the sword as the instrument even though held by a human hand. In the work of baptism by the Spirit, the preposition is probably used in a similar instrumental sense. While the American Standard Version uses "in" the Spirit for both Acts 1:5 and 1 Corinthians 12:13, the Revised Standard uses "with" and "by" respectively, considering both instances instrumental.

It is clear, however, that the entire ministry of the Spirit is being accomplished for the believer at the will of Christ. The Spirit is His agent and doing His work. It can be said, therefore, that we are baptized by Christ in the sense that Christ sent the Spirit. Accordingly, references to baptism of the Spirit as performed by Christ can be interpreted in this light. As the act of the sword in the hands of a disciple (Luke 22:49) is at once the act of the sword and the act of the disciples, so the work of baptism while accomplished by the Holy Spirit is also a work by Christ.

The thought of being brought into the sphere of the ministry of the Spirit by baptism is not excluded by making the Holy Spirit the agent of baptism. The act of bringing the believer into the body of Christ, which is the proper conception of baptism, does by its very nature also bring the believer into the sphere of the ministry of the Spirit. Accordingly, 1 Corinthians 12:13 indicates that we were "all made to drink into one Spirit." It is probable that this refers to participation in the ministry of the Holy Spirit. The work of baptism, however, is just as much a work of the Holy Spirit as regeneration or conviction, and while there is an indissoluble unity in the operation of the Trinity, care must be taken in attributing to each person the proper agency in the undertakings of God, if we are to avoid the errors of Unitarianism.

VIII. The Baptism of Fire

The four Gospels bear the record of the testimony of John the Baptist to the coming baptism by the Holy Spirit (Matt. 3:11; Mark 1:8; Luke 3:16; John 1:33). The testimony of the Synoptic Gospels forms a part of the message of John the Baptist in predicting the coming of Christ. The instance in John bears the additional revelation that Christ would be identified by the descent of the Spirit upon Him. All of the accounts give to Christ the special character of one who baptizes with the Holy Spirit, and all the accounts are prophetic in their nature.

A revelation of special interest is the statement in two of the Gospels that Christ would baptize with the Holy Spirit and with fire (Matt. 3:11; Luke 3:16). Some expositors have pointed to Pentecost as a fulfillment, based on the fact that tongues like as of fire sat on each of them gathered in the upper room. Others have envisioned a possibility of this being a present experience, a second Pentecost. A careful examination of the references in the Gospels, however, would seem to rule out both of these interpretations. The context of the passages points to judgment, the character of which could be fulfilled only at the second coming of Christ and the establishment of the kingdom. While the church age is introduced with a baptism of the Spirit, the kingdom age is to be introduced with a baptism of fire. No reference to baptism by fire is ever found in the Epistles, and the use of fire typically is in reference to future judgment in most instances. While the passages on baptism by fire are not explained definitely in the Word of God, it is safe to conclude that there is no present application of baptism by fire, and that reference is made to the future judgment of the world by Christ Himself at His second coming.

IX. The Abiding Results of Baptism by the Holy Spirit

An examination of the nature of the baptism of the Holy Spirit reveals a number of abiding results which may be numbered among the blessed facts of the Christian's salvation. While the baptism of the Spirit is not experimental in itself, all vital Christian experience flows from the realities which have been brought into being by this work of the Spirit. A full discussion of the body of truth involved cannot be undertaken here, but the leading ideas may be briefly stated.

A new union. The baptism of the Holy Spirit has the permanent result of a new union. The Christian baptized by the Spirit is joined to the body of Christ, a living member sharing its common life. This fact is the ground of all the truth which unites Christians forever. The Christian is not only joined to the body of Christ, but he is joined to Christ Himself in a union of eternal life. The nature of the union is a sound argument for the eternal security of the saint. The baptism of the Spirit, being wholly an act of God, can never be nullified.

A new position. In virtue of the new union effected by the baptism of the Spirit, the Christian is in a new position. This new position embodies most of the wonderful realities of his salvation. Instead of being a child of the world, an instrument in the hands of Satan for his own purposes, the Christian is in a new position in the body of Christ, an instrument which may be used by the Lord to carry out His purposes. The Christian is given every needed gift and provided with every needed enablement to accomplish the purpose of God for his place in the body of Christ. The Christian is also in a new position in Christ. In contrast to his former position in Adam, the Christian is placed in Christ, involving all the standing which this entails, the right to a new inheritance, a new nearness and access to God, and making possible a fullness of ministry of the Holy Spirit in this age which had never been possible before. The new position of the Christian is a challenge and incentive to godly living and the ground of victory over sin.

A new association. Because of the new union and new position of the Christian, through the baptism of the Spirit, he is brought into many new associations. His association with the Trinity is infinitely wonderful, to be realized in full in future ages, but forming an important aspect of his present experience if filled with the Spirit. The Christian's former association with the world is altered, and by grace the Christian may be delivered from the power of the world system, though remaining in the world and being subject to its government. In this new association, the Christian is the object of attack by Satan in the special sense in which Satan is attacking God Himself and all that belongs to God. The Christian needs the delivering power of God as he faces this new enemy. The Scriptures trace many other aspects of the believer's association. His relation to the organized church is stated. The relation of parents and children, husbands and wives, masters and servants, and other similar relationships are noted in Scripture. The particular duties of a Christian as living with other Christians are often mentioned, including the Christian's relation to his sinning brother, to brothers weak in faith or practice, and to brothers who give rebuke or correction. Because of the new association of the Christian baptized by the Spirit, a new standard of conduct based on his position in grace is called for, in keeping with the rich provision of God. In brief, every aspect of the Christian's life is changed because of the baptism of the Spirit. The importance of this doctrine, then, to the Christian and to the theologian is apparent.

CHAPTER XVI

THE INDWELLING OF THE HOLY SPIRIT

I. INDWELLING OF THE HOLY SPIRIT UNIVERSAL AMONG CHRISTIANS

ONE OF the distinctive features of the dispensation of grace in contrast to prior periods is the fact that the Holy Spirit indwells everyone who is regenerated. In the coming period of the kingdom on earth this divine blessing will also be a prominent feature and everyone who is saved will be indwelt by the Holy Spirit. The doctrine of the indwelling Spirit is exceedingly important as the foundation of the many ministries of the Spirit to the saved in this age. The work of the Spirit in filling is made universally available to those yielded to God in virtue of the abiding presence of the Spirit in every heart. The fact of His presence is a rich doctrine in its wide significance.

It is sometimes represented that the presence of the Holy Spirit in the life of the Christian is evidence of unusual powers of yieldedness. On the contrary, the Scriptures represent every Christian as possessing the Spirit. The fact of His indwelling is mentioned in many passages (John 7:37-39; Acts 11:17; Rom. 5:5; 8:9, 11; 1 Cor. 2:12; 6:19-20; 12:13; 2 Cor. 5:5; Gal. 3:2; 4:6; 1 John 3:24; 4:13). On the Day of Pentecost, the Holy Spirit came to make the church His residence, indwelling every believer. A number of considerations point to this doctrine.

Absence of the Holy Spirit proof of unsaved condition. One of the positive evidences for universal indwelling among Christians is the plain statement of Romans 8:9, "If any man hath not the Spirit of Christ, he is none of his." Possession of the Spirit which has been sent by Christ Himself and given to every Christian is necessary in order to be saved and belong to Christ. Accordingly, the unsaved are described as "having not the Spirit" (Jude 19).

Sinning Christians possess the indwelling Spirit. Never in the dispensation of grace are Christians warned that the loss of the Spirit will occur as a result of sin. On the contrary, in the notable case of the Corinthian church, they are exhorted to live a godly life and forsake sin *because* they are indwelt by the Spirit: "Know ye not that your body is a temple of the Holy Spirit which is in you, which ye have from God? and ye are not your own" (1 Cor. 6:19). The inference is plain that the presence of the Spirit abides even in the hearts of Christians who are unyielded and living in sin. While yieldedness remains a condition for the filling of the Spirit, the indwelling of the Spirit is unconditional for genuine Christians.

The Holy Spirit a gift. The Holy Spirit is referred to in many instances as a "gift" (John 7:37-39; Acts 11:17; Rom. 5:5; 1 Cor. 2:12; 2 Cor. 5:5). A gift by its nature is bestowed without merit. The gift of the Holy Spirit is never referred to as a just reward; its only condition is that Christ be received as Savior. It follows, accordingly, that it is a universal gift among Christians.

The high standard of grace requires supernatural enablement. Further proof of the universality of the indwelling Spirit is found in the fact that His presence is presupposed in the high standard of life revealed in the Epistles for Christians. Christ predicted that "rivers of living water" would flow from *within* the Christian (John 7:37-39). The flow of blessing and enablement comes from within the Christian rather than from an external influence. Christ intimated that apostolic teaching would be based upon it, and that the work of the Spirit would be within the Christian. From these several evidences, the Scriptural revelation is plain that the indwelling of the Holy Spirit is a blessing universally possessed by all Christians, just as all Christians are regenerated and baptized by the same Spirit.

II. PROBLEM PASSAGES

The doctrine of the indwelling presence of the Holy Spirit is comparatively simple in statement and in its principal content. The doctrine has been subject to much misapprehension, however, all of which yields to a careful study of every problem passage. A total of seven passages have been subject to serious misinterpretation (1 Sam. 16:14; Ps. 51:11; Luke 11:13; Acts 5:32; 8:14-20; 19-1-6; 1 John 2:20, 27).

Passages dispensationally misapplied. The problem of three passages results from the false assumption that the work of the Holy Spirit is the same in every dispensation. The fact that the Holy Spirit departed from Saul proves only that this was possible in the Old Testament when the Holy Spirit did not indwell all the saints (1 Sam. 16:14). David's prayer (Ps. 51:11) that the Holy Spirit be not taken away from him was in view of the possibility that this might occur as a result of sin, as in the case of Saul. David's prayer is not fitting for the Christian to whom every assurance has been given that the Spirit is an abiding gift. Christ introduced the possibility, apparently limited to His immediate followers during His life on earth, that the Holy Spirit would be given to those who ask for Him (Luke 11:13). We have no record that the disciples ever acted on this promise, and in contrast we have the promise of Christ that the Spirit would indwell them after His departure, implying that they were not indwelt when He gave them the promise. We may conclude that the context of these three passages forbids application to the doctrine of the Spirit indwelling Christians in the present age.

Acts 5:32. Three passages of Scripture are sometimes interpreted to mean that the indwelling of the Spirit is an experience subsequent to new birth, and that therefore it is not a feature of every believer's possessions (Acts 5:32; 8:14-20; 19:1-6). The first of these passages, Acts 5:32, states, "And we are his witnesses of these things; and so is the Holy Spirit, whom God hath given to them that obey him." The inference is sometimes made that obedience or yieldedness to the will of God is a condition of receiving the indwelling Holy Spirit. The context of this passage, however, makes it clear that the obedience required is not in reference to moral commands or to a standard of life, but rather to obedience to the command to believe in Christ. It resolves itself into another statement that God gives the Holy Spirit to those who believe in Christ. The word *obey* in the original (*peitharchousin*) has the meaning of obeying an authority. Hence it involves recognizing the person and authority of Christ as contained in belief in Him.

Acts 8:14-20. The problem of Acts 8:14-20 no doubt presents the most serious difficulty in the support of the doctrine of universal indwelling. According to the record, the believers who had been baptized by Philip had not received the Holy Spirit. The passage reveals that when Peter arrived, they received the Holy Spirit as he laid his hands upon them. From this it has been falsely inferred that receiving the Holy Spirit is a work subsequent to salvation and requiring the laying on of hands.

The problem has a solution in at least three particulars. First, while the delay of the normal indwelling of the Spirit until the arrival of Peter may be admitted, it is clear that this phenomenon was never repeated. The early chapters of Acts are transitional. The normal operations of God for this age are only gradually assumed. There was good reason why the extension of the gospel should be closely identified with the apostles themselves, and for this reason they were given unusual powers, and much blessing hinged on their presence. The full-orbed ministry of the Spirit among the Gentiles began in Acts 10, when the Holy Spirit indwelt at the moment of faith in the gospel. It was made plain to Peter that the working of the Spirit from this time on was not conditioned upon any special act on his part, but only on faith in Christ. This solution to the problem fully supports the doctrine of the universal indwelling of the Holy Spirit.

Two other solutions are possible, however. A second solution is found in the explanation that prior to Acts 10, the indwelling of the Spirit may have been limited to Gentiles ministered to by the apostles themselves, only Jews receiving the Spirit immediately. It is clear, at least, that each new extension of the gospel was attended by the immediate agency of the apostles. A third solution is sometimes offered in which the expression "received the Holy Spirit" (Acts 8:17) is interpreted as the filling of the Spirit, an outward phenomenon rather than indwelling. It is doubtful whether the word *received* is ever used to express the filling of the Spirit. The first two solutions provide a sufficient explanation of the passage. In any event, the phenomenon of a delayed indwelling of the Holy Spirit is never repeated, and to reason from this one event that this is normal for the entire church age is unwarranted.

Acts 19:1-6. The problem of Acts 19:1-6 yields to a careful study of the context and an accurate translation of the text. From the context it can be learned that the disciples at Ephesus were followers of John the Baptist and had not come into contact with the gospel of grace. Upon their baptism and confession of faith in Christ, the Holy Spirit came on them. It is indicated that Paul "laid his hands upon them" (Acts 19:6), either in the act of baptism or otherwise, and the presence of the Holy Spirit was manifested in that they spake with tongues. It is apparent from the narrative that the Spirit both indwelt and filled these disciples, the indwelling being known by the manifestation which accompanied the filling. It cannot be inferred, therefore, from this passage that the Spirit comes to indwell as a work subsequent to salvation, because they had not been saved previous to Paul's visit.

The translation of Acts 19:2 in the Authorized Version, "Have ye received the Holy Ghost since ye believed?" should be translated, "Did ye receive the Holy Spirit when ye believed?" as in the American Revised Version. Instead of being in support of the supposed theory that only some Christians are indwelt, it is actually a refutation. In the fact that they had not received the Holy Spirit, Paul found proof of the lack of regeneration. The absence of the Holy Spirit indicated a lack of salvation. It may be concluded, therefore, that the events of this section of Scripture indicate no departure from the norm of the doctrine that all Christians are indwelt at the moment of regeneration.

The anointing of the Holy Spirit. A further problem is introduced by the passages that refer to the anointing of the Holy Spirit. Some have inferred from these passages that this is a separate work of the Spirit in contrast to indwelling. A careful study of the seven references to the anointing of the Holy Spirit (Luke 4:18; Acts 4:27; 10:38; 2 Cor. 1:21; 1 John 2:20, 27, twice) will reveal that every use of *anoint* in relation to the Spirit may be safely interpreted as the *initial act of indwelling.* The word *anoint* is used in the sense of *apply,* and is especially appropriate in view of the fact that oil is used as a type of the Spirit. The presence of the Spirit is the result of the anointing, and every reference to anointing by the Spirit is used in this sense.

III. The Distinct Character of Indwelling of the Holy Spirit

While the indwelling of the Holy Spirit begins at the same moment as other tremendous undertakings by God for the newly saved soul, a careful distinction must be maintained between these various works of God. Indwelling is not synonymous with regeneration. While the new life of the believer is divine and by its nature identified with God's life, the possession of divine life and divine presence are distinct. The work of baptism by the Spirit is also to be distinguished from indwelling. Baptism occurs once and for all and relates to separation from the world and union with Christ. Indwelling, while beginning at the same moment as baptism, is continuous. As will be indicated in the ensuing material, the indwelling presence of the Holy Spirit does have a most intimate relation to the sealing of the Holy Spirit, the presence of the Holy Spirit constituting the seal.

Probably the most difficult distinction is that of the indwelling and filling of the Spirit. The two doctrines are closely related, yet are not synonymous. Filling relates wholly to experience, while indwelling is not experimental, in itself. In the Old Testament period, a few saints were filled temporarily without being permanently indwelt by the Spirit. While filled with the Spirit, Old Testament saints could in one sense be considered also indwelt, but not in the permanent unchanging way revealed in the New Testament. In the church age, it is impossible for anyone to be filled with the Spirit who is not indwelt. Indwelling is the abiding presence of the Spirit, while the filling of the Spirit indicates the ministry and extent of control of the Spirit over the individual. Indwelling is not active. All the ministry of the Spirit and experience related to fellowship and fruit issues from the filling of the Spirit. Hence, while we are never exhorted to be indwelt, we are urged to be filled with the Spirit (Eph. 5:18).

IV. THE IMPORTANCE OF THE INDWELLING OF THE HOLY SPIRIT

The importance of the abiding presence of the Holy Spirit in the life of the Christian cannot be overestimated. It constitutes a significant proof of grace, and of divine purpose in fruitfulness and sanctification. The presence of the Holy Spirit is our "earnest" of the blessing ahead (2 Cor. 1:22; 5:5; Eph. 1:14). The presence of the Spirit not only brings all assurance of God's constant care and ministry in this life, but the unfailing purpose of God to fulfill all His promises to us. The presence of the Holy Spirit makes the body of the believer a temple of God (1 Cor. 6:19). It reveals the purpose of God that the Spirit be resident in the earth during the present age. To surrender this doctrine or to allow its certainty to be questioned strikes a major blow at the whole system of Christian doctrine. The blessed fact that God has made the earthly bodies of Christians His present earthly temple renders to life and service a power and significance which is at the heart of all Christian experience.

CHAPTER XVII

THE SEALING OF THE HOLY SPIRIT

I. THE HOLY SPIRIT IS THE SEAL

THREE passages of Scripture indicate a work of the Holy Spirit revealed under the symbol of "sealing" (2 Cor. 1:22; Eph. 1:13; 4:30). The context of these passages reveals that the sealing is a ministry of the Holy Spirit. Christ Himself was sealed by the Father, but it is not revealed whether the Holy Spirit is directly related to it (John 6:27).

All the passages make clear that the act of sealing is accomplished entirely by God. It is never given in the form of an exhortation, nor pictured as a goal to which Christians should strive. Rather it is a gracious act by God for those whom He saved.

According to Ephesians 1:13 and 4:30, the believer is sealed by or in the Holy Spirit. No subsequent ministry is traced to this operation. From 2 Corinthians 1:22, it may be inferred that the seal is none other than the Holy Spirit Himself. God in mercy has provided in the presence of the Spirit a seal of greater significance than could be found in anyone or anything else. The figure is that of a finished transaction. As discussed in relation to typology, a seal signifies security, safety, ownership, and authority or responsibility.[1] The seal is provided as the token of what will be brought to its conclusion at the day of redemption.

II. SEALING OF THE HOLY SPIRIT UNIVERSAL AMONG CHRISTIANS

The ministry of the Holy Spirit in constituting the seal of redemption has been misrepresented to be a work of grace subsequent to salvation, and therefore to be coveted and sought. Various experiences are alleged to be related to this ministry as constituting evidence that the individual has been sealed. A careful study of the three references in Scripture will demonstrate, however, that every Christian is sealed by the Holy Spirit at the time of his salvation. The Corinthians, in spite of their many failings, are said to be sealed (2 Cor. 1:22). The

---

[1]Cf. F. E. Marsh, *Emblems of the Holy Spirit*, pp. 29-36.

possibility of only some Christians possessing this blessing is contradicted.

Much of the misrepresentation of this doctrine has arisen from the faulty translation in the Authorized Version in Ephesians 1:13, where it is stated, "After that ye believed, ye were sealed with that holy Spirit of promise." A better translation is found in the American Standard Version, "in whom, having also believed, ye were sealed with the Holy Spirit of promise." The phrase, "having also believed," is not significant of time but of cause. The sealing was immediate upon believing. It was "after that" only in the sense of cause and result.

The third passage, found in Ephesians 4:30, constitutes a reasonable proof that the sealing of the Spirit is universal among Christians. In this passage we are exhorted, "Grieve not the holy Spirit of God," because we are sealed by Him unto the day of redemption. It is assumed that all are sealed, and because of this, all are exhorted not to grieve the Spirit. If the sealing of the Spirit was a reality only for the spiritual, it would not be necessary to exhort such to cease grieving the Spirit. Every reference to sealing, however, contemplates it as a finished act, dependent only upon saving faith. Every Christian, accordingly, can receive by faith the fact of the indwelling Spirit as God's seal, setting him apart to eternal redemption.

III. The Sealing of the Spirit not Experimental

From the fact that all Christians are sealed by the Spirit, it is apparent that sealing is not an experience either at the moment of salvation or later. It occurs once and for all, as demonstrated by the fact that all who are sealed are sealed unto the day of redemption (Eph. 4:30). The Christian therefore needs no unusual experience to confirm the sealing of the Spirit, nor should the Christian pray for the sealing of the Spirit. It is a great truth to be accepted by faith as a token of the unfailing purpose of God in salvation.

IV. The Significance of the Sealing of the Holy Spirit

The point of greatest significance in the sealing of the Holy Spirit is the eternal security of the believer. It is plainly stated that the seal is placed on the Christian with a view to keeping him safe unto the day of redemption—the time of complete deliverance from all sin. The matter is not left in human hands, but is dependent entirely on the power of God. The nature of the seal forbids any possibility of counterfeit or disallowing of the token. The person of the Holy

Spirit, possessing all the attributes of God, by His presence is a token of God's abiding grace which could not be excelled. As God has promised that His Spirit will abide in the believer, so the Spirit Himself as the seal of our salvation brings all assurance to the believer's heart.

PART FIVE

THE WORK OF THE HOLY SPIRIT IN THE BELIEVER

CHAPTER XVIII

THE NATURE OF SPIRITUAL GIFTS

I. IMPORTANCE OF SPIRITUAL GIFTS

FEW SUBJECTS are of more immediate moment in the experience of the believer in Christ than the doctrine of the Holy Spirit in His relation to the spiritual life. Important as other considerations may be from the standpoint of doctrine and accurate interpretation of the Scriptures, the work of the Holy Spirit in the believer has a prior place because it is directly related to every reality of the believer's experience. The believer's sanctification, spiritual understanding, assurance, service, prayer, and worship all spring from the work of the indwelling Spirit. A proper understanding of the doctrine of the work of the Holy Spirit in the believer will do much to unlock the possibilities for spiritual blessing and usefulness, and it is, accordingly, the duty of those who teach and preach to give careful attention to its study and proclamation.

The church from the beginning has been plagued by two opposing extremes in its doctrine of spiritual gifts. From the first, as the Corinthian Epistles bear witness, there was abuse of spiritual gifts. In the course of the history of the church, excesses of the wildest kind are found in relation to this doctrine. On the other hand, there has been an appalling failure to appreciate the importance of spiritual gifts as determining the ministry of the church and as being essential to all its fruitfulness. The proper balance of doctrine is found in the Scriptures, and excesses have been noteworthy in their neglect of what the Scriptures actually teach. In the Scriptural revelation, certain facts are of great importance. First, the nature of the gifts of the Holy Spirit must be determined from the Scriptures. This at once distinguishes the true from the false. Second, spiritual gifts which clearly abide throughout the Christian dispensation must be examined and analyzed. Herein is provided the gifts without which even saved men would find it impossible to minister for God. Third, spiritual gifts as found in the apostolic age must be studied to determine whether, indeed, they are included in the program of God after the apostolic age. In other words, were certain spiritual gifts temporarily given the apostles for specific purposes which ceased to exist after their passing?

II. General Characteristics of Spiritual Gifts

The work of the Holy Spirit in the believer falls into two well-defined categories. The important subject of spiritual gifts as bestowed by the Holy Spirit must be considered first, as the preliminary to all the operations of the Spirit. Second, the work of the Holy Spirit in filling the believer, with consideration of its Biblical conditions and results, must be presented. The two aspects together determine the place and fruitfulness of every believer.

Something of the nature of spiritual gifts is revealed in the various words used in the New Testament to express the idea. The chief passage in the New Testament on the subject of gifts is found in 1 Corinthians 12—14. In the opening verse of the passage, the subject is introduced by the word *pneumatikon,* which with the article indicates the *things of the Spirit,* i. e., spiritual gifts. The word directs attention to the *source,* the Holy Spirit, and the *realm* of these gifts. As so used, the expression has the same reference as *charismaton,* meaning in the singular, a *gift of grace,* and in connection with spiritual gifts, the *"extraordinary powers, distinguishing certain Christians and enabling them to serve the church of Christ, the reception of which is due to the power of divine grace operating in their souls by the Holy Spirit."*[1] This word brings out the ground and nature of spiritual gifts. They are bestowed in grace, are entirely undeserved, and their power and operation is due to God alone. This thought is further emphasized by the use of the verb *didotai* (1 Cor. 12:7 ff.), meaning *to give.* It is clear from these several factors that the whole idea of spiritual gifts necessitates a supernatural work of God quite distinct from any natural powers of man, or even from any spiritual qualities which are universal among the saved. Spiritual gifts by their nature are individual and come from God.

A distinction may be observed in the New Testament between spiritual gifts and gifted men. While the two ideas are inseparable, *spiritual gifts* has reference to the supernatural powers possessed by individuals, while *gifted men* has reference to the sovereign placing of gifted men in the church for the purpose of ministering to the body. While the principal thought of 1 Corinthians 12—14 is that of spiritual gifts, we find reference to the bestowal of gifted men on the church in Ephesians 4:11. The two ideas are not strictly separated as indicated by the references in the Corinthian passage to both spiritual gifts and to gifted men. It may be noted, however, that gifted men are normally

---

[1]J. H. Thayer, *Greek-English Lexicon of the New Testament.* p. 667.

a gift of Christ or of God, while spiritual gifts are a work of the Third Person. The sphere of spiritual gifts is peculiarly a doctrine of the Holy Spirit, and therefore is the primary concern of the present study.

The principal word for spiritual gifts, *charisma,* is found frequently in the New Testament (Rom. 1:11; 5:15, 16; 6:23; 11:29; 12:6; 1 Cor. 1:7; 7:7; 12:4, 9, 28, 30, 31; 2 Cor. 1:11; 1 Tim. 4:14; 2 Tim. 1:6; 1 Pet. 4:10). Most of these instances add little to the central passage of 1 Corinthians 12—14. All except the one passage in Peter are found in the Pauline Epistles. A number of these instances do not have reference to extraordinary powers manifested in spiritual gifts proper. In Romans 5:15-16, the gift in view is that of justification, while in Romans 6:23, eternal life is the gift. The sovereign plan of God for each life, some to marry, some not to marry, is referred to as a gift in 1 Corinthians 7:7. The blessings of God in general as resulting from the prayers of God's people are spoken of as a gift in 2 Corinthians 1:11. In Romans 1:11, Pauls speaks of imparting a spiritual gift to the Romans, either in the sense of a distinct blessing through his ministry, or in the specific sense of imparting a special power, or a spiritual gift properly. The apostle may have had extraordinary authority in this regard as indicated in the impartation of a spiritual gift to Timothy (1 Tim. 4:14; 2 Tim. 1:6), though the act of laying on of hands seems to have been in reality simply a solemn recognition of spiritual gifts already imparted by God, and a setting apart to their full exercise. In any case, there is no warrant to believe that anyone has power to impart spiritual gifts except God in postapostolic times. The other references to spiritual gifts (Rom. 12:6; 1 Cor. 1:7; 12:4, 9, 28, 30, 31; 1 Pet. 4:10) may be taken as reference to spiritual gifts proper, extraordinary powers given by God as tokens of His grace and the means by which the individual's place in the ministry of the body of Christ may be fulfilled.

III. Distinctive Attributes of Spiritual Gifts

Spiritual gifts sovereignly bestowed. Spiritual gifts are revealed to be given sovereignly by God, and as such, they are not properly the objects of men's seeking. To the Corinthians, who were exalting minor gifts to the neglect of more important gifts, Paul wrote, "But covet earnestly the best gifts" (1 Cor. 12:31, A.V.), yet in his other Epistles it is clear from his silence on the subject that seeking spiritual gifts is not a proper subject for exhortation. Because their bestowal is sovereign, it follows that it is not a question of spirituality. A Christian unyielded to the Lord may possess great spiritual value, while one yielded may have relatively minor spiritual abilities. According to the Scriptures, "All these worketh that one and the selfsame Spirit, dividing to every man severally as he will" (1 Cor. 12:11 A.V.). It remains true, of course, that proper adjustment in the spiritual life of the believer is essential to proper exercise of his gifts, but spirituality in itself does not bring spiritual gifts.

The question has been raised whether spiritual gifts are a part of the original bestowal of grace accompanying salvation, or whether they are a subsequent work. The Scriptures give no clear answer, but from the nature of the baptism of the Holy Spirit, which occurs at the moment of new birth, and the resultant placing into the body of Christ, it would be reasonable to infer that spiritual gifts are bestowed at that time in keeping with the place of the believer in the body of Christ, even if these gifts are not immediately observed or exercised. Accordingly, spiritual gifts probably attend the baptism of the Holy Spirit, even though their bestowal is not included in the act of baptism. In the analogy of natural gifts as seen in the natural man, it is clear that all the factors of ability and natural gift are latent in the newborn babe. So, also, it may be true for spiritual gifts in the one born again. In both the natural and spiritual spheres, it is a matter of proper use and development of gifts rather than any additional gifts being bestowed.

Every Christian has some spiritual gifts. According to the Scriptures, "to each one is given the manifestation of the Spirit to profit withal" (1 Cor. 12:7), and "all these worketh the one and the same Spirit, dividing to each one severally even as he will" (1 Cor. 12:11). Christians are "severally members thereof" (1 Cor. 12:27), and "are one body in Christ, and severally members one of another" (Rom. 12:5). However small the gift, or insignificant the place, every Christian is essential to the body of Christ. As the Scripture puts it, "Nay, much rather, those members of the body which seem to be more feeble are necessary" (1 Cor. 12:22). There is divine purpose in the life of every Christian, and spiritual gifts are in keeping with that purpose. It is the challenge of the Scriptures on this subject (cf. 1 Pet. 4:10) that every Christian fulfill the ministry for which he has been equipped by God.

Gifts differ in value. While there is equality of privilege in Christian faith, there is not equality of gift. According to 1 Corinthians 12:28, "God hath set some in the church, first apostles, secondly prophets, thirdly teachers, then miracles, then gifts of healings, helps, governments, diverse kinds of tongues." In the nature of the various gifts, some are more effective and essential than others. Paul contrasts the gift of prophecy and the gift of tongues with the words, "Now I would have you all speak with tongues, but rather that ye should prophesy" (1 Cor. 14:5); and again, "Howbeit in the church I had rather speak five words with my understanding, that I might instruct others also, than ten thousand words in a tongue" (1 Cor. 14:19).

Spiritual gifts to be used in love. As 1 Corinthians 13 bears witness, spiritual gifts to be profitable must be used in love. Spiritual gifts in themselves do not make great Christians. Their use in the proper way motivated by divine love, which is the fruit of the Spirit, is effective and bears fruit to the glory of God.

Some gifts temporary. Another feature of spiritual gifts is that certain gifts were temporary in their bestowal and use. It is clear that the great body of Bible-loving Christians does not have all the spiritual gifts manifested in its midst as did the early apostolic church. On the other hand, certain gifts clearly characterize the entire present dispensation. The considerations leading to the classification of each gift will be noted in its individual treatment.

Contrast of spiritual and natural gifts. A concluding feature of spiritual gifts which is of great importance is the evident contrast between spiritual gifts and natural gifts. While God may choose men of natural ability, it is clear that spiritual gifts pertain to the spiritual birth of Christians rather than their natural birth. The qualities of the spiritual gifts are not evident in the individual before his salvation. The spiritual gifts pertain to his new nature rather than his old. Spiritual gift must not be regarded, then, as an enlargement of natural powers, but a supernatural gift bestowed in keeping with the purpose of God in placing that individual in the body of Christ. It may be frequently observed that individuals with little natural talent are often used mightily of God when those with great natural talent, though saved, are never similarly used. The spiritual gift is not, then, a demonstration of what man can do even under favorable circumstances, but rather it reveals what God can bestow in grace.

CHAPTER XIX

PERMANENT SPIRITUAL GIFTS

AN EXAMINATION of the sixteen spiritual gifts revealed in the New Testament will disclose considerable differences in the character of the gifts. Certain gifts are clearly the possession of the church today as exhibited in their exercise in gifted men throughout the present dispensation. There is little doubt that some men today have (1) the gift of teaching, (2) the gift of helping or ministering, (3) the gift of administration or ruling, (4) the gift of evangelism, (5) the gift of being a pastor, (6) the gift of exhortation, (7) the gift of giving, (8) the gift of showing mercy, and (9) the gift of faith. In contrast to these, as their individual exposition will demonstrate, stand other spiritual gifts known by the early Christians, which seem to have passed from the scene with the apostolic period. Some of these are claimed for today by certain sects, whose neglect of the Scriptural instructions for use of these gifts is in itself a testimony to the spurious quality of their affected gifts. Among these temporary gifts the following can be named: (1) the gift of apostleship, (2) the gift of prophecy, (3) the gift of miracles, (4) the gift of healing, (5) the gift of tongues, (6) the gift of interpreting tongues, (7) the gift of discerning spirits. The purpose of the present discussion is to examine, first, the spiritual gifts admitted by all as the possession of various gifted men throughout the present dispensation, leaving the treatment of the controversial aspects of the doctrine for the discussion to follow.

I. THE GIFT OF TEACHING

The gift of teaching is mentioned specifically a number of times in the New Testament (Rom. 12:7; 1 Cor. 12:28; Eph. 4:11), and it must be considered as one of the major gifts. The foundational character of a teaching ministry is demonstrated in the activities of the apostles. Their principal work was teaching the newborn Christians who had been saved from their heathen estate. The teaching gift consisted in a supernatural ability to explain and apply the truths which had been already received by the church. As such it is related to, but not identical with, illumination, which is a divinely wrought understanding of the truth. Obviously, many Christians are taught of the Spirit, but they do not possess the ability to teach what they know to others as effectively as those who possess the gift of teaching. The teaching gift does not claim any superior knowledge of the truth necessarily, and is distinct from the prophetic gift, in which the prophet speaks as the mouthpiece of God. The teacher must understand the truth and be taught by the Spirit, but the gift of teaching concerns the explanation and application of the truth rather than the method by which the truth was originally received. In the present day, the gift of teaching is exclusively that of teaching the Word of God by means of divinely wrought ability.

II. The Gift of Ministering

A gift possessed universally among Christians, though varying in its qualities, is the gift of ministering or helping (Rom. 12:7; 1 Cor. 12:28). It is difficult to imagine any Christian who does not possess some ability to minister or help in spiritual things. While only to a few is committed the gifts of teaching and leadership, all Christians are able to minister and help. While this ability is universal, it remains a gift sovereignly bestowed according to each individual's place in the body of Christ. The distinctions within the gift are many, different individuals being able to minister in different ways, thereby retaining a peculiar quality to the gift according to the purpose of God in its bestowal. The task of the church would be impossible apart from the gift and its exercise, however greatly endowed might be its leaders.

III. The Gift of Administration

Necessary to the work of the church is the leadership given to it by God. In keeping with this need, the gift of administration and ruling is sovereignly bestowed upon a few (Rom. 12:8; 1 Cor. 12:28). It is clear that all Christians are on the same level of privilege in spiritual things, but in the providence of God some are given places of great authority. To those possessing the gifts of administration and ruling all Christians should give proper heed, being exhorted to observe such gifts and honor them by obedience (Heb. 13:7).

IV. The Gift of Evangelism

Of primary importance in propagating the gospel is the gift of evangelism (Eph. 4:11). By its title it is clear that this gift has reference to effective preaching of the gospel message to the unsaved, and as such it is to be compared to the teaching gift which gives instruction to the saved. It is clear, experimentally, that knowledge of the gospel does not bring with it the ability to preach it with success to others. Men may possess the gift of teaching, for instance, without possessing the gift of evangelism, and vice versa. In some cases, men have possessed both the gift of teaching and of evangelism, as illustrated in the person of the Apostle Paul. While all are called to bring the gospel to the lost by whatever means may be at their disposal, and accordingly, like Timothy, should do the work of an evangelist (2 Tim. 4:5), it is the sovereign purpose of God that certain men should have a special gift in evangelism.

V. The Gift of Being a Pastor

The general care of the Christian flock is the work of a pastor, and to this end some receive the gift of being a pastor (Eph. 4:11). By its very title, it compares to the work of a shepherd caring for his sheep, the word *pastors* being the translation of *poimenas,* a word meaning literally, *shepherds.* A pastor is one who leads, provides, protects, and cares for his flock. As in the natural figure, no small skill is required to care for the flock properly, so in the spiritual reality a pastor needs a supernatural gift to be to his flock all that a pastor should.

A significant insight into the character of a true pastor's work is afforded by the close connection between pastoral work and teaching. In Ephesians 4:11, the use of *kai,* linking pastors and teachers instead of the usual *de,* implies that one cannot be a true pastor without being also a teacher. The principle involved is of tremendous significance. While it is not necessary for a teacher to have all the qualities of a pastor, it is vital to the work of a true pastor that he teach his flock. It is obvious that a shepherd who did not feed his flock would not be worthy of the name. Likewise in the spiritual realm the first duty of a pastor is to feed his flock on the Word of God. Quite apart from being merely an organizer, promoter or social leader, the true pastor gives himself to preaching the Word.

VI. The Gift of Exhortation

As a part of the work of preaching, exhortation fills an important place. Differing from teaching in that it is an appeal for action, exhortation is the practical aspect of a preaching ministry. Some are given special gift in this work, enabling them to lead Christians into the active realization of the will of God. The Greek word translated "exhort" (Rom. 12:8), *parakalon*, in addition to the thought of exhortation embodies the idea of *encouragement, comfort, admonishment*, and *entreaty*.[1] All of these form vital aspects of the preaching ministry which ensue as a manifestation of the spiritual gift of exhortation.

VII. THE GIFT OF GIVING

While the gift of giving borders on the graces which are found universally in all Spirit-filled believers, it has a definite place in the list of spiritual gifts revealed in Romans 12:8, having in view the proper use of temporal means in relation to others. While exercised to some degree by all Christians, and its manifestation is connected somewhat with ability to give, it may be observed as a distinct spiritual gift in some Christians, who demonstrate in the superlative the quality of committing earthly possessions to the Lord for His use.

VIII. THE GIFT OF SHOWING MERCY

The concluding gift revealed in the series of gifts mentioned in Romans 12 is the gift of showing mercy (Rom. 12:8). While the gift of giving had in view the poor and needy in respect to temporal needs, this gift is related to the sick and afflicted and any other who might fall within the sphere of needing succor. In dealing with such, some Christians are given special ability to show mercy with cheerfulness, *hilaroteti*, found only here in the New Testament in the noun form, has in it the thought of *readiness of mind, promptness*. from its root-meaning *propitious*.[2] It is this attitude which is divinely wrought of the Spirit in some Christians, and these may be said to possess this gift.

IX. THE GIFT OF FAITH

In the list of gifts and works of the Spirit in 1 Corinthians 12:8-10, the gift of faith is mentioned. It is found in the context mentioning "the word of knowledge" and "the word of wisdom" as given by the Spirit, which are works of the Spirit rather than gifts of the Spirit. Faith seems to be in a different category, however, and probably refers to the fact that some Christians have outstanding qualities of faith. As a gift, faith is a blessing bestowed

---

[1]*Ibid.*, pp. 482-83.
[2]*Ibid.*, p. 301.

upon some Christians, not all, though all Christians have some faith in God. It is manifested not so much in trust in Christ as Savior as in confidence in God in respect to His power and love working in the details of their lives, supplying their needs and guiding their steps. As such it is an abiding characteristic of the gifts of the Spirit throughout the present age of grace.

Chapter XX

TEMPORARY SPIRITUAL GIFTS

I. The Place of the Miraculous in the Present Purpose of God

IT IS CLEAR from a comparison of present-day Christian experience to that of the apostolic age that certain evident contrasts exist.

The decline of miracles. While the gospel remains unchanged, and many of God's methods of dealing with His own continue throughout the present dispensation, certain factors disappeared with the passing of the apostles and their generation. Different explanations have been offered to account for this. No doubt the church as a whole has drifted from its moorings and is unworthy of the same display of spiritual power. In every generation, however, there has been a faithful remnant of saints true to God, and to these God can continue to reveal Himself in fullness, but even those who have remained close to apostolic doctrine have failed to evince the same outward phenomena.

Purpose of miracles. The best explanation of the passing of certain gifts and their manifestation is found in the evident purpose of God in the apostolic age. During the lifetime of the apostles, it pleased God to perform many notable miracles, in some cases quite apart from the question of whether the benefit was deserved. A period of miracles is always a time when special testimony is needed to the authenticity of God's prophets.

Biblical history of miracles. Three notable periods of miracles are recorded in the Bible as history: (1) the period of Moses; (2) the period of Elijah and Elisha; (3) the period of Christ and the apostles. In each of these periods there was need of evidence to authenticate the message of God. In the case of Moses, the miracles performed witnessed to his office as prophet and leader, causing the people to accept his messages as from God. In the time of apostasy and declension under Elijah and Elisha, there was need for unusual witness to the power of God to call a people back to Himself, especially in lieu of priests who were true to God. In the time of Christ, again there is special need for miracles to witness to His person, to give the proper credentials for the Messiah, and, in the case of the apostles, to demonstrate that their gospel was a message from God.

An unusual display of miracles is, therefore, not an ordinary feature of each generation, to be called down at will even by the godly, but is rather articulated in the purpose of God for its value in promotion of His truth.

Relation to completion of the New Testament. With the completion of the New Testament, and its almost universal acceptance by those true to God, the need for further unusual display of miraculous works ceased. The preacher of today does not need the outward evidence of ability to heal or speak with tongues to substantiate the validity of his gospel. Rather, the written Word speaks for itself, and is attended by the convicting power of the Spirit. It is not a question of the power of God to perform miracles, but simply whether it is His purpose to continue the same form of manifestation of divine power as seen in the apostolic times. Certain sects have clung to the idea that the unusual features of the apostolic age will be reproduced in any age where people truly seek them in faith from God. It is evident, however, that some of the most godly people of recent generations have been entirely without the spiritual gifts which are here classed as temporary. It is evident, also, that some who have claimed these temporary gifts in the present day have shown a gross indifference to the Bible as a whole, to Christian morality, and to the higher claims of a spiritual life. The history of these sects is most convincing in demonstrating that the undue seeking of spiritual gifts results only in excesses of the most unholy kind.

Scripture versus experience. It is impossible in the nature of the case for anyone to cover the whole realm of Christian experience. Not only in the realm of spiritual gifts but also in other fields of doctrine there has been a constant parade of those who justify doctrines on the basis of varied experiences. The final test must always be what the Scriptures actually teach. Experience may serve as a partial test of the conclusions, but in itself the Bible must be taken as the final authority. Experience ever possesses two fatal grounds for error: (1) a misapprehension of the experience itself in its content and divine origin; (2) a faulty conclusion as to the doctrinal meaning of the experience. Hence, on the one hand, an experience supposedly of divine origin may be purely psychological, or worse, a deceiving device of Satan himself. On the other hand, a genuine experience may be misunderstood and mislabeled, as the common denomination of the work of the filling of the Spirit as the baptism of the Spirit. The Christian seeking the truth must come in all humility and dependence on the Spirit to the Word of God, relying on its teachings implicitly, avoiding even by undue emphasis any warping of the truth.

II. The Gift of Apostleship

The extent of the apostolic office. The word *apostle,* a translation of the Greek *apostolos,* means literally, *a delegate, messenger,* or *one sent forth with orders.*[1] According to Thayer (after Lightfoot) it is used 79 times in the New Testament, with 68 of these instances in Luke, Acts, or the Epistles of Paul.[2] Its first use in the New Testament is found in the sending of the twelve to preach the imminency of the kingdom (Matt. 10:2; Mark 3:14; 6:30; Luke 6:13). Among those called to the office of apostle was Paul (Rom. 1:1; 1 Cor. 1:1, etc); Barnabas (Acts 14:14; cf. Gal. 2:9); Matthias (Acts 1:25-26); and possibly James (1 Cor. 15:7; Gal. 1:19); and Apollos (1 Cor. 4:6, 9). To these some have added Silvanus and Timothy (1 Thess. 1:1; 2:6); Epaphroditus (Phil 2:25, cf. Greek and A.S.V. margin); the unnamed brethren (2 Cor. 8:23, cf. Greek); and Andronicus and Junia (Rom. 16:7).

Because of the varied usage, some have taken the position that an apostle was anyone called of God, particularly to missionary endeavor. Hence, J. C. Lambert writes, "The apostolate was not a limited circle of officials holding a well-defined position of authority in the church, but a large class of men who discharged one—and that the highest—of the functions of the prophetic ministry (1 Cor. 12:28; Eph. 4:11)."[3] The more common position is that the word *apostle* had first of all a strict application to those who were witnesses to the resurrection of Christ and were formally called by Christ or the Holy Spirit to this testimony, and, second, had a general application to all those sent of God to witness. In any case it is clear that every minister of the gospel in the apostolic age was not designated by the term *apostle,* nor can it be proved that all the apostles were missionaries, as Lambert contends.[4]

Qualities of the apostolic office. C. I. Scofield has produced a remarkable summary of the qualities entering into a New Testament apostle: "(1) They were chosen directly by the Lord Himself, or, as in the case of Barnabas, by the Holy Spirit (Mt. 10.1, 2; Mk. 3.13,

---

[1]J. H. Thayer, *Greek-English Lexicon of the New Testament,* p. 68.
[2]*Loc. cit.*
[3]J. C. Lambert, "Apostle," *International Standard Bible Encyclopaedia,* pp. 203-4.
[4]*Loc. cit.*

14; Lk. 6.13; Acts 9.6, 15; 13.2; 22.10, 14, 15; Rom. 1.1). (2) They were endued with sign gifts, miraculous powers which were the divine credentials of their office (Mt. 10.1; Acts 5.15, 16; 16.16-18; 28.8, 9). (3) Their relation to the kingdom was that of heralds, announcing to Israel only (Mt. 10.5, 6) the kingdom as at hand (Mt. 4.17, *note*), and manifesting kingdom powers (Mt. 10.7, 8). (4) To one of them, Peter, the keys of the kingdom of heaven, viewed as the sphere of Christian profession, as in Mt. 13, were given (Mt. 16.19). (5) Their future relation to the kingdom will be that of judges over the twelve tribes (Mt. 19.28). (6) Consequent upon the rejection of the kingdom, and the revelation of the mystery hid in God (Mt. 16.18; Eph. 3.1-12), the Church, the apostolic office, was invested with a new enduement, the baptism with the Holy Spirit (Acts 2.1-4); a new power, that of imparting the Spirit to Jewish-Christian believers; a new relation, that of foundation stones of the new temple (Eph. 2.20-22); and a new function, that of preaching the glad tidings of salvation through a crucified and risen Lord to Jew and Gentile alike. (7) The indispensable qualification of an apostle was that he should have been an eye-witness of the resurrection (Acts 1.22; I Cor. 9.1)."[5]

Apostleship a gift. In view of the distinct nature of the apostolic office, it is designated a *gift* in the New Testament (1 Cor. 12:28; Eph. 4:11). It is expressly declared to be the most important gift (1 Cor. 12:28), in that "God hath set some in the church, first apostles . . ." Apostles are distinguished from prophets, teachers, workers of miracles, etc. (1 Cor. 12:28). It is clear, then, that the apostolic gift is given only to those who are apostles in the strict sense of the word. As Scofield indicates, as quoted above, the work of the apostles prior to Pentecost and after Pentecost must be distinguished. The work prior to Pentecost was chiefly in announcing the kingdom as at hand. During the period immediately following Pentecost, they were leaders in introducing the gospel of salvation, having a divine commission and authority in this leadership, and given special revelation as the foundation of their teaching. The apostles in most instances had also the prophetic gift, and the gift of working miracles (2 Cor. 12:12), though not all who had these gifts were apostles. The apostolic office died with the first generation of Christians, there being no provision for successors, nor have there been in the history of the church any who could stand with the apostles. The fact that apostles were chosen from those who were eyewitnesses of the resurrected Christ

[5]C. I. Scofield, *The Scofield Reference Bible*, p. 1008, note 1.

eliminates any possibility of later generations participating in the call to apostleship. The inventions of the Roman church in the attempt to continue the apostolic office have been often refuted.

III. THE GIFT OF PROPHECY

The extent of the gift of prophecy. Classed second in importance in the list of spiritual gifts is the gift of prophecy (1 Cor. 12:28). The importance of this gift is attested by definite mention in other passages (Rom. 12:6; 1 Cor. 12:10; 14:1-40). The gift of prophecy was evidently possessed by many during the apostolic age. Agabus with evident prophetic gift predicted a famine (Acts 11:27-28) and warned Paul of his sufferings (Acts 21:10-11). Barnabas, Simeon, Lucius, Manaen, and Paul are mentioned among the "prophets and teachers" at Antioch (Acts 13:1). The four daughters of Philip possessed the gift of prophecy (Acts 21:9), indicating that in the New Testament as in the Old Testament the prophetic gift was not limited to men. Indication that Paul possessed prophetic insight is apparent in his direct guidance by God (Acts 16:6 ff.; 18:9-10; 22:17-21; 27:23-24). Judas and Silas were evidently prophets (Acts 15:32). In all probability all the apostles possessed the gift of prophecy.

Characteristics of the New Testament prophet. The New Testament prophet partook of some of the characteristics of the Old Testament prophet. Both spoke for God; both warned of judgment upon sin; both delivered their message as from God; both dealt with contemporaneous events as well as predicted events of the future. The Old Testament prophet, however, often had the character of a national leader, reformer, or patriot, and delivered his message normally to Israel. The New Testament prophet has no national characteristics; his message is individual and personal; it revealed the will of God which otherwise might have been unknown, meeting the need which later was to be filled by the written New Testament.

Elements of the gift of prophecy. Three elements were essential to the gift of prophecy: (1) the prophet must have received his message from God in the form of some special revelation; (2) the prophet must have divine guidance in the declaration of this revelation, corresponding to the inspiration of the written Word; (3) the message delivered by the prophet must bear with it the authority of God. It has been often pointed out that the prophet's message was not necessarily of future things—it might be an interpretation of present events or doctrine. This does not destroy the character of his message as from God, however. Mere teaching guided by the Spirit as experienced by many Christians throughout the present dispensation is not evidence of prophetic gift. The prophet, if a true prophet, must necessarily deliver a message free from error, a product not of his own mind, but a revelation from God. While prophets were men who could err in judgment and in conduct, as illustrated in Peter's compromise with legalism, in their prophetic messages they must be kept from error. Accordingly, there is no reference in the New Testament to anyone teaching error who is designated a true prophet.

The need of the prophetic gift in the apostolic church. The need for the prophetic gift in the apostolic period is evident. There had been a tremendous doctrinal transition from what was commonly believed by the Jews to what constituted the Christian faith. The New Testament was not written immediately, and there was imperative need for an authoritative source of revelation of the will of God. Guidance was required in formulating the doctrine of the church as commonly believed. To this end God gave to the church prophets who possessed the supernatural gift of prophecy. To them the church gave heed and was kept in relative doctrinal purity in spite of the fact that many of the first generation of Christians did not live to see the day of the completed canon.

The importance of the prophetic gift is indicated in 1 Corinthians 14, where it is set forth as the greatest gift in respect to edification, exhortation, and comfort (1 Cor. 14:3). In contrast to the gift of speaking in tongues, teaching and exercise of the prophetic gift is declared to be far superior: "Howbeit in the church I had rather speak five words with my understanding, that I might instruct others also, than ten thousand words in a tongue" (1 Cor. 14:19). Prophecy is declared to have special benefit in teaching those who believe (1 Cor. 14:22). In establishing order in the church assemblies, Paul indicates that the prophets should speak in turn, "For ye all can prophesy one by one, that all may learn, and all may be exhorted" (1 Cor. 14:31). Probably related to the prophetic gift is the "word of wisdom" and the "word of knowledge" given to some by the Spirit (1 Cor. 12:8).

Temporary character of the prophetic gift. While it may be freely admitted that men today possess the gift of teaching, the gift of exhortation, and the gift of evangelism, it is a safe conclusion that none possess the gift of prophecy. With the completed New Testament, it is evident that there is no further need for additional revelation. It is the purpose of God to reveal Himself through the Word, rather than beyond the Word. There is no more possibility of anyone possessing the prophetic gift in the present dispensation than there is of anyone writing further inspired books to be added to the canon. It is in this light that we may interpret 1 Corinthians 13:8, where in contrast to the abiding character of love, prophecy and special revelation (knowledge) are said to "fail" and "vanish away." The solemn warning of Revelation (Rev. 22:18-19), the last to be written of the New Testament, is that God's judgment will rest upon those who add to the book, a reference specifically to the Book of Revelation, but embodying the principle which underlies the whole canon.

IV. The Gift of Miracles

Miracles a lesser gift. The gift of miracles (1 Cor. 12:28) is classified as the first of the lesser gifts. While apostles, prophets, and teachers are of primary importance, miracles and other gifts are secondary. The use of "then" (*epeita*) makes it clear that the order is deliberate. The apostle is putting first things first. The word for miracles, *dunameis,* has in it the thought of *inherent power, power residing in a thing by virtue of its nature.*[6] From this idea is drawn the specific application of power to perform miracles. It is the regular word used for the miracles of Christ (Mark 5:30; Luke 5:17; 6:19; 8:46, etc.), and is used in combination with other words to indicate the nature or purpose of the miracles. In 2 Corinthians 12:12, it is grouped with signs (*semeiois*), wonders (*terasin*), and mighty works (*dunamesin*), as the "signs of an apostle." Miracles were, accordingly, a display of divine power with a view of authenticating the apostolic or prophetic gift.

Gift of miracles ceased at end of apostolic age. As has been previously indicated, it was evidently the purpose of God to confine this unusual display of divine power to the apostolic age, as the need for subsequent miraculous works ceased with the advent of the written Word of God with its manifest inspiration of God. Much of the objection to the position that the gift of miracles was confined to the apostolic age arises from the confusion of thought which identifies every miracle with the gift of miracles. The apostolic age is distinct because in it some men had the power to perform miracles at will in the name of Christ. It was not simply that a miracle was performed, but it was rather that men possessed a gift of performing miracles frequently.

Miracles continue though the gift has ceased. In the history of the church there have been occasional miracles, and God has inter-

---

[6]Thayer, *op. cit.*, p. 159.

vened in answer to faith and prayer and performed mighty works. To no one, apparently, since apostolic times, has power been given to heal *all* who are sick, to raise the dead, and in other ways display unusual power to perform miracles. As the gift of apostleship and the gift of prophecy have ceased, with it has ceased the need for the signs of the gift. A Christian can still appeal to God to do wonders, and God does answer prayer. God can still heal and even raise the dead if He chooses, but these miracles are sovereign and individual, not committed to the will of men or bestowed as a spiritual gift. While, therefore, the gift of miracles is not a part of the present program of God, the power of God to perform miracles must be affirmed.

V. The Gift of Healing

The only reference in the Scriptures to healing as a gift is found in 1 Corinthians 12 (vv. 9, 28, 30). In each of the three instances, healing (*iamaton*) is used with *charismata* (gifts). It is an aspect of the gift of miracles, a specific application of the power of God. The gift of miracles, however, in some cases was not displayed in healing, as the blinding of Elymas proves (Acts 13:11). The gift of healing had specific reference to restoring health to the body. Like the gift of miracles, it was designed to be a testimony to the truth proclaimed, and ceased as a gift with the passing of the apostles. The same distinction between the gift of miracles and the possibility of miracles exists between the gift of healing and the possibility of healing. While the gift of healing is no longer bestowed, God is able to heal in answer to prayer and faith. It is possible that some Christians may have unusual experiences in answers to prayer for healing, and yet it seems healing as a gift is not now committed unto men. In every case healing is sovereignly bestowed. No one today, however filled with faith and powerful in prayer, is able to heal in virtue of an abiding gift.

VI. The Gift of Tongues

Throughout the history of the church, no spiritual gift has occasioned as much continual controversy as the gift of tongues. Many solutions have been offered to the problem of the nature of this gift, but every one has some difficulties. A full discussion of the problem can be afforded only in works which deal with this one subject. However, within the limited sphere of the present study, the problem can be stated, the nature of speaking in tongues be examined, and the arguments for concluding that this gift was temporary be set forth.

The problem stated. The starting point in the examination of the doctrine of speaking in tongues is the account of Pentecost (Acts 2:1-13). According to the Scriptures, attendant to the filling of the Holy Spirit (Acts 2:4), all the considerable company gathered together on that day in Christian fellowship, "began to speak with other tongues, as the Spirit gave them utterance." This phenomenon amazed unbelievers who flocked to the scene. They confessed to hearing everyone his own language (Acts 2:8-11), and in their own language the wonderful works of God were extolled. Some accounted for this as an expression of drunkenness, but Peter refuted this by contending it was a predicted sign of the outpouring of the Spirit, quoting Joel 2:29, "Yea and on my servants and on my handmaidens in those days will I pour forth of my Spirit; and they shall prophesy" (Acts 2:18).

The Scriptural account definitely states they spoke with other tongues (*lalein heterais glossais*). In addition to this definite statement, there is the confirming evidence that they were heard and understood in various languages. All naturalistic explanations must be dismissed. It is clearly a supernatural work of God, designed to be a sign of His power attending the events of Pentecost.

In Acts 10:46, in connection with the conversion of Cornelius and his house, a second instance of speaking in tongues occurs. While Peter was bringing the gospel to them, the Spirit fell upon them and "they heard them speak with tongues, and magnify God." Attending the formal extension of the gospel to the Gentiles, speaking with tongues is repeated, as if linking this event definitely with Pentecost. Peter evidently refers to this when, in reciting the event, he states, "And as I began to speak, the Holy Spirit fell on them, even as on us at the beginning" (Acts 11:15).

A third important passage is found in Acts 19:6. Paul had discovered some disciples of John the Baptist who had never heard the gospel of grace and, accordingly, had not turned in faith to Christ. Following their baptism, Paul laid his hands upon them, and "the Holy Spirit came on them; and they spake with tongues, and prophesied" (Acts 19:6). The three instances in Acts constitute the only Scriptural reference to tongues in the New Testament except for the account in 1 Corinthians (12:10, 28, 30; 14:1-40). The passages in Acts do not explain the gift of tongues, nor is there any evidence in Acts that the act of speaking in tongues was ever repeated by those who had part in these three instances. Outside of 1 Corinthians there is no exposition of the doctrine in any of the Epistles. Accordingly, it is the problem of the doctrine of tongues to examine the instances in Acts for clues as to the nature of the gift, and to determine its regulation and extent from the 1 Corinthian passages.

Various solutions to the problem. Before attempting to reach conclusions in the doctrine, note must be taken of the attempts to solve the problem by various simple expedients. Liberal theologians have tried to solve the problem by placing a late date upon the Acts and inventing a theory that these references are textual interpolations. There is, of course, no scholarship to support this view beyond wishful thinking.

There has been a tendency on the part of some writers in all classes of theology to claim a distinction between Acts 2 and the 1 Corinthian passages. While it is allowed by some that in Acts 2 speaking in tongues consisted in utterances in foreign languages which could be understood naturally by those acquainted with them, it is claimed that in 1 Corinthians speaking in tongues consisted in ecstatic utterances in which human language was not used, the strange sounds issuing forth from the tongue being interpreted by others who had the gift of interpretation. Accordingly Thayer defines speaking in tongues in 1 Corinthians as "the gift of men who, rapt in an ecstasy and no longer quite masters of their own reason and consciousness, pour forth their glowing spiritual emotions in strange utterances, rugged, dark, disconnected, quite unfitted to instruct or to influence the minds of others: Acts x. 46; xix. 6; 1 Co. xii. 30; xiii. 1; xiv. 2, 4-6, 13, 18, 23, 27, 39."[7]

In an attempt to repudiate the excesses of the modern tongues movement, it has served the purpose of some writers to minimize the gift of tongues and to deny it the reality of an unknown language. Some, like Thayer, extend this only to the 1 Corinthians passage. Others include the passages in Acts as being simply ecstatic utterances which included some foreign words. Any view which denies that speaking in tongues used actual languages is difficult to harmonize with the Scriptural concept of a spiritual gift. By its nature, a spiritual gift had reality, and being supernatural, needs no naturalistic explanation. The phenomenon of speaking in tongues was accepted by believers as a work of the Holy Spirit. All attempts to relate speaking with tongues with the ravings of heathen mystics and soothsayers, as some do, must be rejected as in effect an attack on the accuracy of the Scriptural revelation.

---

[7]*Ibid.*, p. 118.

There are good reasons for believing that Thayer's position, illustrating the viewpoint of moderate opposition to considering all Scriptural references to tongues as essentially one, is based on an inadequate conception of the gift. By the express statement of Acts 11:15, the phenomenon of speaking in tongues in Caesarea was similar to the experience at Pentecost. If these two instances are essentially the same, Acts 19 would follow. It would be, certainly, arbitrary and strained exegesis to make a distinction when none is made in the text.

The use of identical terms in reference to speaking with tongues in Acts and in 1 Corinthians leaves no foundation for a distinction. In all passages, the same vocabulary is used: *laleo* and *glossa,* in various grammatical constructions. On the basis of the Greek and the statement of the text no distinction is found. The appeal to psychology is at best an *a priori* argument based on presumption.

Some have ignored the problem of Acts and attempted to solve the statements of 1 Corinthians by making all references to tongues a reference to the Hebrew language—i.e., an unknown language to the Corinthians. There is no basis for this in the text, nor does it warrant the designation a *spiritual gift,* if it concerns a language known to the speakers by natural means.

Principles used in the solution of the problem. The only safe principle to follow in discerning the doctrine of speaking in tongues is to assume that basically the gift is the same in its various references. Distinctions there are, as will be noted, but in each case speaking in tongues is real, not simply apparent; supernatural, not natural; a work of the Spirit, not a product of psychology or education; and a sign given particularly for unbelievers.

The problem of whether the gift of tongues was temporary for the apostolic period or permanent throughout the dispensation must be settled on the basis of 1 Corinthians alone. This problem becomes more simple if first the real character of speaking in tongues is determined. An examination of all the facts will substantiate the doctrine that speaking in tongues is not normal for the entire present age.

Speaking in tongues in Acts significant as signs. Previous discussion of the three notable passages in Acts (2:4; 10:46; 19:6) has shown a unity in vocabulary, binding the instances together. It is evident that all are real, as proved both by the direct statement of Scripture, and the confirming evidence of those who heard them. All must have been supernatural in character, a work of the Holy Spirit. It remains to note that all three instances have their significance revealed in their character as signs.

On the Day of Pentecost, all the full-orbed work of the Spirit now enjoyed by believers came into being. In addition to the full reality of regeneration, believers were baptized into the body of Christ, indwelt by the Spirit, sealed unto the day of redemption, and filled with the Spirit. On the Day of Pentecost the church as the body of Christ began by the act of baptism. It is evident that some outward display of the fullness of the Spirit was fitting. In the providence of God, the ability to speak with tongues was given as a confirmation that God had wrought in them and as a token of the ultimate universal extension of the gospel to all nations.

In the preaching of the gospel to Cornelius, a further important step was taken and a sign was needed. The gospel had been preached to Gentiles before, but it was now being revealed that Gentiles could accept the gospel on the same basis as the Jews: they had equal privilege. This was the truth which was impressed upon Peter. Accordingly, God saw fit to endow the occasion with a display of divine power which reproduced to some extent the phenomenon of speaking with tongues manifested at Pentecost. An outward token was needed, and God provided it.

The third instance in Acts 19:6 offers another instance in which an outward sign was needed. The sign was needed not only to convince unbelievers, but also to confirm the faith of the believers who only then had come to know Him of whom John spake.

The question has been raised whether these instances of speaking in tongues ever had repetition. In each case, the phenomenon was present only at the beginning of the Christian experience. The Acts is silent on any other similar instances.

It is apparent from this fact that speaking in tongues was by no means a test of either salvation or spirituality in the early church. Its presence in genuine form was a testimony to the reality of salvation, but it was not indispensable, and was, in fact, rare. Only in the Corinthian church, in the midst of heathen wickedness and idolatry, did God apparently bestow the gift in abundance. It is possible that a distinction obtained between speaking with tongues as an initial testimony of salvation and the gift of tongues as an abiding gift to be enjoyed through Christian experience. The experience of Cornelius, however, is expressly designated a *gift* (Acts 11:17), and there is no Scriptural basis for the distinction, though it may have existed.

Speaking in tongues in 1 Corinthians. The occasion for the exposition of the subject of spiritual gifts in 1 Corinthians may have had its rise in the difficulties within the church which the Epistle reveals. In any case, the exposition is full on all the important gifts. The subject is introduced with an account of the spiritual gifts of the body of Christ and the believer's place in that body. Reference is made to speaking in tongues in 1 Corinthians 12:10, 28, and it is mentioned *last* in a list in verse 28 which is clearly arranged in order of importance. In chapter 13, the important revelation is given that gifts are worthless except as used in love born of the Holy Spirit. Twice the subject of tongues is mentioned: first, tongues are declared to be "sounding brass, or a clanging cymbal" unless used in love (v. 1); second, tongues with prophecy and knowledge are said to be temporary, "whether there be tongues, they shall cease" (v. 8). The entire chapter which follows deals more or less with the problem of tongues and prophecy in the church.

In chapter fourteen, a number of important points are made. First, tongues are declared inferior to prophecy as a means of edification, exhortation, and comfort (1 Cor. 14:1-12). Their inferiority lies in the fact that no one could understand them. In later discussion, Paul states that five words with understanding are of more benefit than ten thousand words in a tongue (1 Cor. 14:19).

Second, tongues should not be used in the assembly unless an interpreter is present (1 Cor. 14:13-20). While the Corinthians are permitted to pray in an unknown tongue in private, Paul indicates that prayer with understanding is better (1 Cor. 14:15).

Third, tongues are declared to be a sign to unbelievers, and not intended primarily for the edification of believers (1 Cor. 14:21-22). Speaking in tongues will fail to convince unbelievers, however, unless there is order (v. 23), but even here prophecy is the greater gift leading to faith and worship (vv. 24-25).

Fourth, tongues as well as the gift of prophecy should be regulated and used only when it will result in edification of the church (vv. 26-38). Only two or three are to be permitted to speak in a tongue, and then only if an interpreter be present (vv. 27-28). Women are not to be permitted to speak as a prophet or in tongues in the church (vv. 34-35). He exhorts them, "Let all things be done decently and in order." It is evident that these rules, if applied, would remove from the modern tongues movements their unscriptural and injurious practices.

Fifth, speaking in tongues must, on the one hand, be not forbidden, but, on the other hand, the gift of prophecy was much superior and to be coveted (v. 39).

Speaking in tongues a temporary gift. It is, of course, impossible for anyone to prove experimentally that speaking in tongues cannot occur today. It may be demonstrated, however, that speaking in tongues is not essential to God's purpose now, and that there are good reasons to believe that most if not all the phenomena which are advanced as proof of modern speaking in tongues is either psychological or demonic activity. A most convincing argument is the history of the tongues movement with its excesses and its obvious evil characteristics. Some earnest Christians, however, are numbered among those claiming to speak in tongues, and it is not possible to examine the experience of everyone. The evils of the tongues movement have not arisen from the belief in speaking in tongues, but rather in the neglect of the Scriptures in their teaching on the subject, their regulation of the gift, and the modern false doctrine of tongues itself.

Four important lines of argument substantiate that speaking in tongues was a temporary gift. First, it is obvious that speaking in tongues began at Pentecost. There is no record of Christ or the disciples ever speaking in tongues before this event. It was a spiritual gift which was not given in the Old Testament period and during the Gospels. If the gift began at Pentecost by the sovereign will of God, it can also be withdrawn at divine pleasure.

Second, tongues had the characteristic of being a sign to Israel. Such a sign was necessary at the inauguration of the age of grace to prove to Israel that the gospel message was from God. It had been predicted by the prophets and this prophecy required fulfillment. Isaiah predicted, "Nay but by men of strange lips and with another tongue will he speak to this people" (Isa. 28:11). This is quoted in 1 Corinthians 14:21-22, "In the law it is written, By men of strange tongues and by the lips of strangers will I speak unto this people; and not even thus will they hear me, saith the Lord. Wherefore tongues are for a sign, not to them that believe, but to the unbelieving." The fulfillment being fully established, there is no further need of the sign.

Third, some other spiritual gifts are temporary, as illustrated in the gift of apostleship, the gift of prophecy, the gift of miracles, and the gift of healing. It was apparently God's purpose to withdraw the unusual signs which attended the ministry of the apostles in the early church after they had served their purpose.

Fourth, it is predicted that tongues would cease (1 Cor. 13:8). In view of the fact that tongues as mentioned in the context refers to the gift of tongues, it is reasonable to conclude that the same reference is here. On the basis of both inference and specific reference, the gift of tongues is revealed to be a temporary provision of God for the apostolic period.

The danger of abuse of the doctrine. It is apparent from 1 Corinthians that speaking with tongues by its very nature is peculiarly liable to abuse. With this in view, certain facts may be restated in conclusion. First, speaking in tongues is the least of all spiritual gifts. It was, therefore, not to be exalted as an evidence of great spiritual power or usefulness. The prominence given to it by certain sects is quite apart from the Scriptures.

Second, speaking in tongues was in no sense a test of salvation. By its very nature as a gift, it is clear that not all Christians possessed it even in apostolic times. The total lack of reference outside of Acts and 1 Corinthians must imply that it was nonessential. If tongues were essential even as an outward sign of inward salvation, it is inconceivable that it should not be given a prominent place in the plan of salvation. It is significant that neither the Gospel of John nor Romans mentions it.

Third, the gift of speaking in tongues was no indication of spirituality. Of all the churches to whom Paul wrote, the Corinthian church manifested the most carnality and gross sin, yet speaking in tongues was more in evidence here than in the other churches. It is a matter of history that the tongues movement has not led in holiness of living, but rather has been guilty of all manner of excesses. Many godly men and women through the centuries have been entirely aloof from any experience of speaking in tongues.

Fourth, speaking in tongues is not inseparable from baptism of the Spirit. According to 1 Corinthians 12:13, every Christian is baptized by the Spirit, but it is obvious that all Christians do not speak in tongues. The attempt to make speaking in tongues a necessary condition for baptism of the Spirit is one of many evils attending abuse of the Scriptural doctrine.

VII. The Gift of Interpreting Tongues

In connection with the bestowal of the gift of speaking in tongues upon some in the early church, there was need for others to interpret what was spoken. It is possible that in some cases speaking in tongues became the vehicle for revelation, though it is sharply distinguished from prophecy. It consisted mostly in ecstatic ascriptions of adoration and worship. The gift of interpreting tongues (1 Cor. 12:10; 14: 26-28) was simply the divinely wrought ability to translate the speech of those speaking in tongues. If speaking in tongues is no longer existent in the church today, it is clear that the gift of interpreting tongues has likewise passed from the present purpose of God.

VIII. THE GIFT OF DISCERNING SPIRITS

In the midst of many forms of oral revelation, it was essential to the early church to have divine assistance in detecting the false amidst the true. Satan then as now attempted every deceiving device. The gift of discerning spirits (1 Cor. 12:10) was apparently the ability given by the Holy Spirit to discern the true from the false sources of supernatural revelation given in oral form. As the New Testament had not been completed, there was no written Word to appeal to except the Old Testament. With the coming of the completed New Testament, the written Word made this work of the Spirit no longer necessary.

The indwelling Holy Spirit no doubt continues to help all believers in detecting error. This is the universal possession of every Christian, as indicated in 1 John 2:27, "But the anointing which ye have received of him abideth in you, and ye need not that any man teach you: but as the same anointing teacheth you of all things, and is truth, and is no lie, and even as it hath taught you, ye shall abide in him."

Because of the ever-present danger of being led into error, believers are exhorted to "prove the spirits, whether they are of God" (1 John 4:1). The test is given: "Every spirit that confesseth that Jesus Christ is come in the flesh is of God" (1 John 4:2). It is probable that by the word *spirit* there is reference to human beings as such. Any teacher, accordingly, is to be tested by the child of God on the issue of whether he confesses that Jesus Christ is come in the flesh. In connection with demon possession, as encountered particularly in heathen lands by missionaries, no doubt the same method of testing can be used. In any case, however, the gift of discerning spirits seems to be no longer bestowed. Christians are dependent now upon the written Word of God as illuminated by the Holy Spirit, and no one is given authority to discern spirits apart from that belonging to all Christians alike.

The doctrine of spiritual gifts as a whole is another testimony to the grace of God, His sovereignty, His wisdom, and His providence. The secret of fulfilling the divine purpose of God encompassed in each life unfolds according to the divine pattern. It can be best traced in love, in dependence upon God and yieldedness to His sovereign will.

CHAPTER XXI

THE NATURE OF THE FILLING OF THE HOLY SPIRIT

I. THE VITAL IMPORTANCE OF THE DOCTRINE

FROM THE standpoint of practical value to the individual Christian, no field of doctrine relating to the Holy Spirit is more vital than the subject of the filling of the Spirit. It has been greatly neglected in the average theology, along with other practical applications of doctrine. The doctrine of the filling of the Spirit demands in addition to theological knowledge an experimental understanding of the truth. It is necessary to bear in mind the important foundation laid in the delineation of the other ministries of the Holy Spirit, and upon this foundation to erect the grand structure of living experience entirely in keeping with the doctrine of the Scriptures on this truth. Many have been the attempts to explain the doctrine without a proper understanding of its background in the baptism, indwelling, regeneration, and sealing of the Spirit. Some have ignored the teachings of Scripture in favor of conclusions based on experience alone. The task before us is to expound this doctrine in the light of the Scriptures accounting as well for the varied phenomena of Christian experience. The subject is here treated from three standpoints: (1) the nature of the filling of the Holy Spirit; (2) the conditions for the filling of the Holy Spirit; (3) the results of the filling of the Holy Spirit.

II. THE PRIMARY SOURCE OF SPIRITUAL EXPERIENCE

A careful study of the nature of the filling of the Holy Spirit will reveal that it is *the source of all vital spiritual experience* in the life of the Christian. As such it is sharply distinguished from experience which precedes salvation, such as conviction, and is distinct from salvation itself, with all the attendant ministries of the Spirit. The facts that sustain these conclusions are found in the Scriptural representation of the filling of the Holy Spirit, including its conditions and results.

III. THE VARIETY OF SPIRITUAL EXPERIENCE

There is no experimental fact more abundantly sustained in the

189

Scriptures than the wide diversity of spiritual experience. Lewis Sperry Chafer has written: "There is an obvious difference in the character and quality of the daily life of Christians. This difference is acknowledged and defined in the New Testament."[1] The Scriptures distinguish fundamentally between the saved and the lost by use of many distinguishing terms. but the spiritual divisions of mankind do not stop there. The Scriptures also distinguish the "spiritual" and the "carnal" (1 Cor. 2:9—3:4); those who walk "worthily of the Lord," and those who "walk after the manner of men" (1 Cor. 3:3; Col. 1:10). The distinction represented in these frequent contrasts is within the fold of the Christian Church and is definitely traced to a difference in relationship to the Holy Spirit. Accordingly, Paul writes to the Galatians, "But I say, Walk by the Spirit, and ye shall not fulfill the lust of the flesh" (Gal. 5:16).

IV. Spirituality Contrasted to Maturity

The diversity of spiritual experience and blessing is contrasted in Scripture to another important aspect of doctrine, the Christian's growth in grace. While any Christian may be spiritual, may walk in the Spirit, and abide in Christ, even though a newborn saint, there is a gradual spiritual growth which issues in maturity and ultimate conformity to Christ when the body of flesh is cast aside in death or at the Lord's coming for His own. This gradual growth while conditioned to some extent upon the spirituality of the individual is nevertheless in the sovereign control of God, and the individual Christian is promised ultimate perfection. Frequent reference to this truth in Scripture assures it a major part in the purpose of God. The wheat and the tares *grow* together until the wheat is mature and ready for harvest (Matt. 13:30). The purpose of the gift of gifted men to the church is "for the perfecting of the saints, unto the work of ministering, unto the building up of the body of Christ: till we all attain unto the unity of the faith, and of the knowledge of the Son of God, unto a fullgrown man, unto the measure of the stature of the fulness of Christ . . . but speaking truth in love, may grow up in all things unto him, who is the head, even Christ" (Eph. 4:12-13, 15). Christians are exhorted, "As newborn babes, long for the spiritual milk which is without guile, that ye may grow thereby unto salvation" (1 Pet. 2:2). We should "Grow in the grace and knowledge of our Lord and Savior Jesus Christ" (2 Pet. 3:18).

There is, however, a vital relation between the Christian's growth

[1] L. S. Chafer, *He That Is Spiritual*, p. 3.

in grace and the Christian's spirituality. While the Christian is assured ultimate perfection in heaven, he is exhorted to grow to spiritual maturity. While it is impossible for any Christian to attain spiritual maturity apart from the gradual process which it entails, any Christian upon meeting the conditions may enter at once into all the blessedness of the fullness of the Spirit. The correspondence of spirituality and maturity to the health and growth of the physical body is obvious. A child may be immature as to stage of growth but at the same time be perfectly healthy. Growth of the body requires time and development, while health is an immediate state of the body which determines its present enjoyment and growth. Likewise in the spiritual realm, a newborn saint may have the fullness of the Spirit, while being nevertheless quite immature, and in contrast a mature saint may lack the fullness of the Spirit. There is an important connection between maturity and spirituality, however. A saint will mature in the faith more rapidly when living in conscious fellowship with God in the fullness of the Spirit than if wandering in the realm of the flesh. A "babe in Christ" is one who has had time to reach some maturity but whose development has been arrested by carnality. What physical health is to the growth of the physical body, the fullness of the Spirit is to spiritual growth.

There has been some opposition to the viewpoint that any Christian, however immature, can attain immediately to a spiritual state upon meeting its conditions. The proof of the possibility is found in the fact that Christians are exhorted to have the fullness of the Spirit. As J. East Harrison states it: "Some Christians who are living on the lower plane of religious experience are not only content to dwell there, but resent the suggestion that there is anything nobler or better; while others go constantly mourning and complaining of the dreary desert way they are treading. In either case the loss is unspeakable, and the harm done to the cause of Christianity by their defective testimony and character is pitiable."[2]

The diversity of spiritual experience can, therefore, be traced to the two factors of the fullness of the Spirit and spiritual maturity. Of the two, the fullness of the Spirit is by far the most important in spiritual experience. All the ministries of the Spirit may be known by the immature Christian if he is living in proper adjustment to the Spirit. The fruit of the Spirit is intended by God to be produced in any Christian in whom the Spirit has full sway. The evident fact that many Christians never know the full-orbed ministry of the Spirit

---

[2] J. E. Harrison, *Reigning in Life*, pp. 42-43.

in their own lives constitutes a challenge to the church and its ministry to proclaim this important aspect of truth.

V. The Unhindered Ministry of the Indwelling Holy Spirit

The work of the Holy Spirit in filling the believer may be simply defined as that ministry which is accomplished in the believer when he is fully yielded to the indwelling Holy Spirit. Every reference to the filling of the Holy Spirit indicates a spiritual condition on the part of the person filled which is brought about by the complete control of the Spirit. There are fourteen references to the filling of the Holy Spirit in the New Testament, including the references in the Gospels. The Greek verb *pimplemi* is found eight times used in this connection (Luke 1:15, 41, 67; Acts 2:4; 4:8, 31; 9:17; 13:9). Another form of the same verb, *pleroo,* is found twice in reference to the filling of the Spirit (Acts 13:52; Eph. 5:18). In addition to the two verbs used to express the idea, the adjective *pleres* is used in four instances (Luke 4:1; Acts 6:3; 7:55; 11:24).

It is clear in all of these instances that the Spirit of God is ministering to the individuals concerned in entire freedom from hindrance. Frequently, there is outward evidence of this ministry in the form of a work for God accomplished in the power of the Spirit. The thought is not that individuals by any process have received more of the Spirit, but it is rather that the Spirit has complete possession of the individual. In the original act of indwelling the believer at the time of salvation, it is clear that each individual received the whole of the person of the Spirit, as well as other members of the Trinity. In the nature of the persons of the Trinity, their personality is undivided, ministering and dwelling in entirety wherever any ministry or presence is indicated at all. Accordingly, it is not a question of securing more of the presence of God but of entering into the reality of His presence and yielding to all the control and ministry for which He has come to indwell. While in this age it is impossible to be filled with the Holy Spirit unless permanently indwelt, it is a sad reflection on the spiritual state of many Christians that though their bodies are the temple of the Holy Spirit they are not yielded to Him and know nothing of the great blessings which His unhindered ministry would bring.

A study of the various passages referring to the filling of the Spirit bring out these aspects in clarity. According to Luke 4:1, Christ was filled with the Holy Spirit, speaking of more than the unity of the persons of the Trinity, extending a definite ministry particularly to His human nature. It is prophesied that John the Baptist should be filled with the Spirit from his mother's womb (Luke 1:15), and

Elisabeth, his mother, and Zacharias, his father, are on occasion filled with the Spirit (Luke 1:41, 67). These references to the filling of the Spirit in the Gospels partook of the character of this ministry found in the Old Testament, being, with the exception of Christ (Luke 4:1), a temporary infilling governed by the sovereign purpose of God, rather than being a universal privilege extended to all yielded saints. The references in the Acts and Ephesians all speak of the normal experience of this dispensation.

The doctrine of the Holy Spirit is subject to gradual unfolding in the Acts, certain aspects of His ministry being subject to the immediate agency of the apostles. In the doctrine of the filling of the Holy Spirit, however, every instance fully sustains the premise that this ministry is found only in Christians yielded to God. Accordingly, in Acts 2:4, on the Day of Pentecost, the company waiting in the upper room was filled with the Spirit. Peter seeking to honor God before the Sanhedrin was filled (Acts 4:8). The early Christians experienced a second filling after prayer (Acts 4:31). An essential quality sought in selection of the first deacons was that they should be "full of the Spirit" (Acts 6:3). Stephen was "full of the Holy Spirit" as he looked to the heavens to see the glory of God before his martyrdom (Acts 7:55). Paul upon receiving the Lord's messenger, Ananias, was filled with the Holy Spirit (Acts 9:17). In this case, an unusual feature was that Paul was not filled until Ananias placed his hands upon him, a temporary restriction designed to authenticate Ananias as a messenger of God. Paul is mentioned as filled with the Spirit again years later (Acts 13:9). Barnabas is described as "full of the Holy Spirit" (Acts 11:24), and all the disciples at Antioch in Pisidia were "filled with joy and with the Holy Spirit" (Acts 13:52). Every historic instance of the filling of the Spirit illustrates the principle that only Christians yielded to God are filled.

VI. The Command to be Filled with the Holy Spirit

The work of the Holy Spirit in filling the believer partakes of the special quality of being commanded of every Christian. According to Ephesians 5:18, all Christians have the responsibility of being filled with the Spirit: "And be not drunken with wine, wherein is riot, but be filled with the Spirit." As such the ministry of the Holy Spirit stands in sharp contrast to other ministries. While all men are commanded to obey the gospel and believe in Christ unto salvation, no one is ever exhorted to be born again by any effort of the flesh, or exhorted to be indwelt, or sealed, or baptized by the Spirit. These ministries of the Spirit come at once upon saving faith in Christ. They pertain to salvation, not to the spiritual life of the Christian. Christians are, however, commanded to be filled with the Spirit. It is, of course, impossible for any Christian to be filled with the Spirit by simply willing it. The Scriptural conditions for this fullness of the Spirit are revealed. It is the responsibility of the Christian to meet these conditions of yieldedness. The fullness of the Spirit will inevitably result.

In the nature of the fact that Christians are commanded to be filled with the Spirit, it is clear also that it is possible to be a Christian without being filled. No Christian is ever warned to seek the other ministries of the Spirit because in their nature they are wrought in salvation. It is apparent, then, that the filling of the Holy Spirit, while possible only for the saved, is not a part of salvation itself. It is also evident that the filling of the Spirit is to be contrasted sharply to the baptism of the Spirit, the former being a quality of spiritual life, the latter the possession of every Christian by which he has become a member of the body of Christ. The filling of the Spirit must also be contrasted to the indwelling of the Spirit as all Christians are indwelt from the moment of salvation (Rom. 8:9), while the filling of the Spirit is found only in some Christians. No Christian can be said to be in the will of God unless he is filled with the Spirit. It is a universal responsibility as well as a privilege, extending equally to all Christians, but never addressed to the unsaved.

VII. The Filling of the Holy Spirit a Repeated Experience

An important contribution to the doctrine of the filling of the Spirit is the tense of the verb in the command to be filled (Eph. 5:18). The verb *plerousthe* is found in the present imperative. The present tense indicates a durative idea, and could be translated, "keep being filled." The contrast with the state of intoxication mentioned in the verse is obvious. Instead of being constantly in a state of being drunk with wine, the entire faculties of the body being subject to its power and influence, the Christian should be constantly filled with the Spirit. The present imperative is regularly used in the New Testament to express this durative idea,[3] and it is of great significance here. Its major contribution is to bring out clearly the contrast between the baptism of the Spirit and the filling of the Spirit, the confusion of which has been the weakness of many studies on the Holy Spirit. A study of 1 Corinthians 12:13 reveals that the word *baptize—ebaptisthemen*—is found in the aorist, an action which takes place once and

---

[3]A. T. Robertson, *A Grammar of the Greek New Testament in the Light of Historical Research*, p. 890.

for all. In contrast to this, there is the continuous ministry of the Holy Spirit in filling.

The use of the present tense in the command to be filled with the Spirit makes it evident that this work of the Spirit is a continuous reality in those who are yielded to God. It is a moment-by-moment relationship which may be hindered by sin. It is not a question of a so-called "second work of grace" or any epochal experience. While the outward evidence of the fullness of the Spirit may vary, the abiding reality is intended by God to be the normal experience of His own. It is only as the Christian experiences the present reality of the fullness of the Spirit that the full-orbed ministry of the Spirit may be realized.

The Scriptures bear a decisive testimony that the filling of the Holy Spirit is a repeated experience. The early church was filled with the Spirit on the Day of Pentecost (Acts 2:4). In Acts 4:8, Peter is mentioned as again being filled with the Holy Spirit, and the entire company gathered at Jerusalem to hear Peter's report of his encounter with the Sanhedrin are again filled with the Holy Spirit (Acts 4:31). Stephen, originally chosen a deacon because he was filled with the Spirit, is revealed to have been "full of the Holy Spirit" immediately before his martyrdom (Acts 7:55). Both Paul and Barnabas are found filled with the Holy Spirit at widely differing periods of their lives (Acts 9:17; 11:24; 13:9, 52). The evidence for the experimental nature of the filling of the Holy Spirit is fully sustained in every instance.

It may be concluded from this study of the nature of the filling of the Spirit that the Scriptures point to this ministry as accounting for, in large measure, the wide diversity of spiritual experience. The filling of the Holy Spirit has been shown to be the ministry accomplished in the believer fully yielded to His control. The universal responsibility on the part of Christians to be filled with the Spirit was found to be substantiated by explicit command of the Scriptures. It was demonstrated that it is possible for any Christian to be filled continuously with the Spirit, the repeated experience of the early Christians being an illustration. The filling of the Holy Spirit in every respect stands in sharp contrast to the ministries of regeneration, indwelling, sealing, and baptism, which are accomplished once and for all at the time of salvation.

CHAPTER XXII

CONDITIONS FOR THE FILLING
OF THE HOLY SPIRIT

IN HIS popular work of the Holy Spirit, *He That Is Spiritual*, and more recently in his *Systematic Theology*, volume six, Lewis Sperry Chafer has directed attention to the simple and effective outline afforded in the Scriptures on the subject of conditions for the filling of the Holy Spirit. Three conditions are specified for the filling of the Spirit. In 1 Thessalonians 5:19, the command is given, "Quench not the Spirit." In Ephesians 4:30, another exhortation is found, "And grieve not the Holy Spirit of God, in [by] whom ye were sealed unto the day of redemption." A third positive command is recorded in Galatians 5:16, "But I say, Walk by the Spirit, and ye shall not fulfill the lust of the flesh."

These three Scriptures provide a divinely inspired outline of the conditions for the filling of the Holy Spirit. While there are many aspects to the spiritual life and experience, all will be found to be related to these simple commands. The importance of these Scriptures as the key to unlocking the truth of the conditions for the filling of the Holy Spirit cannot be overemphasized. It is a sad commentary upon much so-called exhortation that it deals with the externals rather than the primary causes for defeat and spiritual apathy. As one turns to this important subject, it must be with a new realization that herein is one of the most important doctrines of the Scripture.

I. QUENCH NOT THE SPIRIT

Definition. The expression, "Quench not the Spirit," found in 1 Thessalonians 5:19, is nowhere formally explained in Scripture. *Quenching* is often used in the Bible in its proper physical sense, as illustrated in Matthew 12:20, where Christ spoke of not quenching flax, and in Hebrews 11:34, the heroes of the faith are revealed to have "quenched the violence of fire." In Ephesians 6:16, the shield of faith is said to "be able to quench all the fiery darts of the wicked." In 1 Thessalonians, however, it is used in a metaphorical sense, meaning according to Thayer, *"to suppress, stifle."*[1] It is patently impossible

---

[1] J. H. Thayer, *Greek-English Lexicon of the New Testament*, p. 572.

to extinguish the Holy Spirit in the absolute sense, or to put Him out. His abiding presence is assured for all Christians. His person is indestructible. It is, therefore, quenching in the sense of resisting or opposing His will. Quenching the Spirit may be simply defined as being unyielded to Him, or saying, "No." The issue is, therefore, the question of willingness to do His will.

The sin of Satan. In the introduction of sin in God's creation by the original rebellion of Satan, Lucifer is revealed to have opposed the will of God by five "I will's" which are summarized in the fifth, "I will make myself like the most High" (Isa. 14:14). The original rebellion against God is identified with Satan and the wicked angels who fell with him. With the introduction of sin into the human race in Adam, the field of rebellion was extended to man. The Christian who has been reclaimed from spiritual death and condemnation in Adam faces the crucial issue of flesh, the natural tendencies of the sin nature, the power of the world, and the power of Satan. There can be no compromise on the issue if the fullness of the Holy Spirit is to be realized. It is necessary to be yielded to the will of God to have the full blessings of His ministry. The life of yieldedness has several aspects as will be seen.

The initial act of surrender. Every Christian faces the obvious fact that no man can serve two masters or lords (Matt. 6:24). It is impossible to enter into the present joys of salvation without accepting the Savior as Lord, but this is a truth to be apprehended in experience as well as in doctrine. Accordingly Christians are constantly exhorted to yield themselves to God. In Romans 6:13, the exhortation is found, "Neither present your members unto sin as instruments of unrighteousness; but present yourselves unto God, as alive from the dead, and your members as instruments of righteousness unto God." The Greek word for *present* is found in two tenses in this verse which illustrates clearly that the appeal is to a yielding to God which is accomplished once for all.

In the first instance, *present* is found in the present tense, *paristanete,* meaning, "Stop presenting your members as instruments of unrighteousness unto sin." There was a constant and abiding experience of sinfulness. In contrast to this, the exhortation is to present yourself unto God, *parastesate,* in the aorist tense, meaning, "Present yourself to God once and for all." A Christian is called upon to make a definite yielding of his life to God to make possible its full blessing and usefulness just as he was called upon to believe in order to be saved. The familiar exhortation found in Romans 12:1, to "present" ourselves to God, is the same word in the aorist tense, again a definite act of yielding to God. To be filled with the Spirit, a surrender of life and will to His guidance and direction is prerequisite. The original act of surrender is a surrender of our wills to God's will. It is not a question of any particular area of conflict of will.

Lewis Sperry Chafer has summed up the issue concisely: "A yieldedness to the will of God is not demonstrated by some one particular issue: it is rather a matter of having taken the will of God as the rule of one's life. To be in the will of God is simply to be willing to do His will without reference to any particular thing He may choose. It is electing His will to be final, even before we know what He may wish us to do. It is, therefore, not a question of being willing to do some one thing: it is a question of being willing to do *anything,* when, where and how, it may seem best in His heart of love. It is taking the normal and natural position of childlike trust which has already consented to the wish of the Father even before anything of the outworking of His wish is revealed."[2]

The continued life of yieldedness. It is a matter of experience as well as revelation that the issues of yieldedness are not settled by the initial act. The initial act accepts by faith the will of God *before* it is known. In facing the actual leading of the Spirit, the plain teaching of His Word, and the providential dealings of God, there is many a struggle with the inner man. It is in this realm that the precise command, "Quench not the Spirit," applies. The word *quench (sbennute)* is found in the present imperative. The thought may be either *do not quench,* or it may presume that the reader has already been quenching the Spirit, in which case the appeal is to *stop quenching* the Spirit. It is an exhortation to maintain the same attitude as was adopted in the original surrender to the will of God. It is not a *re*consecration, but a call to recognize that the Spirit has the right to rule. The believer must not resist the one to whom he has given his life and surrendered his will.

The continued life of yieldedness to God involves a relationship to the will of God in several aspects. The yielded Christian has an unusual relationship to the Word of God. As its revelation becomes known and its application becomes evident, the issue of being yielded to the truth as made known by the Holy Spirit becomes very real. It is evident that refusal to submit to the Word of God is quenching the Spirit, making the fullness of the Spirit impossible.

---

[2]L. S. Chafer, *He That Is Spiritual,* p. 113.

Quenching the Spirit is closely related to His guidance. There are many spiritual decisions for which the Word of God does not give specific instruction. The general truths of Scripture must be applied to a given life and circumstance. In this aspect of the truth, the Word of God gives the principles, but the Spirit of God gives the instructions. This is a very precious portion of the believer's heritage and a mark of his sonship (Rom. 8:14). Refusal to follow this evident leading is a quenching of the Spirit. Guidance may take various forms and does not follow a regular pattern. The Spirit may lead one into a field of service and exclude another. Guidance usually relates to service and is essential to it. Man was not created with a self-guiding faculty, but is dependent upon God for direction. The Spirit may prohibit a course of action as in forbidding Paul to preach the gospel in Asia and in Bithynia, only later to direct his steps to these very fields and bless in the ministry of the Word (cf. Acts 16:6-7; 19:10). It is essential to effective service and wise action to follow implicitly and trustingly the ordered steps indicated by divine guidance. The fullness of blessing awaits only in the divinely appointed path.

An important field of yieldedness is in relation to providential acts of God, which often are contrary to natural desires of our hearts, and may seem outwardly from the human viewpoint to be a triumph of evil rather than of good. The "thorn in the flesh," whatever its character, must be accepted in faith in the love and wisdom of God. The child of God who desires to live without quenching the Spirit must know the sweetness of submission to the will of God. It may often be observed that the suffering saint evinces a sweetness of testimony and a fullness of the Spirit which is unknown in others. Yieldedness to the Spirit includes, then, submission to the plain teachings of the Word of God, obedience to the guidance of the Spirit, and acceptance in faith of the providential acts of God. All of these are a part of the moment-by-moment experience of living in the will of God with an indwelling Spirit who is unquenched.

The supreme illustration of Christ. As many writers have pointed out, Christ Himself is the supreme illustration not only of one in whom the fullness of the Spirit was manifested at all times, but one who was submissive to the whole will of God. The classic passage of Philippians 2:5-11 reveals not only the glory and victory which belongs to our Lord, but His submission to the humiliation of the cross. Christ was willing to *be* what God chose: "a servant . . . made in the likeness of men." He was willing to *go* where

God chose, into a sinful world which would reject Him and crucify Him. He was willing to *do* what God chose: "obedient even unto death, yea, the death of the cross." The Garden of Gethsemane with its struggle epitomized by the epical words, "Not my will, but thine, be done" (Luke 22:42), has had its lesser counterpart in the lives of all great Christians. The child of God who has "the mind of Christ" is one who is fully yielded to the will of God for his life in every particular as Christ was for the will of God in His life. For the fullness of the Spirit, it is absolutely necessary to be yielded to Him.

II. GRIEVE NOT THE SPIRIT

Definition. The Scriptures often testify to the fact that the Spirit of God is holy and that He is a person. The indwelling presence of this holy person constitutes the body of a believer a temple of God. In the nature of the case, the presence of sin in any form grieves the Holy Spirit. Accordingly, when the Christian is exhorted to "grieve not the Holy Spirit of God, in whom ye were sealed unto the day of redemption" (Eph. 4:30), it is an appeal to allow nothing in his life contrary to the holiness of the Spirit. It is clear that the one cause of grieving the Holy Spirit is sin.

Grieving the Holy Spirit involves several factors. It is a spiritual condition characterizing unyielded Christians. The first step may well be the quenching of the Spirit, i.e., refusing to follow His leading and resisting His will. It is not an issue of salvation, as this is settled once for all when regeneration took place. The persistent resistance of the leading of the Spirit results in further departure from the will of God. The Spirit can no longer direct and bless in fullness as His ministry has been denied. It is this condition which is designated in Scripture as grieving the Spirit.

The fact that the Spirit of God has been grieved may be readily determined in the Christian's experience. There is a loss of fellowship with God and the fruit of the Spirit, and some of the spiritual darkness that engulfs the unsaved descends upon the consciousness. For this reason Christians who have grieved the Holy Spirit may appear outwardly to be living on the same plane of experience as the unsaved.

It is possible, however, to be mistaken concerning the factors of experience. It has been often pointed out by careful writers that physical conditions affect spiritual experience. One who is tired and hungry or one who is sick may fail to have the evidence of an overflowing spiritual life without necessarily living in sin. The issue too is confined to sin which is known to the Christian. The Spirit is grieved by definite sins, not by the presence of the sin nature. It is the duty of the Christian who senses a loss of spiritual fellowship and power to seek the cause in prayer and study of the Word. It is ever true that if we draw nigh to God we may expect God to draw nigh to us.

It may be concluded that sin constitutes the cause for grieving the Spirit. As the cause for grieving the Spirit is definite, so the remedy is specifically set forth in the Word of God.

The remedy: confession of sin. There has been an amazing lack of understanding of the doctrine of grieving the Holy Spirit on the part of theologians. Even such a great work as Kuyper's[3] does not so much as mention Ephesians 4:30, nor the importance of confession of sin as indicated in 1 John 1:9. This neglect is quite common, however, as a survey of most works on the Holy Spirit will substantiate. It is a lamentable deficiency, however, as the heart of the doctrine of the Holy Spirit is its relation to the spiritual life of the believer, and a grieved Holy Spirit makes impossible the fullness of spiritual blessing. The Bible is still the best work on the doctrine of the Spirit, and those who read its pages carefully will find the answer to every problem.

The remedy for a grieved Holy Spirit is summed up in the simple word *confess.* According to 1 John 1:9, "If we confess our sins, he is faithful and righteous to forgive us our sins, and to cleanse us from all unrighteousness." This passage, standing as it does in the center of a revelation of the basis of fellowship with God (1 John 1:5—2:2), is a message to Christians. It avails not to the unsaved to confess their sins, as they have not accepted the Savior who was the sacrifice for sins. For the unsaved the exhortation is likewise summed up in one word, *believe.* For the Christian who stands in all the blessed relationship to God wrought by saving faith in Christ there remains the issue of maintaining fellowship. It is this issue that is in the foreground in 1 John. The promise of forgiveness should not be confused with justification nor the question of the guilt of sin. As far as the judicial aspect is concerned, the sin question was settled at the time of saving faith. The presence of sin in the life of the Christian, however, constitutes a barrier to fellowship. While the Christian's sonship is in no wise affected, the happy family relationship is disturbed. On the human side, confession must come before restoration into fellowship is possible. The cause for grieving the

---

[3]The Work of the Holy Spirit.

Spirit must be judged as sin and confessed. Confession involves self-judgment (1 Cor. 11:31), in which the Christian acts as his own judge, condemns his own sin, and then confesses his sin to his heavenly Father.

Complete assurance is given that this approach to the sin problem is acceptable to God. It is not a question of doing penance nor of inflicting chastening punishments upon oneself. Nor is it a matter of leniency with the Father when He accepts the confession. The whole act is based upon the finished work of Christ, and the question of penalty is not in view. The price for restoration has already been paid. Accordingly, the Father is *faithful* and *righteous* in forgiving, not merely *lenient* and *merciful*. The Father could not do otherwise than forgive the Christian seeking forgiveness, for His own Son has already provided a complete satisfaction for sin. The process from the human side is, accordingly, amazingly simple.

The further promise given to those who confess sin is often overlooked. Not only are the sins forgiven, referring to sins already committed, but the promise is given "to cleanse us from all unrighteousness." While this promise cannot be construed to be a pledge of total eradication of sin, nor to make it impossible for the Christian to sin, it does constitute a revelation of the undertaking of God to *prevent* further sin. Confession by its very nature is a sanctifying force. The Christian who has agonized before God in the knowledge of his own guilt and claimed the cleansing of the precious blood will by this very operation be less prone to return to the paths of sin. The prodigal upon returning to his father no longer desired the life of a prodigal. The act of confession also in effect is an act of dependence upon God, a recognition of human weakness and of the need of divine power. This will be seen, in the discussion of walking in the Spirit, to be an important aspect of victory over sin.

Confession is entirely on the human side. The revelation of 1 John 2:1-2, indicates that on the divine side the adjustment made necessary by sin in the Christian's life is immediate: "My little children, these things write I unto you that ye may not sin. And if any man sin, we have an Advocate with the Father, Jesus Christ the righteous: and he is the propitiation for our sins; and not for ours only, but also for the whole world." It is a blessed fact that when a Christian sins Christ immediately undertakes His work as Advocate, presenting His own righteousness and finished work on behalf of the sinner. The divine side is always in proper adjustment. This remains unknown to the experience of the Christian, however, until confession of sin restores the fellowship. As in an electrical circuit, one break will stop the current, so it is in our fellowship with God. The Scriptures make clear that the break is always on our side. The torn ends of fellowship are quickly united by confession of sin and the full power and blessing of fellowship with God again are realized. It is possible that Christians who have lived long in sin may require a time of heart-searching before all is restored, but the remedy in any case is confession of sin.

The warning against continuing in sin. The problem of human suffering has attracted not only the theologian and the philosopher but the writers of Scripture as illustrated in the Book of Job. Basically, the human race suffers because of Adam's sin by which the human body was blighted, the human senses spoiled, the sin nature imparted, and all creation came under the curse. The introduction of salvation of the soul does not remove all these fundamental causes for suffering. The chastening hand of the Father falls on all of His children as Hebrews 12:5-6 reveals: "My son, regard not lightly the chastening of the Lord, nor faint when thou art reproved of him; for whom the Lord loveth he chasteneth, And scourgeth every son whom he receiveth." Through chastening experiences, the child of God is trained, sin is prevented, knowledge is gained, and the whole life made fit for greater usefulness. It is a maxim that great Christians have had great suffering.

The Scriptures warn, however, that much chastening can be prevented by proper self-adjustment and confession of sin. According to 1 Corinthians 11:31-32, "But if we discerned ourselves, we should not be judged. But when we are judged, we are chastened of the Lord, that we may not be condemned with the world." In these simple words there is divine warning. The Christian is given time and opportunity for self-judgment and for confession of sin to the Father. Neglecting this opportunity, and persisting in sin, the Father intervenes, and by chastisement disciplines the Christian and brings him to confession of sin through trial that he was unwilling to confess before the chastisement was imposed. The Scriptures therefore plainly warn the Christian that it is dangerous to trifle with sin. Experience confirms this doctrine, and all Christians can bear witness to the unprofitableness of forsaking the place of confession and continuing in sin. The loss in any case is unspeakable. Not only is there loss of the positive spiritual blessings that are afforded only by fellowship with God and the unhindered work of the Spirit within, but there is the added sorrow of heartache and trial which might well be avoided. As the apostle who denied his Lord and wept bitterly over it wrote in his inspired epistle, "If ye are reproached for the name of Christ, blessed are ye; because the Spirit of glory and the Spirit of God resteth upon you. For let none of you suffer as a murderer, or a thief, or an evil-doer, or as a meddler in other men's matters" (1 Pet. 4:14-15).

III. WALK BY THE SPIRIT

The subject of this section could furnish a theme for an entire work, instead of being considered merely as an aspect of the work of the Holy Spirit in the believer. It is in this field of doctrine that much misapprehension has arisen and the most dangerous heresies have been advanced. It is, at the same time, an intensely practical doctrine. The two former requirements for a Spirit-filled life were negative in character: We cannot say "no" to the Spirit, quenching Him; and we cannot continue grieving the Spirit, if we desire the filling of the Spirit. The third requirement, of walking in the Spirit, is the positive aspect of the truth, and in content is more important than the other.

Definition. In the command, "Walk by the Spirit" (Gal. 5:16), there is urgent exhortation to walk by the power and presence of the Spirit who dwells within. The Greek is simple and direct: *Pneumati peripateite. Pneumati* is a simple dative, to be translated *by the Spirit* rather than *in the Spirit* as in the Authorized Version. As in Galatians 5:5, the absence of the article does not indicate an impersonal spirit, either human or divine, but the Holy Spirit Himself. Charles J. Ellicott commenting on Galatians 5:5, a similar instance, upholds the interpretation that this is a definite reference to the Holy Spirit.[4]

The exegesis is, accordingly, plain. Christians are commanded to walk by the person and power of the Holy Spirit if they desire to

---

[4]Charles J. Ellicott, *A Critical and Grammatical Commentary on St. Paul's Epistle to the Galatians, with a Revised Translation* (1884 ed.), p. 120. His comment is as follows: "The dative is not equivalent to *en Pneumati* (Copt.), still less to be explained as merely adverbial, 'spiritually' (Middl. *in loc.*), but, as the context suggests, has its definite ablatival force and distinct personal reference; our hope flows from faith, and that faith is imparted and quickened by the Holy Spirit. No objection can be urged against this interpr. founded on the absence of the article, as neither the canon of Middleton (*Gr. Art.* p. 126, ed. Rose), nor the similar one suggested by Harless (*Eph.* ii. 22.),—that *to Pneuma* is the personal Holy Spirit, *pneuma* the indwelling influence of the Spirit (Rom. viii. 5), can at all be considered of universal application; see ver. 16. It is much more natural to regard *Pneuma, Pneuma hagion* and *Pneuma Theou* as proper names, and to extend to them the same latitude in connection with the article; see Fritz. *Rom.* viii. 4, Vol. II. p. 105."

have the lusts of the flesh unfulfilled. It is clear that walking by the Spirit is a continual experience, as *peripateite* is in the present tense, with the thought, *continue to walk* by the Spirit, or *keep walking* by the Spirit. The failure to continue walking by the Spirit will result in immediate spiritual failure.

The Christian standard of spiritual life. The necessity of walking by the Holy Spirit is especially apparent in view of the high standard of spiritual life demanded of the Christian in the Scriptures. The Israelites had a high standard of life suited for their life under the law, but they did not have the universal indwelling of the Holy Spirit nor the universal enablement provided the Christian, and their standards of conduct were, accordingly, elementary in comparison to Christian standards. The standards of the future kingdom are also high, but their requirements are tuned to the special conditions which will obtain at that time—a devil bound, Christ on the throne, universal righteousness and peace throughout the world, a system nevertheless legal in character. The standards which are peculiarly applicable to the present dispensation are found in the New Testament, particularly the Acts and Epistles and part of the Gospels. An examination of these standards will demonstrate that they are attainable only by those walking by the Spirit. While some of the commands of the law of Moses may be taken to be equally impossible standards, there is a distinction. The law of Moses was designed as a means to condemnation. The standards of grace in the present age are designed for sanctification. What man could not do under the law, with the enablement provided then, man can do under grace by the power of the Holy Spirit. The effect of these truths is that the Christian is responsible for a life empowered by the Spirit as the saints were not in previous dispensations, when the Spirit was not as freely bestowed.

A brief study of the standards of this age will make this sufficiently clear. We are commanded to love each other as Christ loves us (John 13:34; 15:12). Even "every thought" must be brought "to the obedience of Christ" (2 Cor. 10:5). We must "be longsuffering toward all," and "always follow after that which is good" (1 Thess. 5:14-15). We should "Rejoice always. Pray without ceasing. In everything give thanks" (1 Thess. 5:16-18). Illustrations can be multiplied of similar standards equally impossible to the flesh. What is impossible for man unaided by the Holy Spirit is possible for the one walking by the Spirit. The utter need of the power of the Spirit in the life of every Christian is one of the great realities of both revelation and experience.

The power of the world system. The Christian standards of spiritual life become all the more difficult to attain in view of the corrupting influence of the present world system. When Christ prayed for His disciples, He did not ask that they be immediately taken out of the world, but rather that they be kept from evil in the world (John 17:15). They were to be in the world bodily, but spiritually "in the heavenlies." The Scriptures spare no words in denouncing the world. Friendship with the world is called spiritual adultery and the friend of the world is the enemy of God (James 4:4). Love of the world excludes love of the Father (1 John 2:15). Union with the world and conforming to the world is forbidden (Rom. 12:2; 2 Cor. 6:14). The whole world is declared worthless in comparison to the value of a human soul (Matt. 16:26). Worldliness is revealed to rob the Christian of fruit, choking the Word (Matt. 13:22). The world is declared crucified by the cross of Christ (Gal. 6:14). The Christian is to be in the world but not of the world, to bear a witness to the world, but not to allow the world to corrupt him. The power of the world is such, however, that this is impossible except for the power of the Holy Spirit.

The power of Satan. The important doctrines of Satanology, so neglected in most theological discussions, make the responsibility of attaining Christian standards of conduct all the more difficult. Satan is revealed in the Scripture to be the greatest power apart from God. The Christian's warfare is essentially with Satan. As Paul knew from both revelation and experience, "For our wrestling is not against flesh and blood, but against the principalities, against the powers, against the world-rulers of this darkness, against the spiritual hosts of wickedness in the heavenly places" (Eph. 6:12). Satan blinds the minds of unbelievers to the gospel (2 Cor. 4:4), making necessary a work of the Holy Spirit to enable them to believe. Christians are exhorted, "Be sober, be watchful: your adversary the devil, as a roaring lion, walketh about, seeking whom he may devour" (1 Pet. 5:8). At the same time, the Scriptures reveal that "Satan fashioneth himself into an angel of light" (2 Cor. 11:14). Satan is a liar and murderer as Christ Himself bears witness (John 8:44). The power of Satan is so great that "Michael the archangel, when contending with the devil he disputed about the body of Moses, durst not bring against him a railing judgment, but said, The Lord rebuke thee" (Jude 9). It is clear from the Scriptural revelation that this enemy of God is also the enemy of every saint and that victory over him is impossible apart from divine power and protection. The walk of the Christian in the will of God is impossible because of this enemy unless he walks by the Spirit. It is significant that Satan the archdeceiver has persuaded many that he does not exist, much less constitutes our greatest enemy. In the light of the modern apathy regarding the field of Satanology, is it any wonder that there is little understanding regarding the issues of walking by the Spirit?

The sin nature. The utter dependence of every soul upon the Spirit for victory is not only a result of the foes without, but is occasioned as well by the weakness within. The Scriptures reveal that every child of Adam possesses Adam's nature, with all its predisposition to sin. Whether designated as the sin nature (Rom. 5:21; 1 John 1:8), the Adamic nature, the *flesh* (Rom. 13:14; 1 Cor. 5:5; 2 Cor. 7:1; 10:2-3; Gal. 5:16-24; 6:8; Eph. 2:3; etc.); the *old man* (Rom. 6:6; Eph. 4:22; Col. 3:9-10), or any other term, the reference is to the human nature, including soul, spirit, and body. When the word *sin* is found in the singular as in Romans six and seven, for instance, it may be understood as a reference to the nature rather than the act. It is the source of all evil within, that which desires sin and gives ear to the devil. A clear understanding of this doctrine is essential to realizing the need for walking by the Spirit.

Practically all heresies characterizing the holiness movement, and false doctrines of sanctification, eradication, or perfectionism have their origin in a failure to comprehend the Scriptural teaching regarding the sin nature. It is impossible within the scope of the present discussion to examine in detail all the truth involved, but the main elements can be presented.

The theory of perfectionism. The doctrine of perfectionism is not always stated in precisely the same terms by its adherents. The definition of Webster's Dictionary is probably fair to all parties: "*Perfectionism: 2. Theol.* The doctrine that a state of freedom from sin is attainable in earthly life."[5] Some perfectionists limit this freedom to willful sin. Others limit the freedom from sin, which they conceive of as attainable in this life, to freedom from known sin, excluding sins of ignorance either on the ground that they are not sin or that they cannot in any case be included in the realm of perfection. Some believe the sin nature itself is eradicated. An examination of the Scriptures will not only sustain the fundamental elements of the doctrine of the sin nature itself, but it will make clear that the doctrine of perfectionism is not taught in the Bible at all as it is held by its advocates.

---

[5]*Webster's International Dictionary* (Second Edition, Unabridged, 1947), p. 1818.

In the Old Testament, while a number of Hebrew words are translated *perfect,* it is clear from the context that the characters involved were *not* sinless (Gen. 6:9; 1 Kings 15:14; 2 Kings 20:3; 1 Chron. 12:38; Job. 1:1, 8; Ps. 37:37; 101:2, 6; etc.). In the New Testament, with which we are primarily concerned, there are thirteen words translated *perfect.* These thirteen are found to reduce to five roots, however, and only two have important bearing upon the doctrine of perfection as related to sin.

The verb *katartizo,* having the thought of *being complete in all details* and therefore *fitting,* or *adjusted,* is found frequently as a verb, noun, and adjective with variations and indicates perfection in the sense of *completeness* (2 Cor. 13:9, 11; Eph. 4:12; 1 Thess. 3:10; 2 Tim. 3:17, etc.). A word of equal or greater importance, found in five different forms, is *teleioo,* meaning *to bring to the end,* or *to bring to the goal* (1 Cor. 2:6; Eph. 4:13; Phil. 3:15; Col. 3:14; 4:12; Heb. 6:1; 7:11; 10:14; etc.). The word has the idea, therefore, of *attainment.*

Other words are found translated *perfect* in the New Testament, but they contribute little or nothing to the doctrine of perfection. One of them relates to perfection in knowledge, *akribeia,* rather than to sin, and is found in adjective form (Acts 22:3) and more often as an adverb (Luke 1:3; Acts 18:26; etc.). Another word, *pleroo,* is found translated in one instance *perfect* (Rev. 3:2), but it means essentially *to fill* or *to make full,* as a vessel might be filled, and is translated *fulfill* fifty-one times, and *to fill* seventeen times. In Luke 8:14, *telesphoreo* is found, meaning, *to bring to the goal,* but it has no bearing on the doctrine of perfection. Practically, the first two words considered, in their various forms, furnish us with all the Scriptural information on the doctrine of perfection.

Perfection as related to sin is found in Scripture in three aspects. First, *positional perfection* is revealed to be the possession of every Christian. In Hebrews 10:14, it is stated, "For by one offering he hath perfected [*teteleioken*] for ever them that are sanctified." The verb is found in the perfect indicative, indicating that the perfection indicated was completed once and for all in past time, an act never to be repeated. It is, therefore, absolute perfection, which Christ wrought for us on the cross. There is no reference here to the quality of the Christian's life. The issue of sinfulness is not in view. All saints (sanctified ones) are partakers of the perfection accomplished by the death of Christ.

Second, *relative* perfection is mentioned frequently in the Scriptures, as indicated by the context. In some instances, *spiritual maturity* is referred to as perfection. Paul writes the Philippians, "Let us therefore, as many as are perfect [*teleioi*], be thus minded" (Phil. 3:15). That he is referring to spiritual maturity rather than sinless perfection is made clear by the reference in the same passage in verse twelve, "Not that I have already obtained, or am already made perfect: but I press on, if so be that I may lay hold on that for which also I was laid hold on by Christ Jesus." The reference in Philippians 3:12 is to ultimate perfection which will include sinlessness, of course, but this Paul denies as a present possession. Spiritual maturity may be compared to physical maturity—full development without, however, absolute perfection. Maturity is viewed in Philippians 3:15 as attained. In other passages, some particular aspect of spiritual maturity may be in view. We may be spiritually mature in respect to the known will of God (Col. 4:12); in love (1 John 4:17-18); in holiness (2 Cor. 7:1); in patience (James 1:4); in "every good work" (Heb. 13:21). In all these instances, there is no indication of a possibility of reaching these attainments once and for all in this life. It is perfection in the relative sense only, an advanced position of attainment.

Spiritual maturity is viewed also as progressive as illustrated by the use of the present tense in 2 Corinthians 7:1, ". . . perfecting holiness in the fear of God," and in Galatians 3:3, "Are ye so foolish? having begun in the Spirit, are ye now perfected [literally, are ye now *being made perfect*] in the flesh?" The gifts of ministry bestowed by Christ upon the church are designed, "for the perfecting [*katartismon*] of the saints . . ." (Eph. 4:12), that is, that they may make the saints complete in every detail. This is obviously a process accomplished through exercise of their gifts and belongs to the progressive spiritual maturity in view in relative perfection. Only an arbitrary system could twist these passages and others like them to fit the idea of present sinlessness. This the Greek does not allow and the whole of revelation and experience denies.

A third aspect of the truth is revealed in passages referring to *ultimate perfection*. A clear instance is found in Philippians 3:12, quoted above, where Paul denies that he is "already made perfect." The verb here is in the perfect indicative (*teteleiomai*). While his position in Christ is perfect (Heb. 10:14), he recognizes that his ultimate perfection is reserved to the time of the resurrection of the dead (Phil. 3:11), when he will be perfect in soul, spirit, and body. The Scriptures do not, therefore, teach that perfection can be attained in this life.

The theory of sanctification. The Bible presents a well-rounded doctrine of sanctification, which, if understood properly, gives much light upon the holiness of our calling. The doctrine of sanctification has been abused, however, and the theory has been advanced that it is possible in this life to be wholly sanctified. Christians are, accordingly, urged to wait on God for this total sanctification. It is described by some as a "second work" of grace, and it is implied that Christians who have failed to attain entire sanctification are guilty of failing to seek the whole will of God.

The word *sanctify* and its other forms *sanctification, holiness, saint* and other less frequent translation, is derived from the Greek word *hagiazo*. Its other English forms are translations of various Greek words derived from the same root. For all essential purposes it may be concluded that *sanctification, holiness,* and *saint* have the same essential meaning, which according to Thayer, is to *"render or declare sacred* or *holy, consecrate."*[6] Among the secondary meanings is found the thought, *"to separate from things profane and dedicate to God,"* and *"to purify."*[7] The three main ideas of consecration, separation, and purification combine in the central idea of holiness. The doctrine has a rich background in the Old Testament offerings and the added revelation of the New Testament truth.

As presented in the New Testament, in brief, sanctification is divided into three main divisions, which correspond roughly to the same divisions in the doctrine of perfection: positional sanctification, experimental or progressive sanctification, and ultimate sanctification. In the doctrine of sanctification the thought is concentrated upon holiness or being set apart for holy use, rather than perfection in its larger sense. Sanctification is, therefore, also extended to inanimate objects, such as the gold sanctified by the temple (Matt. 23:17), to the unbelieving wife or husband where the other party is saved (1 Cor. 7:14), to food sanctified by prayer (1 Tim. 4:5). Sanctification is used in relation to Christ Himself in the sense that He was set apart for holy use (John 10:36; 17:19; 1 Pet. 3:15). Sanctification in these instances does not mean *purify,* but only to separate from the unholy and consecrate to God for holy use.

The most frequent reference in the New Testament is to positional sanctification, that wrought by Christ for every believer, and which is the possession of the believer from the moment of saving faith. All of the approximately sixty-five references to *saints* in the New Testament are to be classified under this division. In addition

---

[6]Thayer, *op. cit.,* p. 6.
[7]*Loc. cit.*

to these, a number of other important references are found (Acts 20:32; 26:18; Rom. 15:16; 1 Cor. 1:2, 30; 6:11; 2 Thess. 2:13; Heb. 2:11; 10:10, 14; 13:12; 1 Pet. 1:2; Jude 1). A particularly significant reference is 1 Corinthians 1:2, where the notoriously worldly Corinthians are declared to be *saints,* this one reference alone making clear that sanctification does not mean sinlessness.

Progressive or experimental sanctification is an important doctrine of the Scriptures, though with less specific reference than positional sanctification. This aspect of sanctification was probably in view in our Lord's prayer in John 17:17, where He prayed, "Sanctify them in the truth: thy word is truth." Another instance of sanctification is mentioned in Ephesians 5:26, where Christ is revealed to have given Himself in sacrifice, "That he might sanctify it, having cleansed it [the church] by the washing of the water with the word." While many have taken this as a reference to water baptism, the text does not warrant the interpretation, and it is more probably a reference to the sanctifying power of the Word of God itself. The blood of Christ is revealed as the cleansing agent in Hebrews 9:13-14. All the work of God in cleansing us from sin in this life, whether or not the word *sanctify* is used, pertains to this aspect of the truth. Saints are exhorted, accordingly, to recognize the need for experimental sanctification (1 Thess. 4:3-4; 2 Pet. 3:18). This aspect of sanctification is the main objective of the work of the Spirit and is accomplished by walking by the Spirit.

As Lewis Sperry Chafer points out in his admirable section on walking in the Spirit,[8] experimental sanctification has three relationships: (1) the believer's yieldedness to God; (2) the believer's deliverance from the power of sin through the power of the Spirit; (3) the believer's growth in grace which is a constant development throughout life.[9] It is the very heart of the doctrine of the spiritual life, and should be the subject of earnest study and prayer by every Christian.

Ultimate sanctification is the expectation of all the work of God in dealing with the believer. Positional sanctification has the promise of issuing in that perfect sanctification which will be the portion of the saints in the eternal state. Experimental and progressive sanctification has its ultimate goal to be realized in the future life. In the Scripture, however, the word *sanctification* is used only in relation to the present life. It is doubtful if any of the many instances in which it is found apply specifically to the ultimate aspect, though all

---

[8]*He That Is Spiritual,* pp. 119-72.
[9]*Ibid.,* p. 136.

anticipate it. The doctrine of ultimate sanctification is derived from the Scriptures which picture the attainment of the goal to which we strive for in this life. In 1 John 3:2, for instance, we read, "Beloved, now are we children of God, and it is not yet made manifest what we shall be. We know that, if he shall be manifested, we shall be like him; for we shall see him even as he is." This Scripture is significant in appointing the time for ultimate sanctification as that glorious future moment when He shall appear. In Ephesians 5:27, our present sanctification is revealed to issue in the future state in perfection: "That he might present the church to himself a glorious church, not having spot or wrinkle or any such thing; but that it should be holy and without blemish." According to Romans 8:29, we shall be "conformed to the image of his Son." According to Hebrews 12:14, every saint will have holiness to perfection when he sees the Lord. These and many other Scriptures combine in anticipating the perfection of the eternal state in every particular. These Scriptures are specific, however, in referring the time of ultimate sanctification to the future life.

The passages which are used in an effort to prove the necessity or possibility of complete sanctification in this life will reveal, upon careful study, a perfect harmony with the truth as it has been here set forth. Misapprehension and resulting false doctrine spring from three sources. First, positional sanctification, which by its nature is perfect even in this life, is construed to mean sinlessness. This view is easily refuted by a study of the passages speaking of this aspect of the doctrine. It is clear in Scripture that *saints* commit sin, even though their position in Christ is perfect. A second cause for misunderstanding is a failure to comprehend the varied uses of the word *sanctification* itself. The word *sanctification,* as used in the Bible, is *never used in the sense of sinlessness,* though in the case of Christ He is, in fact, sinless. Even when used in the sense of separation or purification, it cannot be considered absolute. The third source of misunderstanding has arisen from certain passages which seem to demand sinlessness as a condition of salvation. Here again study will solve the problem of each passage.

An illustration of the false idea that sinlessness is essential to salvation is found in 1 John 3:6-9, "Whosoever abideth in him sinneth not: whosoever sinneth hath not seen him, neither knoweth him. My little children, let no man lead you astray: he that doeth righteousness is righteous, even as he is righteous: he that doeth sin is of the devil; for the devil sinneth from the beginning. To this end was the Son of God manifested, that he might destroy the works of the devil. Whosoever is begotten of God doeth no sin, because his seed abideth in him: and he cannot sin, because he is begotten of God." As given in the English translation, there is room for misunderstanding. In the Greek, however, the difficulty largely vanishes. Throughout the passage the present tense is used. The revelation is that anyone who continually sins, i.e., whose life is characterized as living in sin, is unsaved. Those who abide in Christ and those who are born again cannot by their nature continue without check in a life of sin. It may be difficult for us to judge borderline cases, but the Word of God is specific that God will chastise sinning believers, and will deal with them in other ways to bring them to Himself. From our human standpoint, we have the right to question the salvation of those living in unchecked sin.

Another solution to the problem of this passage has been suggested based on the principle that the subject of this Scripture is the new nature. Under this approach, the teaching would be that the new nature, that which is born of God, does not sin. It is true that the new nature which is given by God does not originate sin in the life of the believer and to this extent the interpretation would be justified. The passage uses the verb in the present tense, however, which implies that while sin is not continuous it actually does occur occasionally. If the thought was that the new nature did not sin at all, it would call for the aorist tense rather than the present. The fact that the present tense rather than the aorist tense is used would point to the first solution as the better one.

In any case the teaching that sinlessness is essential to salvation in this life would destroy the doctrine of grace, the doctrine of security, and place salvation upon a human works level. It is for this reason that the historic church, whatever its failures in apprehending many important doctrines, has been careful to affirm that sinlessness in this life is not essential to salvation. A proper doctrine of sanctification not only gives glory to God but gives to the believer a revelation of his own need of walking by the Spirit. Apart from the power of God salvation in any of its aspects is impossible.

The theory of eradication. The teaching has been advanced that it is possible in this life to reach a point in spiritual development where the sin nature is eradicated and is no longer operative. This idea is, in effect, a combination of the idea of perfection and sinlessness in this life and attempts to set up a radical change in the nature of man. The theory is contradicted by so many plain teachings of Scripture and is so foreign to normal experience that it is not seriously advanced by thinking Christians. The many passages of Scripture which speak of the struggle with the flesh and the universal need for dependence upon God for deliverance are in themselves insuperable obstacles to this teaching.

As Lewis Sperry Chafer writes in discussing the divine method of dealing with the sin nature: "Two general theories are held as to the divine method of dealing with the sin nature in believers. One suggests that the old nature is *eradicated,* either when one is saved, or at some subsequent crisis of experience and spiritual blessing, and the quality of the believer's life depends, therefore, on the *absence* of the disposition of sin. The other theory contends that the old nature abides so long as the Christian is in this body and that the quality of life depends on the immediate and constant control over the 'flesh' by the indwelling Spirit of God, and this is made possible through the death of Christ. In both of these propositions there is a sincere attempt to realize the full victory in daily life which is promised to the child of God. . . . The life that is delivered from the bondservitude to sin is the *objective* in each theory. It is therefore only a question as to which is the plan and method of God in the realization. Both theories cannot be true, for they are contradictory."[10]

After showing that the theory of eradication is not the divine method of dealing with the believer's difficulties and that it is contrary to experience, Chafer lists seven arguments to prove that eradication is not according to divine revelation:

"In the Word of God we have 'instruction,' 'correction,' and 'reproof.' By these we must determine our conclusions rather than by any impression of the mind, or by analyzing any person's experience whatsoever. The Bible teaches:

"(1), All believers are warned against the assumptions of the eradication theory: 'If we say that we have no sin [nature], we deceive ourselves, and the truth is not in us' (1 John 1:8).

"(2), The Spirit has come to be our Deliverer and the whole Bible teaching concerning His presence, purpose and power is manifestly meaningless if our victory is to be by another means altogether. For this reason the eradication theory makes little place for the Person and work of the Spirit.

"(3), The Spirit delivers by an unceasing conflict. 'The flesh [which includes the old nature] lusteth against the Spirit, and the Spirit against the flesh: and these are contrary the one to the other: so that [when walking by the Spirit] ye cannot do the things that ye [otherwise] would' (Gal. 5:17, *cf.* Jas. 4:5). So, also, in Rom.

---

[10]*Ibid.,* p. 165-66.

7:15-24, and 8:2, the *source* of sin in the believer is said to be the sin nature working through the flesh, and the victory is by the superior power of the Spirit. The extreme teachings of the eradication theory are to the effect that a Christian will have no disposition to sin to-morrow and thus the theory prompts one to an alarming disregard for true watchfulness and reliance upon the power of God. The Bible teaches that the latent source of sin remains and, should the 'walk in the Spirit' cease, there will be an immediate return to the 'desires' and 'lusts' of the flesh. So long as 'by the Spirit ye are walking, ye shall not fulfill the lust of the flesh.' We are creatures of habit and may become increasingly *adapted* to walk in the Spirit. We store knowledge through experience as well. Thus the walk in the 'flesh' may cease at a given time; but the *ability* to walk after the 'flesh' abides. In this aspect of it, true spirituality means, for the time, not wishing to sin (Phil. 2:13); but this does not imply the eradication of the ability to sin: it means rather that, because of the energizing power of God, a complete victory for the present time is possible. It remains true that we always need Him completely. He said, 'Apart from me ye can do nothing' (John 15:5). Because the 'infection' of sin is always in us, we need every moment 'the conquering counteraction of the Spirit.' The 'walk' in the Spirit is divinely enabled at every step of the way.

"(4), The divine provisional dealings with the 'flesh' and the 'old man' have not been unto eradication. God has wrought on an infinite scale in the death of His Son that the way might be made whereby we may 'walk in newness of life.' The manner of this walk is stated in such injunctions as 'reckon,' 'yield,' 'let not,' 'put off,' 'mortify,' 'abide'; yet not one of these injunctions would have the semblance of meaning under the eradication theory. The Scriptures do not counsel us to 'reckon' the nature to be dead: it urges us to 'reckon' ourselves to be dead unto *it*.

"(5), The teachings of the eradicationists are based on a false interpretation of Scripture concerning the present union of the believer with Christ in His death. That in the Bible which is held to be *positional* and existing only in the mind and reckoning of God, and which is accomplished once for all for every child of God, is supposed to mean an *experience* in the daily life of a *few* who dare to class themselves as those who are free from the disposition to sin.

"(6), The conclusions of the doctrine of eradication are based on false teachings concerning the Bible use of the word 'flesh.' The advocates of this teaching do not understand that the word 'flesh' refers to *all*,— spirit, soul and body,—of the natural man, and, were it possible, the removal of the sin nature would not dispose of all the problems created by the limitations of the 'flesh.' 'In me (that is, in my flesh,) dwelleth no good thing.' The 'flesh' must, therefore, remain so long as the 'earthen vessel,' the 'body of our humiliation' remains. Certainly the body is not eradicated.

"(7), Eradication teaching is more concerned with human experience than with the revelation of God. It has always been content to analyze experience and attempt to prove its conclusions by such analysis. That which is a normal experience of deliverance by the power of the Spirit may easily be supposed to be an evidence of 'sinless perfection,' 'entire sanctification' and 'eradication.' A human supposition can never take the place of divine revelation.

"The two theories are irreconcilable. We are either to be delivered by the abrupt removal of all tendency to sin and so no longer need the enabling power of God to combat the power of sin, or we are to be delivered by the immediate and constant power of the indwelling Spirit. The Bible evidently teaches the latter."[11]

The theory of dying to self. A companion doctrine to the theory of eradication is the view that a Christian by an act of his will can die to self completely. This idea is often held by many who do not accept the idea of sinless perfection or of eradication of the sin nature. The difficulty arises from a failure to examine the Greek text where the key passages are found bearing upon the subject of self-crucifixion or dying to self. An examination of these passages will reveal them to refer in every case to past time. The believer in Christ died with Christ on the cross. This is a fact of substitution, not a present experience. In Romans 6:6, the American Revised Version is correct when it translates the verb in the past tense: "Knowing this, that our old man was crucified with him," rather than, "is crucified." The verb is in the aorist, referring to the one act of Christ. A reference even more decided is that of Galatians 2:20, where Paul writes, "I have been crucified with Christ; and it is no longer I that live, but Christ liveth in me. . . ." The verb for *crucified* is in the perfect tense, action which took place definitely in past time, but the effects of it continue in the present. In contrast to the tense of *crucified,* Paul states, "It is no longer I that live," with the verb in the present. The present victorious life of Paul was made possible by the fact that he died in Christ on Calvary. The exhortation is not to die to self by our own act but to realize that we did die to self with Christ on the cross and that we should live in the light of this revelation. The important truth is that we must reckon ourselves dead to self, and this should be done continually by the Christian.

The fact that the believer died with Christ on the cross does not remove the sin nature or make it inoperative, however. The important passage in Romans 6 where the believer's death with Christ is discussed includes the exhortation, "Let not sin therefore reign in your mortal body, that ye should obey the lusts thereof" (Rom. 6:12). The Christian should reckon himself dead to the sin nature because by the death of Christ the power of God can triumph over it. It is the important truth that the death of Christ not only atones for the guilt of sin, but it has power to deliver the believer from the bondage and corruption of sin itself.

The utter weakness of the flesh. The discussion of the doctrines of perfection, sanctification, eradication, and dying to self, upon being understood in the light of the revelation of the Word of God bear a powerful testimony to the weakness of the flesh and the dependence of every believer upon the Spirit for victory. The doctrine of the sin nature combined with the truth concerning the high standard of Christian life revealed in the Scriptures, the power of Satan and the forces of darkness, and the corrupting influence of the world bring out in stark relief the utter need of the believer in Christ for the empowering ministry of the Holy Spirit. The forces against the Christian and the latent inability of the Christian to cope with them allow no alternative for a spiritual life in the will of God other than by walking by the Spirit.

The power of the Holy Spirit appropriated. There can be no doubt that the average Christian is only vaguely aware of the nature of the difficulties which prevent a normal Christian victory in his spiritual life. There is the imperative need to make known the nature of the forces of evil and the hopelessness of facing them without help from God. The first step in waging warfare is to know the enemy and to know one's own resources. In spiritual warfare, the many aspects involved are reduced in simple terms to the Scriptural admonitions to "quench not the Spirit," "grieve not the Spirit," and "walk by the Spirit." This is not simply a matter of education. The truth must be apprehended and the full will of God must be sought. The believer seeking the power of the Spirit must submit himself to the searching of the Word of God in its revelation of God's will. There must be waiting on God in prayer that we may be made willing to do His will. The inspiration of fellowship with God's people and sharing with them the blessings of God is an important source of help. Walking by the Spirit presumes activity; it is not a defensive stand against the enemy, but a positive approach to the problems of the spiritual life, endeavoring to be active in the will of God as well as resting in His sufficiency. The heart of the matter remains in the continued dependence upon the Spirit to do for us what we cannot do for ourselves, to be yielded to the Spirit in all His guidance, to confess every known sin, and to seek from the Spirit in faith that ministry which will work in us "both to will and to work for his good pleasure" (Phil. 2:13). The walk by the Spirit is a delight to the heart of the believer in which the intimate joys of fellowship with God are known and the fruit of the Spirit is produced in the heart and life. Here, indeed, is a foretaste of the unstinted and unhindered blessings that will be ours when we see the glorious face of Him who suffered and rose in triumph from the tomb that we might have victory in a world over which He Himself has triumphed.

CHAPTER XXIII

RESULTS OF THE FILLING
OF THE HOLY SPIRIT

THE EFFECT of being filled with the Holy Spirit is manifest in all aspects of the Christian life and experience. Obviously, a life empowered and directed by the Holy Spirit will evince a distinct quality of spiritual life. A search of the Scriptures will reveal that the entire present program of God in sanctification, spiritual experience and service is qualified by the factor of the filling of the Holy Spirit. There are at least seven results of the filling of the Spirit.

I. PROGRESSIVE SANCTIFICATION

Previous discussion has brought out that sanctification is in three aspects: positional, progressive, and ultimate. The work of the Holy Spirit is especially related to the present aspect of progressive sanctification. The Christian controlled by the Spirit and empowered to do the will of God manifests a fundamental change in character. While his former sin nature is still present, it has been reckoned dead, and the new nature energized by the Spirit is producing the fruit of the Spirit. According to Galatians 5:22-23, the effect of the filling of the Spirit is that His fruit is produced: "But the fruit of the Spirit is love, joy, peace, long-suffering, kindness, goodness, faithfulness, meekness, self-control; against such there is no law." This passage of Scripture is worthy of the closest study. It has been considered by some to present a trilogy, as C. I. Scofield indicates: "Christian character is not mere moral or legal correctness, but the possession and manifestation of nine graces: love, joy, peace—character as an inward state; longsuffering, gentleness, goodness—character in expression toward man; faith, meekness, temperance—character in expression toward God. Taken together they present a moral portrait of Christ, and may be taken as the apostle's explanation of Galatians 2:20, 'Not I, but Christ,' and as a definition of 'fruit' in John 15:1-8. This character is possible because of the believer's vital union to Christ (John 15:5; 1 Cor. 12:12-13), and is wholly the fruit of the Spirit in those believers who are yielded to Him (Gal. 5:22-23)."[1]

[1] C. I. Scofield, Scofield Reference Bible, p. 1247.

219

Another view of the passage is that the fruit of the Spirit is love, from which flows the evidences of love: joy, peace, long-suffering, kindness, goodness, faithfulness, meekness, self-control. While the method of approach is relatively unimportant, the central fact is that progressive sanctification does not proceed from self-effort or from the will of the natural man, nor does it proceed from the new nature in itself. It is a product of the Holy Spirit wrought in a yielded life. The all-important fact is that true Christian character cannot be produced apart from the work of the Holy Spirit. The appeal of the Scriptures, accordingly, is for right adjustment to the Spirit of God first, with the promise that through the filling of the Spirit the longings of the new nature for a holy life in the will of God may be satisfied.

II. TEACHING

The teaching ministry of the Holy Spirit was predicted by Christ as a means of providing the necessary revelation for the ministry of the apostles (John 16:12-15), and its fulfillment is found first in them. The teaching of the Holy Spirit is extended, however, to all Christians, having the peculiar character of illuminating the written Scriptures. The work of the Spirit in teaching is characteristic. The Word of God is written by inspiration of the Holy Spirit, and its divine author, the Spirit of truth, is its best teacher. Facing the problem of the ignorance of the disciples, Christ told them, "I have yet many things to say unto you, but ye cannot bear them now. Howbeit when he, the Spirit of truth, is come, he shall guide you into all the truth: for he shall not speak from himself; but what things soever he shall hear, these shall he speak: and he shall declare unto you the things that are to come" (John 16:12-13). Prior to the cross it was impossible for Christ to teach His disciples the great truths concerning His death, resurrection, and the purpose for the present age, as they were in no position to understand His teachings. The postresurrection ministry of Christ no doubt dealt with some of these truths, but the Spirit of God was the chief agent of teaching after the death of Christ.

To Christians who are spiritual, i.e., filled with the Spirit, it is possible for the Spirit to reveal the deep things of God. In the extended revelation of this truth in 1 Corinthians 2:9—3:2, it is made clear that the deeper things of spiritual truth can be understood only by those who are spiritually qualified to be taught by the Spirit. The natural man is unable to understand even the simple truths understood by those who are Spirit-taught. The appalling ignorance of many Christians concerning the things of the Word of God is directly traceable to their carnality and failure in seeking the blessings of a life filled with the Spirit. The teaching work of the Spirit also extends to warning against error, and we are told in 1 John 2:27, that the anointing of the Spirit, i.e., His indwelling, makes it possible for us to be taught the truth even without human teachers. While it is impossible to extend the treatment of this important subject here, it is obviously a most important factor in Christian experience and knowledge, and an important revelation explaining at the same time the causes of spiritual knowledge and spiritual ignorance.

III. Guidance

Closely related to the teaching work of the Holy Spirit is the work of the Spirit in guiding the Christian. Guidance is a most important element in Christian experience, and it is essential to a life in the will of God. Guidance while similar to the teaching work of the Spirit has a distinct character. While the teaching ministry of the Spirit in this age is directed to making clear the content of the Word of God, guidance is the application of the truths thus known to the individual problems of life. Guidance is always deductive, that is, the application of general Biblical principles to the particular problem at hand. While the Word of God may reveal the purpose of God to preach the gospel throughout the world, only the Spirit of God can call an individual life to an appointed field of service. In the many details of each life, only the Spirit of God can provide the necessary guidance.

An important point in this aspect of the truth is that guidance is given especially to those who are already walking in the will of God. According to Romans 12:1-2, surrender to God is necessary, "that ye may prove what is the good and acceptable and perfect will of God." Even in Old Testament times, the servant of Abraham could bear witness, "I being in the way, the Lord led me to the house of my master's brethren" (Gen. 24:27, A.V.) To the one who is filled with the Spirit of God, guidance becomes the personal direction of the life in the will of God. That it is an essential part of God's provision for the Christian is made clear in the Scriptures. According to Romans 8:14, guidance is an evidence of genuine salvation: "For as many as are led by the Spirit of God, these are the sons of God." Guidance is the present sphere of Christian obligation, providing liberty from the impersonal and more arbitrary requirements of the law for Israel, as is indicated in Galatians 5:18, "But if ye are led by the Spirit, ye are not under the law."

IV. Assurance

While assurance of salvation is not essential to genuine salvation, it is nevertheless the privilege of every Christian. The possession of assurance, however, is dependent upon a proper understanding of revelation and of the witness of the Spirit. One of the important reasons why some Christians do not have assurance of salvation is their failure to meet the conditions for the filling of the Spirit and the resultant ministry of the Spirit to their own hearts. One of the precious realities of fellowship with God is the assurance that He is ours and we belong to Him. To this important fact the Spirit bears His witness. Romans 8:16 speaks specifically, "The Spirit himself beareth witness with our Spirit, that we are the children of God." Other passages bear out the same idea (Gal. 4:6; 1 John 3:24; 4:13). While human reason operating without an understanding of grace and apart from the ministry of the Spirit may arrive at a different conclusion, it is the ministry of the Spirit to assure the child of God of his eternal relationship to his Father in salvation through Christ, of which the Spirit Himself is the seal. It is one of the penalties of carnality and sin in the Christian's life that many lose the blessing of assurance and are robbed temporarily at least of this blessing.

V. Worship

In the minds of some Christians, worship is associated with earthly houses of worship, ritual, and other common features of public worship. According to the Scriptures, however, worship is the adoration of God by those who know Him. Important in its content is the wholehearted praise and thanksgiving that can arise only in a heart in proper spiritual adjustment with God. Accordingly, in Ephesians 5:18-20, immediately following the command to be filled with the Spirit, there is mention of the praise and thanksgiving which is the fruit of a life lived in fellowship with God, and which is at the same time a result of the Spirit producing in the heart the joy, peace, and assurance of which He is the source. The soul which is living in unhindered fellowship with God cannot only perceive the content of God's priceless blessings but has every cause to praise the God whom he adores. To him it is a blessed reality that "to them that love God all things work together for good" (Rom. 8:28), and in all of the providential dealings of God there abides the sweetness of confidence in His love and power, and the assurance that the wisdom of God prevails. True worship in the fullest sense of the word is possible only for those who are filled with the Spirit.

VI. PRAYER

The prayer life of the believer is inseparably integrated with his spiritual life. The teaching ministry of the Spirit reminds of the many promises of the Word of God. The guidance of the Spirit is essential to intelligent prayer, asking for the revealed will of God. Prayer is vitally related to the progressive sanctification of the Christian, prayer being the very breath of the spiritual life and development. In praise and thanksgiving, which are an important part of prayer, the ministry of the Spirit is also apparent. There is hardly an aspect of the spiritual life which does not have a relationship to both prayer and the ministry of the Spirit. The prayer life will prosper in proportion to the spiritual life of the believer in Christ.

The Scriptures reveal in addition to these obvious factors in prayer the ministry of the Holy Spirit in intercession. According to Romans 8:26, "In like manner the Spirit also helpeth our infirmity: for we know not how to pray as we ought; but the Spirit himself maketh intercession for us with groanings which cannot be uttered." There is no explanation of the nature of this ministry, nor is it related to the intercession of Christ. The context of the passage, however, indicates that it is a ministry undertaken in view of our own inability to pray as we ought to pray, and it may be concluded that the Holy Spirit as the Third Person ministers in His own sphere, interceding for us from His position in us. His ministry no doubt includes a revelation of our own prayer needs and the guidance of our prayers to ask for needs which are above human wisdom. The ministry of the Holy Spirit in all its aspects is inseparable from any vital prayer life.

VII. SERVICE

In the extended discussion of spiritual gifts, it was demonstrated that the natural man cannot serve God, and even the believer in Christ who possesses spiritual gifts can exercise them fully only in the power of the Spirit. It is apparent, accordingly, that all service for God is dependent upon the power of God for its fruitfulness. The possibility of unlimited blessing through the power of the Spirit was revealed by Christ Himself: "He that believeth on me, as the scripture hath said, from within him shall flow rivers of living water. But this spake he of the Spirit, which they that believed on him were to receive" (John 7:38-39). The figure used speaks eloquently of the insufficiency of the natural man, of the source of all service and blessing, of the bountiful nature of the supply—"rivers of living water." The spring of all blessing within must, of course, be unhindered in its flow, and this condition obtains when the believer is filled with the Spirit. It is then, and only then, that the believer in Christ fulfills the good works for which he was created in Christ (Eph. 2:10).

The service accomplished in the power of the Spirit, like other results of the filling of the Spirit, is interrelated. Service and our progressive sanctification, our knowledge of the Word of God, our guidance, assurance, worship, and prayer life are not elements which fall into separate categories, but rather are the varied lights of all the colors of the spiritual life, which combined form a holy life in the will of God. Far removed from any human philosophy of self-development or self-achievement, the Scriptural doctrine points to the indwelling Spirit as the source of the experience and fruitfulness of any Christian's life and pleads with every Christian to walk by the Spirit in intimate fellowship possible only when He is unquenched and not grieved.

PART SIX

ESCHATOLOGY OF THE HOLY SPIRIT

CHAPTER XXIV

THE HOLY SPIRIT IN THE TRIBULATION

I. THE NEGLECT OF THIS DOCTRINE

THE DOCTRINE of the future work of the Holy Spirit has attracted practically no attention in existing works on theology and in books on the Holy Spirit. No exposition of this doctrine is given in standard theologies such as Hodge, Strong, Shedd, Alexander, Watson, Wardlaw, Dorner, Dick, Miley, Gerhart, Valentine, Buel, and the recent work of Berkhof. In works on the Holy Spirit such as Kuyper, Smeaton, Moule, Cummings, and Simpson there is practically no mention of the eschatology of the Spirit.

The chief factor causing this defect is the three-way division in the treatment of eschatology itself. The postmillennial theory holds that the prophesied millennium will be fulfilled in the present age through preaching the gospel or a "spiritual" return of Christ. If this theory be held, of course, the present ministries of the Spirit will continue through the age and culminate in the conclusion of all things in the final judgment. There is, in this theory, no need of treating the eschatology of the Holy Spirit. A similar situation is found among the writings of those of the so-called amillennialist view, i.e., that the present age will continue and issue into the eternal state without any millennium. Only the premillenarian, who anticipates a millennium on earth after Christ returns to set up His kingdom, can be expected to consider the doctrine and furnish an exposition of it.

In the writings of premillennial teachers and theologians there is also, however, a surprising neglect of this doctrine. Among the older premillennialists, such as Van Oosterzee, there is little exposition and defense of the premillennial position, and practically no attention is given the prophesied ministries of the Spirit in the millennial period. More attention has been given to the other great themes of prophecy. The result has been that there has been little comprehension of the nature of the ministries of the Spirit in the prophesied period of the tribulation and in the millennium which follows.

The usual premillennial position is assumed as the basis for the discussion. The Scriptures prophesy that after the return of Christ for the church a period of unprecedented trouble will follow, a period of approximately seven years according to Daniel 9:27, shortened a little (Matt. 24:22), and divided into two halves of three and one-half years each. The latter half is known as the great tribulation and in it is an unprecedented display of sin and of divine judgment upon sin. The return of Christ to set up His kingdom abruptly closes the tribulation, and the millennium follows in which Christ will rule and establish universal righteousness and peace. The millennium itself closes with another outbreak of sin and the final judgment of the wicked, and the establishment of the new heavens and new earth brings in the eternal state. It is amidst these stirring events that the Holy Spirit ministers in fulfillment of prophecy. It is clear that in the nature of the circumstances His work will be quite different than His present undertaking for the church. While the body of Scripture is not large, it does speak with certain voice on important points.

II. The Work of the Holy Spirit in Salvation

Many will be saved in the tribulation. One of the popular misconceptions of the prophesied period of tribulation is that all who enter this period are irrevocably lost. It is true that individuals who have had opportunity to hear the gospel and receive Christ during this present dispensation of grace are unlikely to accept Christ in the difficult days of tribulation. On the other hand, it is obvious that many souls will be saved, some of them surviving the horrors of the tribulation to enter the millennium, and others to die the death of martyrs. The translation of the church before the seven-year period of tribulation removes every Christian from the world. Immediately, however, Israel's blindness is removed at least in part (Rom. 11:25), and thousands among Israel turn to their long-neglected Messiah. Among Gentiles, too, there will be conversion from every nation and tongue (Rev. 7:9-17). While the tribulation period is characterized by wickedness and apostasy, it will nevertheless be a period of great harvest of souls. In the light of these facts, it is essential that the Holy Spirit minister during this period.

The prophecy of Joel. A notable prophecy of the Old Testament is quoted in the New Testament by Peter in the opening of his sermon on the Day of Pentecost: "But this is that which hath been spoken through the prophet Joel: And it shall be in the last days, saith God, I will pour forth of my Spirit upon all flesh: and your sons and your daughters shall prophesy, and your young men shall see visions, and your old men shall dream dreams: yea and on my servants and on my handmaidens in those days will I pour forth of my Spirit; and they shall prophesy. And I will show wonders in the heaven above, and signs on the earth beneath; blood, and fire, and vapor of smoke: the sun shall be turned into darkness, and the moon into blood, before the day of the Lord come, that great and notable day: and it shall be, that whosoever shall call on the name of the Lord shall be saved" (Acts 2:16-21; cf. Joel 2:28-32). The prophecy is first of all related to the present age and the phenomenon of the Day of Pentecost. A careful study of the passage will reveal that this is only a partial fulfillment. The prophecy of Joel will have its ultimate fulfillment in the consummation of God's purpose for Israel. The wonders in heaven and in earth (Acts 2:19-20) obviously did not occur on the Day of Pentecost or any succeeding day of the Christian dispensation. It remained for the tribulation period as described in Revelation to fulfill these details.

An important aspect of this passage is found in Acts 2:21, "And it shall be, that whosoever shall call on the name of the Lord shall be saved." This is the order during the dispensation of grace, and it will continue throughout the tribulation period. In view of the natural blindness of the human heart, and the inability of the natural man to understand the gospel sufficiently to believe, apart from the convicting work of the Holy Spirit (John 16:7-11), it must be assumed that there is a continued work of the Holy Spirit in revealing to the lost the way of salvation. This ministry of the Holy Spirit is especially needed in the spiritual darkness which will characterize the tribulation period. We can expect that there will be mighty conviction, especially among Israel, that Christ is indeed the Savior and the Messiah.

Israel's hope. The discourse of Christ with Nicodemus (John 3:1-21) may be understood to confirm that there will be salvation during the tribulation, and that it will be a work of the Holy Spirit. For an Israelite, entrance into the kingdom was more than becoming a part of the spiritual kingdom of God. The kingdom idea for Israel anticipated a reign of Christ on earth in which there was political, visible, and moral government as well as spiritual elements. Israel's hope was not in heaven. We look in vain for such a hope in prophecies of the Old Testament prophets. Their hope was the kingdom of righteousness on earth, a new earth, but not a spiritual existence in heaven. While their conception was not without the realization of the need for being within the fold of salvation and spiritual regeneration, this was conceived of as a means to the end of entering the future earthly kingdom.

The advocates of postmillennialism and amillennialism would eliminate the thought of a political kingdom in favor of a purely spiritual kingdom, such as now exists in the present mystery form of the kingdom in the age of grace, but the many Scriptures which speak eloquently of a kingdom on earth cannot be really explained away (cf. Isa. 11). When, therefore, Christ told Nicodemus that it was necessary that he be born again to enter the kingdom, and expressed surprise that Nicodemus did not already know this fact, He was referring not only to the immediate necessity of the new birth to enter the spiritual kingdom of all true believers, but to the necessity of regeneration for entrance to the millennium itself. Accordingly, it may be deduced that the Spirit of God will not only convict men of their need of Christ and reveal the way of salvation, but He will also regenerate those who believe. They will immediately receive eternal life, and will enter the millennium if they survive the tribulation period.

Israel, in particular, is given the blessed promise of regeneration as a part of the blessing of her restoration into favor with God. That only those who believe will receive this blessing is evident from the judgments which fall on Israel during the tribulation, in which two-thirds of Israel are killed and only one-third survive (Zech. 13:8-9).

III. The Work of the Holy Spirit in Believers in the Tribulation

Much of the revelation concerning the ministry of the Holy Spirit to those saved in the tribulation is based on inference, but a continued ministry of the Holy Spirit to believers in this period, though somewhat restricted, is evident. There is little evidence that believers will be indwelt by the Spirit during the tribulation. The possibility of a universal indwelling of all believers in the tribulation is opposed by the revelation of 2 Thessalonians 2:7, that the one re-straining the world from sin, i.e., the Holy Spirit, will be "taken out of the way" during the tribulation. Unrestrained evil characterizes the tribulation, though the lack of restraint is not total (cf. Rev. 7:3; 12:6, 14-16). The indwelling presence of the Holy Spirit in the saints in itself would contribute to the restraint of sin, and it, therefore, is taken away. The tribulation period, also, seems to revert back to Old Testament conditions in several ways; and in the Old Testament period, saints were never permanently indwelt except in isolated instances, though a number of instances of the filling of the Spirit and of empowering for service are found. Taking all the factors into consideration, there is no evidence for the indwelling presence of the Holy Spirit in believers in the tribulation. If believers are indwelt during the tribulation, however, it also would follow that they are sealed by the Spirit, the seal being His own presence in them.

Even if the Spirit does not indwell all believers of this period, it is clear that some are filled with the Spirit and empowered to witness. This is evident, first, from the fact that there will be world-wide preaching of the gospel of the kingdom during the tribulation (Matt. 24:14). The power to bear witness has ever been a result of the ministry of the Holy Spirit, and is related to the filling of the Spirit, which may be temporary, not necessarily to His indwelling, which by nature is permanent. The spiritual victory achieved by the martyrs to the faith in the tribulation could hardly be accomplished apart from the spiritual enablement of the Holy Spirit. The general phenomena of the tribulation make any sort of spiritual achievement unthinkable apart from the power of God.

IV. THE WORK OF THE HOLY SPIRIT IN THE TRIBULATION LIMITED

The characteristics of the tribulation period are not conducive to an unlimited manifestation of the Spirit's ministries. In contrast to the age of grace which precedes and the millennium which follows, the tribulation is a period of unprecedented sin and rebellion against God. While salvation is possible for those who believe, it must be concluded that the saved will be in much greater minority than at present. False doctrine will reach new heights of deception. Apostasy will reach its acme. The restraining work of the Holy Spirit will be almost totally removed (2 Thess. 2:7).

A notable lack in the ministries of the Holy Spirit is the work of the Spirit in baptism. It is highly significant that the baptism of the Holy Spirit is always regarded in Scripture as future until the Day of Pentecost when the believers were baptized by the Spirit; that the baptism of the Holy Spirit is never found after the translation of the church either in the tribulation period or in the millennium. We search the prophetic Scriptures in vain for any reference to baptism of the Spirit except in regard to the church, the body of Christ (1 Cor. 12:13). While, therefore, the Spirit continues a ministry in the world in the tribulation, there is no longer a corporate body of believers knit into one living organism. There is rather a return to national distinctions and fulfillment of national promises in preparation for the millennium.

Chapter XXV

THE HOLY SPIRIT IN THE MILLENNIUM

I. The Holy Spirit in Restraining Sin

THE MILLENNIAL kingdom will undoubtedly be the most glorious of all the dispensations. There will be the fullest display of righteousness, and universal peace and prosperity will characterize the period. Christ will rule all the earth, and every nation will acknowledge Him. The knowledge of the Lord will be from sea to sea. Throughout the millennium, Satan will be bound, and there will be no demonic activity. Man will continue to possess a sin nature with its inherent weakness, but there will be no outside temptation to arouse it. The ministry of resurrected saints in the earth will add its distinctive touch to the unusual situation. It is manifest that in such a period the Holy Spirit will have a ministry which exceeds previous dispensations in its fullness and power, even though the millennium will be legal in its government instead of gracious as in the present dispensation.

From the general nature of the period it may be learned that there will not be the spiritual conflict with forces of darkness which characterizes the present period. The work of the Holy Spirit in restraining sin will operate only against the manifestation of sin which is latent in the human heart. If all who enter the millennium in the flesh are saved, as the Scriptures seem to indicate, the Spirit will empower from within and, accordingly, will have little need for His general ministry of restraining sin as exercised in the wicked world of today. As the curse upon creation will be lifted at the beginning of the millennium, human life will be greatly extended especially for those who are born in the millennial age. By the end of the first century it is reasonable to assume that those born after the beginning of the millennium will constitute the bulk of human population on the earth. Those born in the millennial age will need to be saved through willing faith in Christ even as their parents exercised before them. Conditions in the world will be such that any open rebellion against Christ will immediately be put down, and all will make at least outward profession of faith in Him. It is from this professing element that the rebels of the final outbreak of sin at the close of the millennium will be drawn. The work of the Holy Spirit will no doubt be correlative to the sovereign rule of Christ. There is little Scripture, however, upon which to base the doctrine of the restraint of the Spirit in the millennium, and inference must be drawn from the characteristic activity of the Spirit in previous dispensations.

II. The Work of the Holy Spirit in Salvation

As previously indicated, there will be need of salvation from sin in the millennium on the part of the children born during the period. There can be little doubt that a larger percentage of the world's population will be saved during the millennium than during any other period. Many Scriptures indicate the fullness of that salvation. Ezekiel 36:25-31 pictures the fullness of salvation for Israel. They will be cleansed from sin, given a new heart, and saved from the power of sin. The universality of salvation, particularly at the beginning of the millennium, is pictured in Jeremiah 31:31-34, and many other references support the same view (Isa. 44:2-4; 60:21; Jer. 24:7). The blessing will also extend to the Gentile world (Zech. 14:16).

The nature of salvation will clearly include regeneration, as indicated in Ezekiel 36:25-31, and in John 3:1-21. The condition of salvation will be faith in Christ, whose visible presence and power will make it easy to understand His power to save. The work of the Spirit remains necessary to saving faith, however, as even in the millennium men before salvation are subject to the same limitations inherent in men today, though freed from the hindering power of Satan. The millennium will be the final display of the power of God to save souls.

III. The Holy Spirit in the Believer in the Millennium

The prophecies picturing the millennium, to which reference has already been made, unite in their testimony that the work of the Holy Spirit in believers will be more abundant and have greater manifestation in the millennium than in any previous dispensation. It is evident from the Scriptures that all believers will be indwelt by the Holy Spirit in the millennium even as they are in the present age (Ezek. 36:27; 37:14; cf. Jer. 31:33).

The fact of the indwelling presence of the Holy Spirit is revealed as part of the glorious restoration of Israel depicted in Ezekiel 36:24 ff. In this section Ezekiel predicts: "For I will take you from among the nations, and gather you out of all the countries, and will bring you into your own land. And I will sprinkle clean water upon you, and ye shall be clean: from all your filthiness, and from all your idols, will I cleanse you. A new heart also will I give you, and a new spirit will I put within you; and I will take away the stony heart out of your flesh, and I will give you a heart of flesh. And I will put my Spirit within you, and cause you to walk in my statutes, and ye shall keep mine ordinances, and do them" (Ezek. 36:24-27). In Ezekiel 37:14, it is stated, "And I will put my Spirit in you, and ye shall live, and I will place you in your own land...." This apparently related to Jeremiah's prediction that God would put His law in their hearts (Jer. 31:33). In view of the personal, glorious presence of Christ in the millennium, it would be most fitting for the Holy Spirit also to be much in evidence in the saints.

The filling of the Holy Spirit will be common in the millennium, in contrast to the infrequency of it in other ages, and it will be manifested in worship and praise of the Lord and in willing obedience to Him as well as in spiritual power and inner transformation (Isa. 32:15; 44:3; Ezek. 39:29; Joel 2:28-29). In contrast to present-day spiritual apathy, coldness, and worldliness, there will be spiritual fervor, love of God, holy joy, universal understanding of spiritual truth, and a wonderful fellowship of the saints. The spiritual unity and blessings which characterized the early church assemblies are a foreview of the fellowship of saints throughout the world in the millennium. The emphasis will be on righteousness in life and on joy of spirit.

The fullness of the Spirit will also rest upon Christ (Isa. 11:2) and will be manifest in His person and in His righteous rule of the earth. The millennium will be the final display of the heart of God before the bringing in of the eternal state. In it God is revealed again as loving and righteous, the source of all joy and peace, and in the period also, at its close, man is revealed as at heart in rebellion against God and unwilling to bow even before such glorious evidence of His power.

From such revelation as is found in the Scriptures, all the ministries of the Spirit known to us in the present age will be found in the millennium except the baptism of the Spirit—which has already been shown to be peculiar to the dispensation of grace, from the Day of Pentecost to the rapture. Though in the midst of growing apostasy in the world and indifference to the Spirit even among those in whom He dwells, we can envision the coming day; and as we wait for Him whose right it is to reign, we can by yieldedness and by dependence on the indwelling Spirit find in our own hearts and manifest in our own lives the fragrance of the fruit of the Spirit.

PART SEVEN

HISTORY

CHAPTER XXVI

A BRIEF HISTORY OF THE DOCTRINE
OF THE HOLY SPIRIT

THE STUDY of the doctrine of the Holy Spirit is predominantly a search of the Scriptures themselves. The notable lack of understanding of the doctrine even among learned men cannot be traced to a lack of scholarship in general, but to the failure to deduce the plain teachings of all Scriptural passages on the subject of the Holy Spirit. The study of the history of the doctrine is illuminating *after* a careful study of the revelation of the Scriptures. A considerable literature on the subject of the history of the doctrine of the Holy Spirit has accumulated, of which the more important and helpful can be noted.[1]

The present treatment is a summary of the labors of others, giving only the more important conclusions and salient facts which may prove helpful to those who are not able to read all the major works.

The history of the doctrine of the Holy Spirit is not easily divided into historic periods. It is a sea of many waves, with one aspect of the doctrine gathering momentum for its moment of strength while others are in various stages of growing or receding prominence. To label any period as predominantly dealing with His person or with some aspect of His work is only to pick out the more prominent features. From the beginning, the major aspects were in the mind of the early Fathers and found expression in various ways, but their technical terms were only gradually formulated, and many confessedly were groping for fuller light on the doctrine which they believed

---

[1]Literature on the history of the doctrine of the Holy Spirit: *The Holy Spirit in the Ancient Church*, H. B. Swete, 429 pp. (a scholarly, unusually complete study). *The Doctrine of the Holy Spirit*, George Smeaton, pp. 291-414 (an excellent analysis of the whole subject). *The Holy Spirit of God*, W. H. Griffith Thomas, pp. 77-117 (a concise and workable summary, especially accurate in its theological insight). *The Early History of the Doctrine of the Holy Spirit*, H. B. Swete, 98 pp. (an earlier, brief work, later expanded in *The Holy Spirit in the Ancient Church*). *History of Christian Doctrine*, George P. Fisher, pp. 11, 45, 95, 109, 144 *sq.*, 146, 147, 205, 280, 299, 323, 338, 339, 342, 346, 378, 392, 518 (factual and brief on important points). Introduction to Kuyper's, *The Work of the Holy Spirit*, by B. B. Warfield.

but had not brought to theological statement. The history of the doctrine may be, however, divided into eight divisions, each of which has its own characteristics: (1) the Ante-Nicene period (100-300); (2) the Nicene period (300-325); (3) the Post-Nicene period (325-451); (4) the Middle Ages (451-1100); (5) Pre-Reformation (1100-1517); (6) the Protestant Reformation (1517-1600); (7) Post-Reformation period (1600-1800); (8) Modern Times (1800-   ).

I. The Ante-Nicene Period

The period prior to the Council of Nicea (325) bears a considerable testimony to the deity of the Holy Spirit, though the period as a whole is characterized as a formulative and preparatory era. While there are controversies involving the doctrine of the Holy Spirit, there was more interest in the practical and spiritual aspects of the truth than the theological. The proper doctrine of the Holy Spirit was generally accepted as witnessed by (1) the baptismal formula, (2) the Apostles' Creed, (3) early hymns and liturgies, and (4) the prompt revolt of the church against early errors. While the language of the early writers in the second and third centuries was not always technically correct, it is obvious that their aim was to remain close to the Scriptures and attribute all praise and honor to the Holy Spirit, as well as to the Father and the Son. While there were always those who held heretical opinions, such as the gnostics, the ebionites, and the followers of Simon Magnus, they were excluded from fellowship with Christians generally and may be considered *outside* the church.

The early witnesses to the deity of the Holy Spirit are numerous. According to Fisher, "The personality and distinct office of the Holy Spirit are clearly set forth in Ignatius."[2] Clement of Rome (c. 100) wrote: "Have we not one God, and one Christ, and one Spirit of Grace that was shed for us?"[3] Justin Martyr, according to Smeaton, "is an emphatic witness to the distinct personality of the Holy Spirit."[4] Irenaeus, while affirming that the Holy Spirit is subordinate to the Father and the Son even as the Son is subordinate to the Father, nevertheless asserted the deity and eternity of the Spirit.[5] Clement of Alexandria (150-c. 215) speaks of the Father, Son and Holy Spirit as the "Holy Triad,"[6] and affirms that the Holy Spirit is a "distinct

---

[2]George P. Fisher, *History of Christian Doctrine*, p. 46. Cf, Ignatius, *Ephes*, 9.
[3]*Epistle of Clement of Rome to the Corinthians*, ch. 46, v. 6.
[4]George Smeaton, *The Doctrine of the Holy Spirit*, p. 293.
[5]Fisher, *op. cit.*, p. 85.
[6]*Ibid.*, p. 95.

hypostasis."[7] Smeaton states, "Theophilus of Antioch about 175 A. D., speaks of a Triad in the Godhead."[8] To Tertullian (160-220) we are indebted for the first use of the word *Trinity* to describe the Godhead.[9]

In addition to direct quotations from early scholars, an important contribution is found in the devotional literature. Griffith Thomas states, "But the strongest confirmation of the true doctrine of the Holy Spirit in this non-reflective period is found in connection with the devotional life of the Church. Experience has often proved the best witness to what is in reality doctrinally implicit in the Christian community, and all the evidences we possess of the life of the Church of these days bear unquestioned testimony to the reality of the Holy Spirit of God."[10] Swete gives witness to the same conclusion, "The devotional language of the early Church was in fact on the whole in advance of its doctrinal system. . . . The worship of the Trinity was a fact in the religious life of Christians before it was a dogma of the Church."[11]

The rising tide of heresy in the second and third centuries forced consideration of doctrine that might otherwise have been neglected. The gnostics and other early heretics forced attention to the person of Christ even more than the person of the Holy Spirit, a movement which culminated in the formal statement of the Nicene Creed. The rise of Montanism (151-171) brought about one of the early decisive victories for those upholding a Biblical doctrine of the Holy Spirit. Montanus claimed for himself and his associates the Holy Spirit which had animated the apostles, and with Him, the spiritual gifts and powers of the apostles and the ability to receive special revelations. The movement was a reaction against the early organization of the church, and it won many followers, among whom was Tertullian. In relation to the doctrine of the Holy Spirit, it was the occasion for establishing the truth that the Scriptures were closed, that the work of the Spirit was illumination of the Scriptures rather than bestowing a new revelation apart from the Scriptures. It laid the foundations for distinguishing true from false mysticism. Smeaton sums up the chief question and its answer thus: "Is the Church—since the canon of Scripture was closed—warranted to expect any further immediate revelations or prophetic visions? The ancient Church,

---

[7] *Loc. cit.*
[8] Smeaton, *op. cit.*, p. 296.
[9] *Ibid.*, p. 296.
[10] Griffith Thomas, *The Holy Spirit*, p. 82.
[11] H. B. Swete, *The Holy Spirit in the Ancient Church*, p. 159.

as against the Montanists, answered in the negative. It was a question not what God can do, but whether He will, besides the written word, communicate any further revelations of the counsel of His will."[12] An important contribution of this period to the doctrine of the Holy Spirit lies in its sane conclusions regarding spiritual gifts and super-natural revelation. The church early took its stand "that extraordinary gifts were never promised to the Church as a permanent inheritance."[13]

Most important to the doctrine of the Spirit in this period were the controversies regarding the person of the Holy Spirit. While most of the discussion and argument concerned the Second Person, the Son, an error regarding the Second Person usually involved an equal error regarding the Third Person. Two phases of error arose, the first being Sabellianism and its earlier forms, the second being Arianism.

Sabellianism denied that God is in three persons, affirming that the Father, Son, and Holy Spirit are merely modes of manifestation. Arianism, on the other hand, while affirming the distinct personality of the Son, followed the early errors of gnosticism which gave to the Son and the Spirit the place of created beings. Sabellianism was named after its principal advocate, Sabellius, who came into public eye at the beginning of the third century. He took up the modal idea of the Trinity earlier given the title *Monarchianism* by Tertullian.[14] They had appeared under the name of *Alogi*[15] in 170 in Asia Minor, who had held that Christ was only a man, chosen of God and made a Son of God by adoption. This "humanitarian" form of modalism died out in the second century, however.[16] Another type of modalism which has persisted seems to have originated in Praxeas about 200 A. D., holding that the three persons are merely modes of manifes-tation. Because this led to the idea that the Father was crucified, they were known as *patripassianists*.[17]

The Sabellian heresy is not only important as a forerunner of mod-ern unitarianism, but it is unusual in that it was the first major error on the doctrine of the Trinity to gain a large following in the church. As Smeaton put it, "It was the first, or one of the first, errors on the Trinity *that got a footing within the Church,* and it is an error to

---

[12]Smeaton, *op. cit.*, p. 302.
[13]*Ibid.*, p. 303.
[14]Fisher, *op. cit.*, p. 98.
[15]*Ibid.*, p. 100.
[16]*Ibid.*, p. 102.
[17]*Loc. cit.*

which modern thought discovers a decided inclination to return."[18]

There was much opposition to these modalistic views, and Tertullian violently opposed them, partially because they opposed Montanism. Dionysius, bishop of Alexandria, also exerted his influence against it,[19] warning the leaders and finally writing a treatise against it, though in such moderate terms that he himself was charged with Arianism. Sabellius was finally excommunicated in 261 with the result that the movement was greatly checked. It remained for the church to deal with equal decision with the Arian view of the Trinity, and later to refute the Semi-Arians, known as Macedonians, who assailed the deity of the Holy Spirit.

II. THE NICENE PERIOD

Arius (c. 336), after whom the Arian controversy was named, was a presbyter teaching at Alexandria. While he refused the Sabellian explanation of the Trinity, he held that the Son and the Holy Spirit were created, and emphasized the subordination of the Son and the Holy Spirit denying their consubstantiality with the Father. Smeaton sums up the viewpoint of Arius, "He violently contended that Deity and derivation from another person involved contradictory idea. The numerous arguments propounded by Arius, and especially by Eunomius,—who was by far the ablest of the Arians,—as these are stated and referred to by Athanasius, Basil, and Gregory Nazianzen, may all be reduced to two—that the same ETERNITY and the same INDEPENDENCE cannot possibly be possessed by a person who is OF or FROM another. . . . He dismissed in the most abrupt way the whole array of Biblical evidence, which goes to prove that the divine essence, numerically one, is possessed in common by Father, Son, and Spirit."[20] In relation to the doctrine of the Spirit, Arius seems to have held that the Spirit is created by the Son, i.e., the creature of a creature. Smeaton says, "It is stated, both by Epiphanius and Augustine, on evidence that seems liable to no suspicion, that Arius regarded the Holy Ghost as a creature of the Son, that is, as the creature of a creature; because, according to his beliefs, the Son of God occupied no higher position than that of a creature."[21]

The extended discussion of the Nicene Council in 325 led to an open declaration by Arius that the Holy Spirit was but a creature,[22]

---

[18]Smeaton, *op. cit.*, p. 304.
[19]*Ibid.*, p. 305.
[20]*Ibid.*, p. 307.
[21]*Ibid.*, pp. 307-8.
[22]*Ibid.*, p. 308.

based on the proof that all things were made by the Son. The Nicene Creed, while including a definite statement about the deity and eternity of the Son as consubstantial with the Father, merely said of the Holy Spirit, "I believe in the Holy Spirit." While many explanations have been offered to account for this simplicity, it seems that the council was content in establishing the main doctrine under dispute, relating to the Son. It is possible, too, as the next fifty years showed, that the church was not mature in its understanding of the doctrine of the person of the Spirit, and it required further controversy and another outbreak of heresy to bring the final statement.

III. The Post-Nicene Period

The Post-Nicene period divides into two parts, the first extending from the Nicene Council in 325 to the second general council at Constantinople in 381, the second from 381 to the council at Chalcedon in 451. The fifty years between the Nicene Council and the Council of Constantinople were years of turmoil and uncertainty in respect to the doctrine of the person of the Spirit. It was a transition period, and the rise of the Macedonians, a sect founded by Macedonius, added to the confusion. Macedonius maintained that the Holy Spirit was only a creature, though he does not seem to have arrived at any complete exposition of his viewpoint. The attack on the deity of the Holy Spirit drew forth a mighty array of defenders of the faith in the persons of Athanasius, Basil, Gregory Nazianzen, and Gregory Nyssen.[23] Smeaton states that they proved the deity of the Spirit by ascribing omniscience, omnipotence, omnipresence, and divine majesty to the Spirit, with special attention to the baptismal formula which unmistakably implies the equality of the Holy Spirit with the Father and the Son.[24] By some, however, the Scriptures were not deemed clear on the subject, and a certain voice was needed to settle the difficulty.

The Council meeting at Constantinople in 381 added to the Nicene Creed the additional statement in reference to the Holy Spirit: "The Lord and Giver of Life, who proceedeth from the Father, who, with the Father and Son together, is worshipped and glorified, who spake by the prophets."[25] While the statement did not say that the Holy Spirit is God, nor that He is consubstantial with the Father and the

---

[23]*Ibid.*, pp. 309-10.
[24]*Ibid.*, p. 310.
[25]*Ibid.*, p. 312.

Son, it nevertheless refuted the heretical Macedonians and in fact settled the question of the deity of the Holy Spirit as far as the church was concerned.

The second period, from 381 to 451, witnessed the further spread of the doctrine of the deity of the Spirit. The Council of Chalcedon in 451, which included the Sees of Rome, Jerusalem, Constantinople, and Antioch, confirmed the findings of the previous councils on these points. During this period, in fact, the discussion of the doctrine of the Holy Spirit turned from the question of His deity to that of His procession from the Son as well as the Father—in which His deity is assumed.

IV. THE MIDDLE AGES

The Council of Constantinople in 381 had stated that the Holy Spirit proceeded from the Father, that is, received His person from the Father, but the Council had said nothing concerning the procession of the Spirit from the Son, though this was commonly believed. Prior to the Council of Ephesus in 431, the leaders of the Christian church seem at one on this subject, believing in the procession of the Holy Spirit from the Father and the Son. Athanasius, Didymus, Epiphanius, Gregory Nyssen, Basil, Augustine, and others united with one voice in teaching this doctrine, as Smeaton has proved by quotations from their writings.[26] Smeaton concludes, "The Greek Church never had any scruple in her best days, and when she had her greatest divines in the fourth century, in speaking of the procession of the Spirit from the Son as well as from the Father."[27]

The first voice raised against this doctrine which has come down to us is that of Theodoret, who beginning in 431 adopted a resolute opposition to the thought that the Spirit is of the Son. The controversy continued until it broke out violently after the Council of Toledo in 589. This council, representing only the western church, undertook to add to the creed formulated in the councils at Nicea and Constantinople the phrase "and the Son," to the statement of procession, making it read, "who proceedeth from the Father and the Son."

This controversy regarding *filioque* immediately antagonized the eastern church as it felt with good ground that the western church was tampering with a creed which should be changed only by consent of the entire church. The western church, however, almost immediately included the addition in their liturgy, even though the Roman popes themselves were slow to accept the change. The Greek

---

[26]*Ibid.*, pp. 317-319.
[27]*Ibid.*, p. 318.

Church from this time on as a body denied the procession of the Spirit from the Son, though affirming His procession from the Father. Photius (867) attempted to support the Greek position thereby offending the western church with the result that their differences on this doctrine were one of the major causes for the division of the East and the West in 1054.

An attempt to formulate a statement of the doctrine acceptable to both churches was made in 1439, but its conclusions were ill-received, and were rendered fruitless by the collapse of the eastern empire in 1453. The Greek Church has continued to this day its stand declaring the western doctrine a heresy. The controversy on the procession of the Holy Spirit was one of the most fruitless and unnecessary controversies of the ancient church as neither party denied the deity of the Holy Spirit nor that He is equal in power and glory with the Father and the Son. After the decline of this controversy, the history of the doctrine is concerned chiefly with the work of the Holy Spirit rather than His person.

The attention of the Christian church was turned particularly to the subject of efficacious grace as the principal work of the Holy Spirit by Augustine (354-430). The anthropology of the western church as well as its hamartiology was greatly influenced by Augustine. While the eastern church held weak views of sin and attributed natural ability to the human will, the western church enlarged the conception of the depravity of man and his need of grace in order to believe and be saved. Smeaton has pointed out that the eastern church was unduly influenced by Greek philosophy throughout its history, tending to exalt man and minimize sin.[28] The great Chrysostom may be taken as an example of typical eastern theology along with Cyrill of Jerusalem, Gregory Nazianzen, Basil and others.[29] In the West, however, Augustine took a firm stand for the doctrine of grace which reappeared so strongly in the Protestant Reformation.

The Pelagian controversy tended to bring out the difficulty into the open. Pelagius, a British monk, came to Rome (c. 400) and advocated his theory which denied original sin, asserted man is able to do good apart from divine grace, and affirmed that Adam's sin concerned only himself. Augustine's experience with sin and his theological studies enabled him to attack this heresy. The debate raged from 411 until it was finally settled by the Council of Ephesus in 431, in the condemnation of Pelagius, and Coelestius and other adherents

---

[28]*Ibid.*, pp. 328-30.
[29]Smeaton, *loc. cit.*

of Pelagianism.[30] The history of the controversy illustrates the fact, however, that many in the church, particularly in the East, while rejecting the viewpoint of Pelagius, were not willing to go as far as Augustine, thus preparing the way for Semi-Pelagianism which ultimately was the position of the Roman church, and anticipated the synergism which followed in the wake of the Protestant Reformation. The condemnation of Pelagius, however, restored to prominence the work of the Holy Spirit in salvation.

In the action of the Synod of Orange (529), a further step was taken in opposing Semi-Pelagianism, minutely condemning its theological position point by point. Smeaton's quotation of the first seven canons of this council makes the theological position of this council clearly against Semi-Pelagianism.[31] The church officially lined up on the side of Augustine, affirming the work of the Holy Spirit in awakening faith and in turning the unsaved to Christ.

V. The Pre-Reformation Period

The church, having condemned Pelagianism, and later, Semi-Pelagianism, made little further progress in the doctrine of the Spirit, if any, until the time of the Reformation with its new study of doctrine. Augustine's views were commonly considered the views of the church, though held by some with considerable reservation. Unfortunately, they were twisted to serve the purpose of advancing the Roman Church. Augustine is noted for his doctrine of predestination with its attendant doctrine of efficacious grace and the total depravity of man. Along with these doctrines, which could be fitted into the sacramentarian concept of the church, there was recognition of the church as the authority in doctrine and the administrator of the sacraments—the means of grace. The church easily soft-pedalled the doctrines of predestination and the necessity of a work of the Holy Spirit and emphasized the authoritative concept of the church and the necessity of the sacraments. Instead of progressing in the doctrine of the Holy Spirit, grace was reduced to partaking of the sacraments and to some extent to hearing the Word of God. The result was an increase in formalism and the abuses which forced Martin Luther to break with Rome.

A few bright lights adorn the dark centuries before the Reformation. Bernard of Clairvaux (1091-1153) is noted for his fresh emphasis upon the necessity of grace, as found in his work, "Grace and Free-Will." The corruption of the church, too, drove souls seek-

---

[30]Fisher, *op. cit.*, pp. 104-95.
[31]Smeaton, *op. cit.*, pp. 340-42.

ing spiritual rest to mysticism of various sorts, including the monastic orders. Some went to excesses of one sort or another in an attempt to supplant the cold formalism and moral indifference of the church with a spiritual experience which was warm and vital. Undoubtedly, many spiritual giants lived in those dark centuries, in spite of all the hindrances. Counteracting these mystical elements was the influence of humanism and much of scholasticism. The failure of the crusades dulled spiritual aspiration, and the revival of philosophy under the banner of the church hindered any growth in the doctrine of the Holy Spirit.

The Middle Ages on the whole were dark spiritually as well as intellectually, with few attaining any balance of doctrine acceptable to the earnest Bible student of today. Of the doctrine of the Holy Spirit in its entirety, there was practically no conception. Few grasped the need for personal conversion and the work of the Spirit in regeneration. Practically no attention was given to such subjects as the indwelling Spirit, the baptism of the Spirit, and the filling of the Spirit. It was expressly denied that the Spirit could teach all Christians through the Word of God. Earthly priests were substituted for the Holy Spirit. The "things of the Spirit of God" were lost in the wilderness of sacramentarianism, ignorance of the Word, superstition, humanism, and scholasticism.

VI. The Protestant Reformation

The Protestant Reformation was a revolt against the abuses and the authority of the Roman Church. While the way had been prepared by increasing independency of thought in the centuries before, the real causes of the revolt lay in the decadence of the established church. While the spiritual and political conditions of southern Europe made impossible a Protestant Reformation there, the attitude of northern Europe and the political conditions in this section were conducive to a support of Luther and the other Reformers.

In relation to the doctrine of the Spirit, the Protestant Reformation renewed the teaching of the Augustinian doctrine of predestination, total depravity, and efficacious grace. The Reformers were united on these points with little defection until 1600. Their united witness revived the doctrine of the necessity of the work of the Holy Spirit in man to make possible saving faith. Along with efficacious grace, there was attention given to the doctrine of regeneration by the Spirit —in contrast to the indifference of the Roman Church to personal conversion. Luther unfortunately never was able to forsake the sacramentarian idea that grace came through the eucharist, and added to it an unbalanced doctrine of the power of the Word of God to bestow grace—a power within the Word, not of the Holy Spirit. This did not hinder the Lutheran doctrinal symbols from giving voice to the necessity of the work of the Spirit, however.

Another important contribution of the Reformation was the doctrine of illumination—the Holy Spirit revealing the teaching of the Word of God. In contrast to the Roman conception that only the priest could interpret the Word, the Reformers openly advocated reading the Bible, affirming that all believers could be taught the Word by the Holy Spirit directly. While this element was somewhat hindered by the persistence of the authoritative state church concept, it was nevertheless present.

The work of the Holy Spirit was not, of course, the major issue of the Reformation, but it shared some of the renewed attention that Bible doctrine as a whole enjoyed. All the major Reformers seem to have embraced the central concepts of the depravity of man, the need of grace, and the necessity of personal conversion. In their writings, Luther, Zwingli, Calvin, Knox and others sound the same note of man's need and the work of the Spirit in accomplishing the sovereign purpose of God.

Smeaton's survey of the doctrinal symbols of various portions of the reform movement bears an irrefutable confirmation of the contribution of the Reformation. In the Lutheran Church, the *Augsburg Confession* and the *Concordiae Formula* agree on this point. Smeaton quotes the *Concordiae Formula* as follows: "It is rightly said, however, on the contrary, that *in conversion, God, through the drawing of the Holy Spirit, makes willing men out of the obstinate and unwilling;* and that *after such conversion the regenerated will* of man does not remain inactive in the daily exercise of repentance, but *co-operates in all the works of the Holy Spirit which He performs through us.*"[32]

Smeaton quotes the Helvetic Confession along the same lines: "In regeneration the understanding is *enlightened by the Holy Spirit* to understand both the mysteries and the will of God, and *the will itself is not only changed by the Spirit,* but also furnished with powers both to will and to do good spontaneously (Rom. viii. 5, 6)."[33]

The Westminster Confession is most explicit, not only affirming the procession of the Holy Spirit from the Father and the Son, as do the other confessions, but affirms the work of the Holy Spirit in persuading and enabling faith, in persuading and enabling obedience,

---

[32]*Ibid.*, pp. 350-51.
[33]*Ibid.*, p. 351.

in illuminating the Scriptures, in applying the benefits of redemption, in effecting regeneration, in working sanctification, in giving assurance, and in insuring perseverance.

All the important Protestant creeds such as the Scottish Confession, the Thirty-Nine Articles of the Church of England, the French Confession, the Confession of Basil, and the catechisms of the Protestant churches give particular attention to the depravity of man and the need of efficacious grace to enable him to believe and be saved.[34] As the early church gave its contribution in the form of the doctrine of the person of the Holy Spirit which has remained the doctrine of the western church as a whole through the centuries, so the Reformation outlined the work of the Holy Spirit in efficacious grace, in regeneration, spiritual enablement, and in illumination of the Scriptures. The church at large has not improved to any great extent this contribution of the Reformers.

VII. The Post-Reformation Period

Following the triumphs of the Reformation, there was a sad declension from the great doctrines of the Reformers during the seventeenth and eighteenth centuries, not without, however, signal triumphs for the truth. Under the faulty leadership of Melanchthon, the controversy concerning synergism began in the Lutheran Church. Melanchthon believed that the will *cooperated* with the Spirit, a viewpoint known as synergism. The ensuing controversy beginning in 1555 in which Melanchthon was aided by Strigel of Jena had on the opposing side among others an ardent supporter of Luther's view in Flacius, who however went to extremes affirming that *"sin had become the very substance of man."*[35] The outcome was fortunately a return to Luther's doctrine in the *Formula Concordiae*, but the spirit of controversy continued with such an active defense of Lutheran doctrine as it then was that its doctrine crystallized and ceased to manifest any further progress in the doctrine of the Spirit.

A more serious threat to the doctrine of the Holy Spirit was the rise of the Arminian theology, led by Arminius (1560-1609) who held that the human will decided the matter of salvation, not the work of the Holy Spirit. The Synod of Dort (1618-1619) reaffirmed the viewpoint of the Reformers, and Arminianism had a severe setback, continuing, however, to influence Protestantism in Holland and France.

---

[34]*Ibid.*, pp. 351-52.
[35]*Ibid.*, p. 354.

In England, meanwhile, the Puritan movement which began in the sixteenth century, continued in the seventeenth. It is to this movement which sought a holy life and study of the Word of God that we are indebted for a further advance in the doctrine of regeneration and further clarity in the work of the Holy Spirit in teaching the Word of God. The period was not without excesses of a mystical sort, however, in which appeal for revelation was made directly to the Holy Spirit without the means of the Word of God—false mysticism.

The Reformation which had freed the church from the bondage of the Roman system also freed philosophy to pursue its independent course. After the Reformation had become established, we see, therefore, a number of currents, all of which tended to hinder further advance in the doctrine of the Spirit. The false mysticism which swept away some led to excesses of spiritual and emotional experience unsteadied and undirected by the teachings of the Scriptures. At the other extreme, a growing tendency toward rationalism, which had its roots in the humanism begun centuries before in Italy, had the effect of denying the Scriptures entirely and with them the work of the Holy Spirit. English rationalism took the form of deism, a denial of the immanence and providence of God, and with it all possibility of a work by the Holy Spirit. In the English Church there was a definite trend to formalism, coldness, and indifference to doctrine, even though theoretically they were still guided by the same doctrinal formula. The same deterioration can be observed in other countries. Lutheran churches resisted all progress in doctrine, tending to become formal and sacramentarian. In France, Protestantism was overwhelmed by Catholicism, and in its intellectual life, the growing rationalism led to atheism and skepticism. From France the same spirit overtook Germany where rationalism flourished and fathered many of the philosophic children which form the family of liberal theology today. Under such circumstances, the work of the Holy Spirit could not prosper.

The seventeenth and eighteenth centuries were not without their bright spots, however. Among the important contributions of the Puritans, is the work of John Owen (1616-1691), *Discourse Concerning the Holy Spirit*. Of this work Kuyper writes, "The work of John Owen on this subject is most widely known and still unsurpassed. In fact, John Owen wrote three works on the Holy Spirit, published in 1674, 1682, and 1693."[36] The revival under Philip Spener (1635-1708) in Germany which resulted in the development of the

---

[36]Abraham Kuyper, *The Work of the Holy Spirit*, p. ix.

later Moravian or Pietist movement did much to turn attention to
the doctrine of the Holy Spirit and the spiritual life, though not
without its errors. The fruits of this movement spread to the
Scandinavian countries and to America.

It was partly through the influence of the Moravians in England
and in particular Spangenburg, who was leader of the American
aspect of the Moravian movement, that John Wesley (1703-1791)
was turned into the path which made him a great revivalist and
founder of the Methodist Church in England. The revival under
Wesley and Whitefield which carried much of England and Scotland
and spread to America is a definite epoch in the teachings of the
Holy Spirit. Wesley, in particular, taught the necessity of the work
of the Holy Spirit in regeneration and His witness in the believer.
He was fond, unfortunately, of the theology of Chrysostom, and
accordingly revived the ancient Greek weakness of the doctrine of
human ability. His Arminianism, however, was quite different than
the dead Arminianism which was current on the continent at that
time and which tended toward Socinianism. He insisted on the
necessity of the work of the Holy Spirit in regeneration and in the
spiritual life.

Wesley unhappily pressed his idea of the possibility of attaining
immediate spiritual perfection in this life, confusing as he did the
ideas of spiritual maturity and the "filling of the Holy Spirit," and
contributing to the confusion on this aspect of the doctrine of the
Holy Spirit which has persisted to the present day. Wesley's contribution, coming as it did in the midst of formalism in the church
and rationalism outside the church, is the high point of the eighteenth
century. It availed little however to stem the tide. The bulk of Protestantism continued untouched, and the early zeal of the Methodist
Church was not maintained even as the Pietist movement on the
continent was undermined by Junckheim.[37] England did not suffer
the fatal blow that the church on the continent, in particular in Germany, received, however, and was due to rise again.

VIII. THE HOLY SPIRIT IN MODERN TIMES

The nineteenth century is a rich field of investigation in the
doctrine of the Holy Spirit, though only a few major elements may
be considered here. On the continent, there is little progress to be
observed in the doctrine of the Spirit, though the work of Abraham
Kuyper, appearing in the Dutch in 1888, is an important contribution

---

[37]Cf. Smeaton, *op. cit.*, 373-78.

to its theological statement. Rationalism for the most part nullified any progress. The influence of Schleiermacher (1768-1834), who denied the personality of the Holy Spirit, did much to undermine any sound theology which remained. The work of Ritschl (1822-1889), while turning attention to the practical aspects of Christianity, is notably lacking in the doctrine of the Holy Spirit. The only German contribution on the doctrine of the Spirit was the work by K. A. Kahnis, *Die Lehre vom heiligen Geiste,* a work which was never finished and was treated with disdain by contemporary German theologians.[38]

In England, the Tractarian movement, while an attempt to counteract liberalism, accomplished nothing in the doctrine of the Holy Spirit. The Irvingite group, founded by Edward Irving in Scotland, revived the ancient heresy of immediate revelation, and brought disrepute to the doctrine of the Holy Spirit by its excesses. In Plymouth Brethrenism there were some notable contributions to the doctrine, however, though they are marred by what Griffith Thomas calls, "its fissiparous tendency."[39] It is to this movement that we owe a proper definition of the baptism of the Spirit, the distinct nature of the New Testament church, the importance of Bible study and expositional preaching (a concept not new but revived by them), and the imminent coming of Christ with its attendant study of the whole prophetic Word. The works of Darby and Kelly, notable scholars of the movement, remain a positive contribution to premillennial eschatology and ecclesiology.

The latter part of the nineteenth century witnesses what may be the high point in the study of the doctrine of the Holy Spirit. It was a period of revival beginning particularly with the evangelistic efforts in England, Ireland, and America in 1856-1859 and following. Various holiness movements with both good and bad features sprang up—all of which gave full attention to the doctrine of the Spirit. Among the permanent benefits of these has come the Keswick movement in England, and the corresponding work in America. The work of D. L. Moody is well known with its impact upon the church and its attention to the power of the Holy Spirit.

The nineteenth century, particularly in its latter half, enjoyed a constant flow of books on the subject of the Holy Spirit. Among these can be mentioned Smeaton's *The Doctrine of the Holy Spirit,* to which this brief history of the doctrine has made repeated allusions; *Through the Eternal Spirit,* by J. E. Cummings; *Veni Creator,* by

---

[38]Warfield, Introduction of Kuyper's *The Work of the Holy Spirit,* pp. xxx-xxxii.
[39]Thomas, *op. cit.,* p. 111.

H. C. G. Moule; *The Holy Spirit or Power From on High,* by A. B. Simpson; and, *The Gifts of the Holy Spirit,* by Vaughan. None of these works are a satisfactory exposition of the whole doctrine, but each has its important contribution.

The twentieth century has witnessed another decline in attention to the doctrine of the Holy Spirit. The subject has not been neglected, but few works have made any further contribution. This is attributable to an undermining of confidence in the Scriptures, a result of the permeation of liberal theology of the German universities. The doctrine of inspiration has been not only questioned, but the subject is largely brushed aside today as already beyond the place where it can be defended, in spite of the able and convincing works in apologetics and in the exposition of inspiration.

A few works have survived the deterioration of the last two decades. Griffith Thomas' *The Holy Spirit of God* is a concise and scholarly presentation of the doctrine of the Holy Spirit. A distinct contribution which is remarkable for its clarity and incisive analysis is the work of Lewis Sperry Chafer, *He That Is Spiritual,* which has accomplished the notable task of clarifying such important truths as the baptism of the Holy Spirit as separate from the filling of the Spirit, in defining the nature and extent of sanctification, and in distinguishing spiritual maturity and the filling of the Spirit. The eight-volumed *Systematic Theology,* the crowning literary effort of Chafer, develops the doctrine further in volume six, which is entirely devoted to it. It is to these works and the other teachings of Chafer that the writer is indebted for his introduction to the doctrine of the Holy Spirit.

The history of the doctrine of the Holy Spirit reveals the many pitfalls in the understanding of this important aspect of theology. One can heartily agree with the solemn words of Smeaton written before the history of this century had been enacted, "The doctrine of the Spirit not less than the doctrine of justification by faith in Christ's merits, is THE ARTICLE OF A STANDING OR FALL-ING CHURCH, and without the recognition of it no religious prosperity exists or can exist."[40]

---

[40]Smeaton, *op. cit.,* p. 410.

APPENDIX

THE HOLY SPIRIT IN CONTEMPORARY THEOLOGY

In the preceding study of the Holy Spirit attention has been directed almost exclusively to views which are held by those who accept the inerrancy of Scripture. In contemporary theology, however, much of the current discussion assumes that Biblical inerrancy is no longer tenable and that Scripture must be subject to human judgment. A brief analysis of this approach to the theology of the Holy Spirit as embraced by theological liberals, crisis theologians such as Karl Barth, and adherents of the neo-orthodox view as held in America seems to be necessary. The contribution of liberals has been greatly overvalued in contemporary discussion and it is doubtful if anything at all has been added to the Biblical doctrine. An understanding of these developments, however, is necessary if current literature on the subject is to be understood.

I. THE HOLY SPIRIT IN LIBERAL THEOLOGY

The person of the Holy Spirit. The doctrine of the Trinity defined by the early fathers according to the Scriptures is one of the first points of departure for the liberalism which characterized the first third of the twentieth century. The concept of three persons in one God seems to contemporary liberalism a fundamental contradiction and a concept which is unacceptable to reasoned theology. The tendency has been inevitably to a unitarian position, that God is one though His manifestations be many. The crux of the Trinitarian problem, viz., the incarnation and person of Christ, is no problem to the liberal because he does not accept the deity of Christ in the orthodox sense anyway.

The problem of the Trinity is to liberal theologians one of the misapprehensions of orthodox theology resulting from its being bound too closely to the Scriptures. Having dispensed with the Trinitarian problem involved in the Second Person, there is little hesitancy to dispose of the doctrine of the Holy Spirit in a similar way, and to ascribe to the Holy Spirit the function of a divine manifestation without the quality of personality. The arguments of Scripture to the contrary are not considered seriously.

Emphasis on the immanence of God. Among many liberals

253

the departure from the Scriptural point of view on the personality of the Spirit is linked with a denial of the transcendence and personality of God and emphasizes the immanence of God. By philosophic reasoning many liberals conclude that God in this present evil world cannot be either transcendent or omnipotent for then He would not permit sin, suffering, and injustice as it exists in human history. To them God must be a finite, limited being, supremely good, but struggling ineffectively against evil.

The deists of the eighteenth century had explained the relation of a good God to an evil world by the postulate that God was transcendent but not immanent, that the world set in motion by God was not under His direct control. The modern liberal has chosen the opposite explanation, an immanent rather than a transcendent God, but one who is not omnipotent, and is therefore contending without success against injustice and sin. To them it is transparent that God cannot be both good and omnipotent for in their reasoning a good and omnipotent God would not permit the world to be evil.

Denial of the supernatural. In this liberal context, the Holy Spirit is the manifestation of divine influence in the world, sometimes little removed from a pantheistic concept of God identified with nature. The tendency, accordingly, is to reduce the operation of God to the nonmiraculous, to make the spiritual life a psychological experience within the limits of natural explanation. The function of the Christian religion is to inculcate and cultivate natural religious tendencies in man, using the ritualistic, aesthetic, and ethical forms of religion, and not rising above a naturalistic humanism. Though all liberals do not carry their departure from Biblical theology to these extremes, the resultant doctrine of the Spirit leaves little basis for a true divine person of the Spirit, and tends to remove the supernatural and transcendent character of the Spirit from their understanding of the doctrine.

Supernatural revelation reduced to human discovery. It is implicit in this approach that the concept of supernatural revelation is eliminated, and revelation is reduced to the human discovery of God. The inspiration of the Scriptures, the supernatural new birth, along with other supernatural aspects of the Christian faith are discarded. The Biblical presentation of the person and work of the Spirit is totally eclipsed.

II. The Theology of Karl Barth

The events of the first half of the twentieth century including the impact of two world conflicts had an inevitable effect upon theological and philosophical thinking. Theories which flowed from the pens of liberal thinkers did not help much in a world of suffering and death. The reaction to the theoretical and impractical pronouncements of liberals was inevitable. Surely there must be something more than a philosophy that man must lift himself by his own bootstraps. The horrors of war forced a reappraisal of sin in more Biblical terms, and with the increased realization of the incompetency of man to solve his own problems there came a reexamination of Biblical theology to see if, after all, there was not a divine answer to human need.

Though the movement of thought toward a reappraisal of theology was widespread, one of its principal spokesmen was the Swiss theologian, Karl Barth. In the darkness and despair that gripped Europe during World War I, Karl Barth, steeped in the tenets of extreme liberal theology, found his faith and his message completely inadequate for the human need of the desperate hearts of his congregation. Groping for some answer to satisfy the hunger for a divine intervention in the human scene, he gradually came to the conclusion that the error lay in the denial of the transcendence and omnipotence of God. When Barth's *Epistle to the Romans* first appeared in 1918, it fell as a thunderclap in a theological drought. Written in all the intricacies of dialectical theology and without departing from liberal denials of the inspiration of the Scripture, Barth's work met liberals on their own ground. He solved the human predicament by attributing to God the power of immediate divine revelation to man and direct intervention in supernatural ways into human problems. Though far from the old faith of orthodoxy, it recovered some of the precious truth that was lost and pointed the way to restudy of the whole theology of today among those still unprepared to accept the inerrancy of Scripture.

Barthian view of the person of the Holy Spirit. Barth's studies led him to reexamine the views of the early fathers on the Trinitarian problems. The key to his contribution lay primarily in a new doctrine of the work of the Holy Spirit and this led to examination of the definition of His person. Faced with a choice between the definition of the Holy Spirit as a distinct person of the Trinity as opposed to the concept that the Spirit is a mode of manifestation, Barth rejected both concepts. On the one hand, he rejected the word *person* as implying tritheism or three Gods. On the other hand, he rejected ordinary modalism or divine manifestation in three ways as an inadequate explanation.

His definition of the Spirit, therefore, though usually assumed rather than stated, is that the Trinity is a threefold mode of divine existence or being, less than that of distinct persons but more than that of mere modes of manifestation. As Weber states: "On account of its history Barth has misgivings about the concept of Person. Instead he would prefer to speak about three 'modes of existence.' "[1]

Barth's definition is an attempt to circumvent the admitted problem in orthodox creeds of using the term *person* to designate the members of the Trinity, and his view is accordingly acceptable even to some who are formally orthodox. Barth believes in the absolute deity of the Spirit. He declares: "The Holy Ghost is God the Lord in the fullness of Deity, in the total sovereignty and condescension, in the complete hiddenness and revealedness of God."[2]

Barthian view of the Holy Spirit as Creator. The supernatural character of the work of the Holy Spirit in man is brought out clearly by this summary of the Holy Spirit as Creator from Barth's own pen: "1. Man's being in the image of God only becomes actual fact when the Holy Ghost comes on the spot on man's behalf. This likeness to God is, therefore, not, and will not be, a property of the human spirit created, but it is and remains the free work of the Creator upon His creature: a work only to be understood as grace, and never to be comprehended by man (p. 11). 2. Christian life is human life that has been made open by the Holy Ghost to receive God's Word. Thus the Holy Ghost, by virtue of His being present and at work, is the subjective aspect when revelation occurs. Man's knowledge, which is imparted to him by Scripture and experience, concerning what his Creator demands from him (i.e. 'the orders of creation'), is not man's own but becomes his in the Holy Ghost, when that information has been given through the Word (p 18)."[3]

It is clear from this summary that Barth regards the transcendent and omnipotent God as entering into the human scene supernaturally and sovereignly to impart to man a true revelation of God. The key to Barth's view is the concept that the Spirit in thus acting in creation makes real to man knowledge imparted "by Scripture and experience. . . ." Barth does not affirm orthodox concepts of the inerrancy and infallibility of Scripture. On the contrary he accepts the extreme higher critical views.   For him the Scriptures, however short of infallibility, are joined to religious

---

[1]Otto Weber, *Karl Barth's Church Dogmatics*, translated by Arthur C. Cochrane, p. 36; cf. Barth, *Church Dogmatics*, I, 374 ff.
[2]Karl Barth, *The Holy Ghost and the Christian Life*, p. 11.
[3]*Ibid.*, p. 9.

experience and made the vehicle of divine revelation by the Holy Spirit. The authority is not in either the Scripture or the experience but in the immediate divine revelation given through them by the Spirit.

This definition of revelation is Barth's most important contribution to contemporary theology. It is a dogmatic and irrational answer to the problem of authority. The divine and supernatural experience of the divine impartation of revelation is essentially inscrutable and not subject to normal tests. It is a modern form of that method of divine revelation which was experienced by the prophets before the Scriptures were written as the final and complete revelation of the will of God.

Barthian view of the Holy Spirit as the Reconciler. Coupled with his doctrine of revelation is Barth's concept of the Holy Spirit as the Spirit of grace reconciling hostile man to God. Barth summarizes his view as follows: "1. Being the Spirit of grace, the Holy Spirit strives against man's hostility to grace, in other words, man's seeking to justify himself by works; for this is the characteristic, unique sin which man cannot get rid of, nor escape thinking of. The Holy Spirit strives against this (p. 28). 2. Christian life is man's actual life in the Holy Ghost; man is accounted as righteous through the Word, or for Christ's sake; man's righteousness is by faith on his part, seen in repentance and trust. Because this righteousness—this being accounted as righteous—attaches to the actual man, it coincides with his sanctification. Man's own obedience to his own true reality as one being sanctified is in the Holy Ghost, and is only actual when it responds to the Holy Ghost (p. 39)."[4]

Without denying the work of Christ on the cross, Barth ascribes to the Holy Spirit the function of the reconciler of man to God —in a word, the ministry of sanctification. In taking this position, Barth is opposing liberal theology with its denial of the supernatural and infinite work of the Spirit. His view, though not coinciding entirely with the orthodox concept, is at least an approximation and does honor to the Spirit as the Spirit of grace.

Barthian view of the Holy Spirit as Redeemer. In referring to the Holy Spirit as "Redeemer" Barth is not thereby surplanting the redemptive work of Christ, but is rather speaking of redemption in its application to man. Barth defines his view as follows: "1. The Holy Ghost is present to man in God's revelation as Spirit of promise. In the Holy Ghost, i.e. in the finality and futurity of what, in principle, is transcendent of man's existence (on earth), man is a new creature: God's child (p. 72). 2. Christian

---

[4]*Ibid.,* pp. 9-10.

life is the new life in hope, begotten of the Holy Ghost. Seeing that the Christian man is hidden with Christ in God, he has always a conscience that is leading him into all truth; he is always bound to God in thankfulness, and therefore in freedom; He prays and because he prays he is always being heard (p. 80) ."[5]

In his view of the Holy Spirit Barth believes the Holy Spirit is the divine agent of the believer's new life in Christ. He is the effector of the constitutional change in man in conversion and the source of the new life in hope. As in other areas of the doctrine of the Spirit, though Barth does not precisely state the doctrine in terms acceptable to orthodoxy, it is, in essence, its equivalent and stands in contrast to liberal unbelief.

Shortcomings of Barthianism. In many essentials of the Christian faith Barth hues closely to orthodoxy. This is especially brought out in his volume on *Dogmatics in Outline,* in which he affirms point by point the doctrines contained in the Apostles' Creed. Nevertheless, by standards of orthodoxy Barth fails in many important particulars to be acceptable as an exponent of true Biblical orthodoxy. Barth does not accept the infallible inspiration of the original writings of Scripture. He embraces some of the extreme findings of higher criticism though rejecting others. He expressly denies the historicity of Adam and Eve and though giving more reverence to Scripture than modern liberals he regards it as only *a* source of divine revelation. As a body of divine truth he considers it as authoritative only as it is made alive and understood by the work of the Holy Spirit. The Bible rather than *the* Word of God is a channel through which the immediate transmission of the Word to men is given.

Like the modern liberal, Barth finds religious authority in revelatory experience rather than the written Word. Unlike the extreme liberal, for Barth this experience is supernatural rather than purely natural. The weakness of his doctrine of revelation becomes especially evident in areas of divine revelation which are remote to immediate human experience, such as the doctrine of creation and in the realm of prophecy. Barth is very weak in his concepts of divine judgment, eternal punishment, and in the fulfillment of unfulfilled prophecies. Though definitely a move toward orthodoxy from an original liberalism, Barthianism is in many respects a subtle and confusing counterfeit of orthodoxy.

III. The Holy Spirit in Neo-Orthodox Theology

The term *neo-orthodoxy,* though sometimes used to include Barth's views, is more commonly related to the American and

---

[5]*Ibid.,* p. 10.

British counterpart of Barthianism. In many respects it is not an accurate term and its tenets are far from orthodox. Many of its basic ideas are new in context only, not in content. Usage, however, has justified this designation of the broad area in contemporary theology to the right of extreme liberalism and to the left of orthodoxy.

Origin of the neo-orthodox movement. Like Barthianism, neo-orthodoxy is a theological reaction to the extreme liberalism which characterized the period between World War I and World War II. The trend away from liberalism actually began in World War I, but the liberal tendency in theology already set in motion was not finally overtaken and reversed until World War II. By 1940 the trend toward realism in both philosophy and theology had arrested the advance of liberalism. A new day had arrived in which a more realistic approach to Bible study and theological discussion would point the way to a new recognition of the divine voice in a desperate human situation. In America the reaction against liberalism was less pronounced partly because liberalism itself had not taken hold as much as in Europe and partly because America had not been shocked out of its self-sufficiency to the same degree.

Among the chief spokesmen for the neo-orthodox movement are Emil Brunner, Reinhold Neibuhr, and Paul Tillich, with many others contributing to the discussion. Brunner, though a native of Switzerland like Barth, has contributed to the American discussion both by his writings and his teaching ministry in this country, and to some extent provides the bridge between Barth and American theologians. Reinhold Neibuhr represents the neo-orthodox movement as a whole and is considered its most authoritative spokesman. Tillich provides the connection between neo-orthodoxy and the old liberalism and represents left-wing neo-orthodoxy.

Neo-orthodox theology in general. Because neo-orthodoxy is bound to no creed and includes many diverse elements, it is difficult to establish norms for its theology. In general, however, it is a revival of a form of supernaturalism like Barthianism. The old liberal tendency to naturalize religion and deny the miraculous is replaced by a concept of a supernatural and transcendent God. Though neo-orthodoxy perpetuates the old distrust of the miraculous as far as Scriptural miracles are concerned, the work of God in extending grace to man and in revealing Himself is regarded as supernatural.

Another similarity of Barthianism and neo-orthodoxy is the tendency to contrast God and man. Man is regarded as a sinner standing in utter need of God. The transcendence of God being re-established, man's need is considered to be met by divine grace. The orthodox doctrine of substitutionary atonement, however, has no place in neo-orthodoxy and the concept of a realistic redemptive act in which the death of Christ is the price of salvation is considered unacceptable. The same tendency to follow the old liberalism is found in their definition of the resurrection of Christ. Unlike Barth who does not seem to question the historicity of the resurrection of Christ, it is common in neo-orthodox theology to find questions raised concerning bodily resurrection as pertaining to Christ and to the resurrection of all men. Barthians and neo-orthodox alike raise doubts concerning divine judgment to come while at the same time affirming some form of immortality for at least a portion of the human race. In respect to the deity of Christ, it is not uncommon for neo-orthodox theologians to define it in terms either vague or contradictory to orthodox creeds. All neo-orthodox theologians, like Barth, repudiate the idea of infallible inspiration of Scriptures which they equate with a mechanical or dictation method.

Within the confines of neo-orthodoxy a variety of emphases can be observed. As Charles C. Ryrie has noted in his analysis of neo-orthodoxy, Barth may be classified as emphasizing the sovereignty of God. Brunner starts with the nature of man as being in the image of God. Neibuhr's approach begins with man as a member of society with the transformation of society the goal of religion.[6] Tillich follows closely to Niebuhr. With the exception of Barth, the viewpoint of neo-orthodoxy on most important theological issues is little removed from the old liberalism except that a degree of supernaturalism has replaced the more naturalistic liberal emphasis.

Neo-orthodox doctrine of the person of the Holy Spirit. As a group, neo-orthodox theologians have little clear delineation of a doctrine of the person of the Holy Spirit. Most neo-orthodox scholars do not follow Barth in his support of the deity of the Holy Spirit. Almost to a man they deny the distinct personality of the Spirit and affirm His deity only in the unitarian sense that the Spirit is a divine manifestation. There is little actual discussion of the point in neo-orthodoxy. George S. Hendry who belongs to the right wing of neo-orthodoxy is the exception.[7] Hendry denies that the doctrine of the Trinity is the teaching of the New Testament. He admits, however, that some of the elements

---

[6]Cf. Charles C. Ryrie, *Neo-orthodoxy: What It Is and What It Does,* pp. 21-34.
[7]Cf. George S. Hendry, *The Holy Spirit in Christian Thought,* pp. 11-52.

of the teaching are found.[8] His discussion on the person of the Spirit rehearses the problems inherent in the doctrine of the Trinity and the many factors which make a real explanation of the Trinity an impossibility. The gist of Hendry's point of view is that the relation of the Trinity is primarily of a functional nature . . . . The distinction between them relates to their respective spheres of activity . . . the names of the three 'persons' are interchangeable."[9] Later, Hendry makes an effort to extricate himself from pure modalism, however, when he affirms ". . . the personality of the Spirit is important for faith . . . this is not because faith is concerned to affirm that the Spirit is a person in relation to God, but because it is concerned to affirm that the Spirit is a person in relation to us, i.e., that the Spirit is not merely a divine influence or force. . . . ."[10]

Brunner's point of view on the person of the Holy Spirit is no less explicit than his fellow Swiss, Barth, and stands in contrast to American neo-orthodoxy. He affirms that God is properly Father, Son, and Holy Spirit, in much the same sense as the early fathers. The human experience of the Holy Spirit is personal.[11] Brunner states further: "Hence there can be no question whether the Holy Spirit also is *Person*: in the New Testament such a question cannot arise; it would indeed be tantamount to asking whether God Himself were Person."[12] After pointing out that in some passages of the New Testament certain manifestations of the Spirit might be construed to be impersonal, he goes on to affirm: "But in the writings of the great teachers of the Primitive Church, in Paul and John, there is no doubt at all about the personal character of the Holy Spirit. Indeed, John does not shrink from placing this personality on a level with the psycho-physical personal reality of the Lord as a parallel in the form of the Paraclete . . . the Holy Spirit is God Himself . . . . He is the Giver, not only a gift; a personality, who speaks, creates, judges, guides, and plans. The Spirit bears witness, teaches, punishes, works, imparts, wills, prays, He can be blasphemed, He can be grieved."[13] From this clear statement it is evident that Brunner, if anything, is more emphatic in his concept of the personality of the Spirit than Barth.

Tillich, by contrast, rejects the personality of the Spirit. His treatment of the doctrine of the Trinity pertains largely to Christ-

---

[8]Cf. *Ibid.*, p. 30.
[9]*Ibid.*, p. 36.
[10]*Ibid.*, p. 42.
[11]Cf. Emil Brunner, *Revelation and Reason*, pp. 47, 114, 236, 318, 369-70.
[12]Emil Brunner, *The Christian Doctrine of God, Dogmatics*, I, 216.
[13]*Ibid.*

tology.[14] He leaves no doubt that he rejects the deity of Christ in the orthodox sense. His concept of the person of the Holy Spirit though less explicitly stated is definitely unitarian and modalistic. His references to the Holy Spirit deal with the work of the Spirit as one who reveals truth and constitutes the activity of God.[15]

Niebuhr is no more orthodox than Tillich. Occupied largely with the Christian and the social order, he himself makes no claim to being a systematic theologian. In his important work *The Nature and Destiny of Man*, considered to be his *magnum opus*, he dwells at length upon the relation of man to the person and work of Christ as the pivotal point in anthropology. Because of his occupation with Christology as opposed to the doctrine of the Holy Spirit, Paul Lehman suggested he might be "binitarian."[16] As Lehman points out, Niebuhr's discussion of the Holy Spirit[17] takes up mysticism but never constructs a doctrine of the Holy Spirit in the Trinitarian sense.

These representative neo-orthodox spokesmen demonstrate that neo-orthodoxy as such does not approach a clear statement of belief in the person of the Holy Spirit as expressed in the historic creeds of the church. The Holy Spirit is rather the activity of God, supernatural and gracious, but not as a person of the Trinity in the orthodox sense. Their writings, with the exception of Barth and Brunner, indicate that they are unconcerned with the theology of the person of the Spirit. Their primary interest is how the Spirit reaches man.

The neo-orthodox doctrine of revelation. The key to the neo-orthodox movement as a whole lies principally in their doctrine of the revelation of God to man. The fundamental problem of how an infinite God can communicate with finite man is a principal item in neo-orthodox literature. The answer given is determined by the role of the Holy Spirit in divine revelation. The neo-orthodox theologians of course reject alike the concept that the Spirit of God speaks with authority either through the church, as held by the Roman Church, or in the Scriptures, as held by the Reformers. It is rather that the Spirit of God projecting divine revelation through both the church and the Scriptures finds a meeting place with human experience beyond the pronouncements of either the Bible or the church. The Spirit of God uses the theologi-

---

[14]Cf. Paul Tillich, *Systematic Theology*, Vol. II.
[15]Cf. *The Theology of Paul Tillich*. Edited by Charles W. Kegley and Robert W. Bretall, pp. 253, 279, 288.
[16]*Reinhold Niebuhr, His Religious, Social, and Political Thought*, edited by Charles W. Kegley and Robert W. Bretall, p. 277.
[17]Cf. *The Gifford Lectures*, II, 98-115.

cal symbols of Scripture and church creeds and translates them into authoritative revelation through supernatural experience.

Hendry has expressed the neo-orthodox point of view of the Spirit and the Word as follows: "To sum up, the testimony of the Spirit in the Word is registered, not in any properties of the Scriptural record, but where the Church receives the testimony of the Word and repeats it in the testimony of its own faith. It occurs, so to speak, at the point where the testimony of Scripture and the testimony of the Church converge . . . . This point is the presence of the living Lord in the power of his finished work."[18]

Weber in his condensation of Barth's *Church Dogmatics* finds the crux of the Barthian doctrine of revelation in the proposition that "God reveals himself as the Lord."[19] He further states: " 'The Fact of his revelation itself' declares that 'it is peculiar to him to distinguish himself from himself.' "[20] Barth summarizes this according to Weber: " 'God's Word is God himself in his revelation. For God reveals himself as the Lord, and according to Scripture that means, for the concept of revelation, that God himself is the Revealer, the Revelation and the Revealedness in indestructible unity, but also in indestructible distinction.' "[21] Barth considers a major part of the act of revelation the incarnation of Christ. As Weber states it: "The 'objective reality' of God's revelation for us is Jesus Christ. It is the incarnate Word."[22] Again: "Revelation has taken place. The Word has become flesh . . . . Revelation is an 'objective' reality, and hence a possibility . . . . The Holy Spirit is the 'subjective reality of revelation and thereby also its 'subjective possibility.' "[23] By this he appears to mean that God is revealed by the Spirit. Stripped of Barthian distinctions and technicalities it means that God reveals Himself to man supernaturally and that this revelation though still leaving God shrouded in mystery is the Word of God, the revelation of what God is. Whether channeled through the church, the Scriptures, or any other means, the resultant revelation becomes man's. The ultimate authority of this revelation is its own character rather than that of a written infallibility.

Brunner's concept of revelation is similar to Barth's view but is stated in less dialectical fashion. According to Brunner: "Revelation always means that something hidden is made known, that a mystery is unveiled. But the Biblical revelation is the absolute

[18]Hendry, *op. cit.*, p. 95.
[19]Weber, *Karl Barth's Church Dogmatics*, p. 34.
[20]*Ibid.*, p. 34.
[21]*Ibid.*, p. 35, cf. Barth, *Church Dogmatics*, I, 311.
[22]*Ibid.*, p. 41.
[23]*Ibid.*, p. 50.

manifestation of something that had been absolutely concealed. Hence it is a way of acquiring knowledge that is absolutely and essentially—and not only relatively—opposite to the usual human method of acquiring knowledge, by means of observation, research, and thought. Revelation means a supernatural kind of knowledge—given in a marvelous way—of something that man, of himself, could never know."[24] In thus defining revelation, Brunner is close to the orthodox doctrine. His point of departure like Barth's is that revelation is essentially God revealing himself, rather than a historic posit of truth in the Holy Scriptures. As Brunner himself says: "Finally, all that has been said leads up to this point: The real content of revelation in the Bible is not 'something,' but *God Himself. Revelation is the self-manifestation of God*."[25]

Brunner goes on to point out that revelation is supremely a divine act which must be received by man to constitute a real revelation. Man receives revelation by faith and submission. Whatever may be said of Scripture or the church as sources of truth, divine revelation is a "divine-human encounter," to use Brunner's own expression, which is used as a title of one of his important books. The Word of God is heard through the Scriptures and the church, but is revealed through the ministry of the Holy Spirit. It is the Spirit which testifies to the truth. Brunner writes: "When the Holy Spirit testifies within me that the Word *Christ* is the Truth, I know, *myself*, that it is true. I do not need any further human guarantee."[26] Man receives divine revelation by faith in this testimony of the Spirit: "True faith, on the other hand, the *fides viva*, is no human achievement on the basis of a human command; it is not a belief on authority, a *sacrificium intellectus;* it is not an act of servile obedience to a law; but it is the divinely effectual miracle that man, through the illumination of the Holy Spirit, becomes able to see the truth of God in Jesus Christ"[27] The revelation of truth is therefore a direct act of God toward man, its authority and testimony depending upon the Spirit of God rather than any confidence in the Scriptures or the church.

For Tillich, divine revelation is also a divine-human encounter but with less overtones of the supernatural. The test of divine truth is not so much the testimony of the Spirit of God as the testimony of the "new being," i.e., what we are as Christians. Tillich states: "If I were asked to sum up the Christian message for our time in two words, I would say with Paul: It is the message of a

[24]Brunner, *Revelation and Reason*, p. 23.
[25]*Ibid*, p. 25.
[26]*Ibid.*, p. 178.
[27]*Ibid.*, p. 184.

'New Creation.' We have read something of the New Creation in Paul's second letter to the Corinthians. Let me repeat one of his sentences in the words of an exact translation: 'If anyone is in union with Christ he is a new being; the old state of things has passed away; there is a new state of things.' "[28] This new being is reason raised to the nth degree which he calls a "numinous astonishment" or an "ecstasy."[29] When a "sign event," i.e., the subjective divine revelation, causes this ecstatic reason or the objective human experience, the resulting situation is revelation.[30] For Tillich revelation, though containing a supernatural and inscrutable element, is little removed from reason in the ordinary sense. Like other neo-orthodox theologians, the result is to remove from Scripture all intrinsic authority and transfer it to the human judgment.

Niebuhr does not dwell upon the experience of revelation but rather its result. Tillich analyzes Niebuhr's epistemology, that is, how he can know divine revelation, in these words: "The difficulty of writing about Neibuhr's epistemology lies in the fact that there is no such epistemology. Neibuhr does not ask, 'How can I know?'; he starts knowing. And he does not ask afterward, 'How could I know?', but leaves the convincing power of his thought without epistemological support."[31] Neibuhr regards the Christian faith as beginning with the historical event of the life, death, and resurrection of Christ. The revelation of the meaning of this is accomplished by divine grace on the part of God and faith and repentance on the part of man.[32] While different than either Barth or Tillich, with both of whom he disagrees, Niebuhr, like them, transfers the judgment of the truth of revelation to man in his total divine-human context. He admits that revelation is only imperfectly comprehended[33] and does not attempt to defend its absolute validity.

IV. Conclusion

Taken as a whole, contemporary theology in relation to the doctrine of the Holy Spirit can be described as a reaction against the extreme liberalism which characterized the first third of the twentieth century. Its main contribution has been the revival of the doctrine of supernatural revelation. Some like Barth and Brunner have returned to a more Biblical form of Trinitarianism and have affirmed the personality of the Holy Spirit in one way or another. There

---

[28]Paul Tillich, *The New Being*, p. 15.
[29]Cf. *Theology of Paul Tillich*, p. 211.
[30]*Ibid.*
[31]*Reinhold Niebuhr, His Religious, Social and Political Thought*, p. 36.
[32]Cf. *Ibid.*, p. 294.
[33]Cf. *Ibid.*

has been also a more realistic appraisal of human sin and need, and of divine sufficiency and power.

The shortcomings of modern liberalism are still more obvious than any gains in the direction of orthodoxy. There has been no disposition to recognize the infallibility of Scripture. While some have returned to a belief in the true deity of Christ, others obviously have not. Their main contribution, supernatural revelation, is a faulty doctrine, a revival of the concept of immediate revelation which according to the orthodox view ceased with the completion of the written Word. Their concepts of the atonement, the indwelling power and presence of the Spirit, and the work of the Spirit in filling the believer are far short of the Biblical revelation.

As compared to the theology of orthodoxy, the contemporary approach to the doctrine of the Spirit represents a movement in the right direction only in isolated factors. The main emphasis of contemporary thought is toward a pseudo-Christianity, governed by reason and human judgment instead of the infallible written Word of God. Evangelicals have tended to underestimate the errors latent in neo-orthodoxy. Contemporary theology has contributed little to the advance of understanding the truth as it is in the Scriptures. Neo-orthodoxy instead of being a modern form of orthodoxy is a modern form of error, destructive of the true doctrine of the Spirit as well as theology as a whole.

BIBLIOGRAPHY

The books listed in this bibliography are representative of the literature available in this field. Inclusion of any work does not imply theological agreement with its contents.

ARMISTEAD, J. S., "The Work of the Holy Spirit, on the Hearts of Men," *Presbyterian Tracts*. Vol. IV. Philadelphia: Presbyterian Board of Publication. Originally published in Edinburgh Presbyterian Review, 1843.

BARTH, K., *The Holy Ghost and the Christian Life*. London: Frederick Muller, 1938. 86 pp.

BIEDERWOLF, W. E., *Help to the Study of the Holy Spirit*. New York: Fleming H. Revell Co., 1903. Fourth edition. 127 pp.

BOETTNER, LORAINE, *The Inspiration of the Scriptures*. Grand Rapids: Wm. B. Eerdmans Publishing Co., 1937. 88 pp.

BROOMALL, WICK, *The Holy Spirit*. New York: American Tract Society, 1940. 207 pp.

BROWNVILLE, C. C., *Symbols of the Holy Spirit*. New York: Fleming H. Revell Co., 1945. 140 pp.

BUCHANAN, JAMES, *Office and Work of the Holy Spirit*. Edinburgh: John Johnstone, 1842. 415 pp.

CALVIN, JOHN, *Institutes of the Christian Religion*. Translated by John Allen. Philadelphia: Presbyterian Board of Christian Education, 1936. 2 vols.

CANDLISH, JAMES S., *Work of the Holy Spirit*. Edinburgh: T. & T. Clark, 1883. 118 pp.

CARROLL, B. H., *The Holy Spirit*. Grand Rapids: Zondervan Publishing House, 1939. 174 pp.

CHAFER, L. S., *Grace*. Wheaton: Van Kampen Press, 1928. 373 pp.

————, *He That is Spiritual*. Wheaton: Van Kampen Press, 1918. 193 pp.

————, *Systematic Theology*. 8 vols. Dallas: Dallas Seminary Press, 1947-48.

CHAPMAN, J. WILBUR, *Received Ye the Holy Ghost?* New York: Fleming H. Revell Co., 1894. 127 pp.

CUMMING, J. E., *After the Spirit*. London: S. W. Partridge & Co., n.d. 251 pp.

————, *Through the Eternal Spirit*. London: S. W. Partridge & Co., n.d. 384 pp.

DAVIDSON, W. T., *The Indwelling Spirit*. London: Hodder and Stoughton, 1911. 340 pp.

DENIO, FRANCIS B., *Supreme Leader*. Boston: Pilgrim Press, 1900. 264 pp.

DILLISTONE, F. W., *Holy Spirit in the Life Today*. Philadelphia: Westminster Press, 1947. 126 pp.

DIXON, A. C., *Person and Ministry of the Holy Spirit*. London: R. D. Dickinson, 1891. 188 pp.

———, *The Holy Spirit in Life and Service*. New York: Fleming H. Revell Co., 1895. 144 pp.

DOLMAN, D. H., *Simple Talks on the Holy Spirit*. New York: Fleming H. Revell Co., 1927. 182 pp.

DORNER, I. A., *A System of Christian Doctrine*, 4 vols. Translated by Alfred Cave and J. S. Banks. Edinburgh: T. & T. Clark, 1888.

DOUTT, NORMAN F., *Filled with the Spirit*. Findlay, Ohio: Fundamental Truth Publishers, n. d. 83 pp.

DOWNER, ARTHUR CLEVELAND, *Mission and Ministration of the Holy Spirit*. Edinburgh: T. & T. Clark, 1909. 347 pp.

EDWARD, HENRY, *The Internal Mission of the Holy Ghost*. New York: Catholic Publishing Society, 1875. 494 pp.

ELLICOTT, CHARLES J., *A Critical and Grammatical Commentary on St. Paul's Epistle to the Galatians, with a Revised Translation*. Andover: Warren F. Draper, 1884. 192 pp.

ERDMAN, C. R., *Spirit of Christ*. New York: George H. Doran Co., 1926. 119 pp.

FABER, GEORGE STANLEY, *Practical Treatise on the Ordinary Operations of the Holy Spirit*. Fifth edition. London: J. G. & F. Rivington, 1834. 222 pp.

FISHER, GEORGE PARK, *History of Christian Doctrine*. New York: Charles Scribner's Sons, 1896. 583 pp.

FROST, HENRY W., *Who Is the Holy Spirit?* New York: Fleming H. Revell Co., 1938. 124 pp.

GAEBELEIN, A. C., *The Holy Spirit in the New Testament*. New York: Our Hope, n. d. 113 pp.

GAUSSEN, L., *Theopneustia*. Revised edition, David Scott's translation. Chicago: Bible Institute Colportage Association, 1912. 365 pp.

GOODMAN, M., *The Comforter*. London: The Paternoster Press, 1938. 135 pp.

GORDON, ADONIRAM JUDSON, *Ministry of the Spirit*. New York: Fleming H. Revell Co., 1894. 225 pp.

GREEN, JAMES B., *Studies in the Holy Spirit*. New York: Fleming H. Revell Co., 1936. 126 pp.

GREEN, PETER, *The Holy Ghost: the Comforter*. New York: Longmans, Green & Co., 1934. 124 pp.

HALDEMAN, I. M., *Holy Ghost Baptism and Speaking with Tongues.* New York: Haldeman, n. d. 32 pp.

HARE, JULIUS CHARLES, *Mission of the Comforter.* Fourth edition. London: Macmillan & Co., 1877. 454 pp.

HARRISON, J. EAST, *Reigning in Life.* Grand Rapids: Zondervan Publishing House, 1937. 212 pp.

HART, J. H. A., *Expositor's Greek Testament, First Peter.* 5 vols. Edited by W. Robertson Nicoll. Grand Rapids: Wm. B. Eerdmans Publishing Co.

HODGE, A. A., *Outlines of Theology.* Chicago: The Bible Institute Colportage Association, 1878. 678 pp.

HODGE, CHARLES, *Commentary on the Epistle to the Romans.* New edition. New York: A. C. Armstrong and Son, 1909. 716 pp.

———, *Systematic Theology.* 3 vols. New York: Scribner, Armstrong and Co., 1877.

HUMPHRIES, A. LEWIS, *Holy Spirit in Faith and Experience.* London: W. A. Hammond, 1911. 368 pp.

IRONSIDE, H. A., *Mission of the Holy Spirit.* New York: Loizeaux Brothers, n. d. 64 pp.

———, *Praying in the Holy Spirit.* Oakland, Calif.: Western Book & Tract Co., n. d., 61 pp.

JACOBS, H. E., *A Summary of the Christian Faith.* Philadelphia: The United Lutheran Publication House, 1905. 637 pp.

JAMIESON, ROBERT, A. R. FAUSSET, AND DAVID BROWN, *A Commentary, Critical, Experimental, and Practical, on the Old and New Testaments.* 6 vols. Glasgow: William Collins Sons and Company, 1868.

JENNINGS, F. C., *The Holy Spirit.* New York: Our Hope Publication Office, n.d. 15 pp.

JOHNSON, E. H., *Holy Spirit, Then and Now.* Philadelphia: The Griffith and Rowland Press, 1904. 305 pp.

KELLY, WILLIAM, *Lectures on the New Testament. Doctrine of the Holy Spirit.* London: Morrish, 1915. 331 pp.

KENYON, JOHN B., *The Bible Revelation of the Holy Spirit.* Grand Rapids: Zondervan Publishing House, 1939. 159 pp.

KLUEPFEL, P., *The Holy Spirit in the Life and Teachings of Jesus and the Early Christian Church.* Columbus: Lutheran Book Concern, 1929. 145 pp.

KUYPER, ABRAHAM, The *Work of the Holy Spirit.* Translated from the Dutch by Henri de Vries. New York: Funk and Wagnalls Co., 1900. 664 pp.

LAMBERT, J. C., "Apostle," *International Standard Bible Encyclopaedia.* 5 vols. Chicago: Howard-Severance Co., 1937.

LAW, WILLIAM, *Power of the Spirit.* Second edition. London: James Nisbet & Co., 1896. 218 pp.

MACKINTOSH, C. H., *Notes on Genesis.* New York: Loizeaux Brothers, n.d. 334 pp.

MANNING, HENRY EDWARD, *Temporal Mission of the Holy Ghost.* Fourth edition. London: Burns and Oates, Limited, 1892. 260 pp.

MARSH, F. E., *Emblems of the Holy Spirit.* New York: Alliance Press Co., 1911. 257 pp.

MASSEE, J. C., *The Holy Spirit in Scripture and Experience.* New York: The Book Stall, 1917. 69 pp.

MATHESON, GEORGE, *Voices of the Spirit.* London: James Nisbet *?.* Co., 1888. 241 pp.

McCLURE, A. D., *Another Comforter.* New York: Fleming H. Revell Co., 1897. 127 pp.

McCONKEY, JAMES H., *Threefold Secret of the Holy Spirit.* Harrisburg, Pa.: Fred Kelker, 1897. 123 pp.

MILES, F. J., *The Greatest Unused Power in the World.* Minneapolis: Wilson Press, 1944. 102 pp.

MOBERLY, G., *The Administration of the Holy Spirit in the Body of Christ.* Second edition. New York: Pott and Amery, 1870. 338 pp.

MORAN, KIERAN P., "The Holy Ghost and Our Lady," *Discourses on the Holy Ghost.* Lester M. Dooley, editor. New York: Joseph F. Wagner, Inc., 1942. 248 pp.

MORGAN, G. CAMPBELL, *Spirit of God.* London: Hodder & Stoughton, 1900. 246 pp.

MOULE, H. C. G., *Veni Creator.* London: Hodder & Stoughton, 1890. 253 pp.

MULLINS, E. Y., "Holy Spirit." *International Standard Bible Encyclopaedia.* 5 vols. Chicago: Howard-Severance Co., 1930.

MURRAY, ANDREW, *Aids to Devotion.* London: James Nisbet & Co., 1910. 134 pp.

———, *Back to Pentecost.* London: Oliphants, n.d. 106 pp.

———, *Full Blessing of Pentecost.* London: James Nisbet & Co., 1908. 182 pp.

———, *Spirit of Christ.* London: James Nisbet & Co., 1888. 394 pp.

NUTTALL, GEOFFREY F., *The Holy Spirit in Puritan Faith and Experience.* Oxford: Basil Blackwell, 1946. 192 pp.

O'REAR, ARTHUR T., *Nativity of the Holy Spirit.* Louisville: Pentecostal Publishing Co., 1929. 188 pp.

Owen, John, *A Discourse concerning the Holy Spirit*. From *The Works of John Owen*. Edited by William H. Goold. 4 vols. Philadelphia: Protestant Episcopal Book Society, 1862.

Pache, Rene, *La Personne et l'OEuvre de Saint-Esprit*. Vennes sur Lausanne, Switzerland: Emmaus Institute, 1942. 140 pp.

Parker, Joseph, *The Paraclete*. London: Henry S. King & Co., 1874. 402 pp.

Parry, Thomas, *Indwelling Spirit*. New York: The Christian Alliance Publishing Co. 1906. 230 pp.

Redford, R. A., *Vox dei*. London: James Nisbet & Co., 1889. 344 pp.

Rees, Thomas, *Holy Spirit in Thought and Experience*. New York: Charles Scribner's Sons, 1915. 221 pp.

Ridout, Samuel, *Person and Work of the Holy Spirit*. New York: Loizeaux Brothers, n.d. 224 pp.

Robertson, A. T., *A Grammar of the Greek New Testament in the Light of Historical Research*. Fifth edition. New York: Richard R. Smith, Inc., 1923. 1454 pp.

Scofield, C. I., *Plain Papers on the Holy Spirit*. New York: Fleming H. Revell Co., 1899. 80 pp.

Scofield Reference Bible. New York: Oxford University Press, 1945. 1362 pp.

Shedd, William G. T., *Dogmatic Theology*. 3 vols. New York: Charles Scribner's Sons, 1891. Third edition.

Simpson, A. B., *The Holy Spirit or Power from on High*. 2 vols. New York: The Christian Alliance Publishing Co., 1895.

Smeaton, George, *The Doctrine of the Holy Spirit*. Second edition. Edinburgh: T. & T. Clark, 1889. 418 pp.

Smith, O. J., *The Enduement of Power*. London: Marshall, Morgan & Scott, n.d. 119 pp.

Soltau, George, *Person and Mission of the Holy Spirit*. Philadelphia: Philadelphia School of the Bible, n.d. 128 pp.

Stowell, William H., *On the Work of the Spirit*. London: Jackson and Walford, 1849. 468 pp.

Strong, A. H., *Systematic Theology*. Unabridged edition. Philadelphia: The Judson Press, 1907. 1163 pp.

Swete, H. B., *The Early History of the Doctrine of the Holy Spirit*. Cambridge: Deighton Bell & Co., 1873. 98 pp.

———, *Holy Spirit in the Ancient Church*. London: Macmillan and Co. 1912. 429 pp.

———, *Holy Spirit in the New Testament*. London: Macmillan and Co., 1909. 412 pp.

THAYER, J. H., *Greek-English Lexicon of the New Testament.* New York: American Book Company, 1889. 727 pp.

The Constitution of the Presbyterian Church in the U. S. A. Philadelphia: Board of Christian Education of the Presbyterian Church in the U. S. A., 1946. 532 pp.

THIESSEN, H. C., "Will the Church Pass through the Tribulation?" *Bibliotheca Sacra,* 92:301. Dallas: Evangelical Theological College.

THOMAS, W. H. GRIFFITH, *The Holy Spirit of God.* Chicago: Bible Institute Colportage Association, 1913. 303 pp.

TORREY, R. A., *Baptism of the Holy Spirit.* New York: Fleming H. Revell Co., 1897. 77 pp.

VALENTINE, MILTON, *Christian Theology,* 2 vols. Philadelphia: Lutheran Publication Society, 1906. 476 pp.

VAUGHAN, C. R., *The Gifts of the Holy Spirit.* Richmond: Presbyterian Committee of Publication, 1894. 415 pp.

WARFIELD, B. B., "Inspiration," *International Standard Bible Encyclopaedia.* 5 vols. Chicago: Howard-Severance Co., 1930.

———, *Revelation and Inspiration.* New York: Oxford University Press, 1927.

WATSON, RICHARD, *Theological Institutes.* 2 vols. Twenty-ninth edition. New York: Nelson and Phillips, 1850.

WEBB, A. B., *The Presence and Office of the Holy Spirit.* London: Skeffington, 1889. 179 pp.

Webster's New International Dictionary. Springfield, Mass.: G. & C. Merriam Co., 1945. 3210 pp.

WESTCOTT, B. F., *The Epistle to the Hebrews.* Third edition. London: Macmillan and Co., 1906. 506 pp.

WILDER, R. P., *Studies on the Holy Spirit.* London: Student Christian Movement, 1909. 31 pp.

WINSTANLEY, E. W., *Spirit in the New Testament.* Cambridge: University Press, 1908. 166 pp.

WOLSTON, W. T. P., *Another Comforter.* Second edition. London: James Nisbet & Co., 1900. 330 pp.

WOOD, IRVING F., *Spirit of God in Biblical Literature.* London: Hodder and Stoughton, 1904. 280 pp.

YOUNG, ROBERT, *Literal Translation of the Bible.* Revised edition. Grand Rapids: Baker Book House, 1953.

TOPICAL INDEX

A

Apostleship, 175-77.
Arius, 5, 8, 241-42.
Arminianism, 248, 250.
Arminius, 248.
Articles of English Church on procession, 13.
Athanasian Creed on procession, 13.
Augsburg Confession, 247.
Augustine, 244; influence on Reformers, 245-46.

B

Baptism by fire, 21, 148-49.
Baptism of the Holy Spirit, 138-50; abiding results, 149-50; an act of the Third Person, 147-48; an instantaneous act of God, 147; as expounded in Acts, 143-44; begins at Pentecost, 139; coextensive with salvation, 139-40; into body of Christ, 140-41; into Christ, 141-43; lack of exhortations related to, 140; never repeated, 145-46; not experimental, 146-47; occurs at moment of salvation, 145; only in this dispensation, 143-46; related to baptism of fire, 148-49; related to identification with Christ, 142; related to new union of life, 142-43; related to position, 141-42, 149; related to positional truth, 146-47; related to tongues, 144-45; related to union in Christ, 149; relation to dispensationalism, 143; results in new associations, 150; sources of

confusion in understanding, 138-39; universal among believers, 146; universal among Christians, 139-40.
Bernard of Clairvaux, on necessity of grace, 245-46.

C

Calling, cf. common grace, 107-18; cf. efficacious grace, 119-27.
Church, formed by Holy Spirit, 34.
Clothing, type of Holy Spirit, 18-19.
Common grace, 107-18; importance of 108-9; limitations of, 116-18; Lutheran view, 111-12; man's need of, 109-10; nature of, 110-14; related to Christian experience, 117; related to efficacious grace, 110; related to irresistible grace, 110; related to mysticism, 112; related to rationalism, 112; related to restraint of sin, 114-16; related to revelation to world, 112-14; related to sufficient grace, 110: relation to the Word of God, 111-12; scope of, 107-8.
Concordiae Formula, 247.
Confession of Basil, 248.
Conversion, view of creeds, 247-48.
Council at Constantinople, adds to Nicene Creed, 242-43.
Creation, design of, 40-41; designed for God's glory, 42; life of, 41-42; order of, 40-41; preservation of, 42-43; renewal of, 42-43.

tongues, in Acts, 183-84; tongues, in I Corinthians, 184-85; tongues, interpretation of, 187; tongues, problem of, 181-83; tongues, temporary, 185-86.

Synod of Dort, 248.

T

Thirty-nine Articles, 248.

Tongues, 180-88.

Tribulation, neglect of work of Spirit in, 227-28; relation to Holy Spirit, 227-31; salvation in, 228-30; work of Spirit in, 230-31;

work of Spirit limited in, 231.

Types, of the Holy Spirit, 18-25.

U

Unitarianism, 5.

W

Water, type of Holy Spirit, 23-24.

Wesley, John, related to Holy Spirit, 250.

Westminster Confession, 247-48; on procession, 13.

Wind, type of Holy Spirit, 24-25.

Wisdom, gift of Holy Spirit, 74

INDEX TO SCRIPTURES

2 CORINTHIANS